Corporations and Citizensh

It is widely … ven social roles. Yet … preciated. *Corporatio* … g the concept of cit … ensions of corporatio … d responsibilities a … and their governing … and multifaceted pi … rporations as citizens … rations as arenas of … temporary reconfigur … ogical and cosmopol … our understanding … allocating power an…

ANDREW … thics at the Schulich …

DIRK MA … kard Chair in Corpo … iness, York Universit…

JEREMY … nd Director of the … nsibility at Nottingh…

Business, Value Creation, and Society

Series editors
R. Edward Freeman, *University of Virginia*
Stuart L. Hart, *Cornell University* and *University of North Carolina*
David Wheeler, *Dalhousie University, Halifax*

The purpose of this innovative series is to examine, from an international standpoint, the interaction of business and capitalism with society. In the 21st century it is more important than ever that business and capitalism come to be seen as social institutions that have a great impact on the welfare of human society around the world. Issues such as globalization, environmentalism, information technology, the triumph of liberalism, corporate governance, and business ethics all have the potential to have major effects on our current models of the corporation and the methods by which value is created, distributed, and sustained among all stakeholders – customers, suppliers, employees, communities, and financiers.

Published titles:

Fort *Business, Integrity, and Peace*
Gomez & Korine *Entrepreneurs and Democracy*

Forthcoming in this series:

Painter-Morland *Business Ethics as Practice*
Doh & Yaziji *NGOs and Corporations*
Rivera *Business and Public Policy*

Corporations and Citizenship

ANDREW CRANE
York University
DIRK MATTEN
York University
JEREMY MOON
University of Nottingham

CAMBRIDGE UNIVERSITY PRESS
Cambridge, New York, Melbourne, Madrid, Cape Town, Singapore, São Paulo, Delhi

Cambridge University Press
The Edinburgh Building, Cambridge CB2 8RU, UK

Published in the United States of America by Cambridge University Press, New York

www.cambridge.org
Information on this title: www.cambridge.org/9780521612838

First published 2008

Printed in the United Kingdom at the University Press, Cambridge

A catalogue record for this publication is available from the British Library

Library of Congress Cataloging in Publication data
Crane, Andrew, 1968–
Corporations and citizenship / Andrew Crane, Dirk Matten, Jeremy Moon.
p. cm.
Includes bibliographical references and index.
ISBN 978-0-521-84830-5
1. Business and politics. 2. Corporations–Political activity. 3. Business ethics.
4. Social responsibility of business. I. Matten, Dirk. II. Moon, Jeremy, 1955–
III. Title.
HD3611.C73 2008
322′.3–dc22

2008019385

ISBN 978-0-521-84830-5 hardback
ISBN 978-0-521-61283-8 paperback

Contents

Figures

Tables

Foreword

Andrew Crane, Dirk Matten and Jeremy Moon have provided business thinkers and scholars a great service. They have systematically analyzed the idea that we see corporations as citizens. While both 'corporation' and 'citizenship' have been problematic terms for political theory, Crane, Matten and Moon identify a discrete number of important interpretations of these ideas, and they show how the resulting 'theories' can be linked into a systemic whole.

Their starting point is that in the 21st century we need a more robust understanding of the political role of corporations in society. They propose the idea of 'corporate citizenship' and 'global corporate citizenship' as ways forward. As the world gets even 'flatter', understanding how corporations play a political role, as well as economic, social and moral roles, is central to the dialogue of how we govern civil society. Citizenship is simply at the heart of the global debate on societal governance, and the main institution that we use to create value for each other, business, must be nearby. Alternatively, seeing corporations as citizens lets us understand 'citizenship' for people in more interesting terms. For instance, Crane, Matten and Moon suggest that we need to see the corporation–stakeholder relationship in citizenship terms. Corporations become places where people can engage in the citizenship process. Such a view is much more interesting than the usual debate about the limits of corporate power, and the constant griping of 'too much' or 'too little' government.

In short, Crane, Matten and Moon have proposed a new starting point for an important debate about the role of capitalism and its sister institutions: government and the rest of civil society. By focusing on 'citizenship' they give us a way to tie these ideas together and to pave the way for meaningful reform. Crane, Matten and Moon have given us a complex and multi-layered argument that continues to set the direction for a new conversation about business and its role in society. Indeed, it is a perfect volume for the series on *Business, Value Creation, and Society*.

The purpose of this series is to stimulate new thinking about value creation and trade, and its role in the world of the 21st century. Our old models and ideas simply are not appropriate in the '24/7 Flat World' of today. We need new scholarship that builds on these past understandings, yet offers the alternative of a world of hope, freedom and human flourishing.

R. Edward Freeman
Olsson Professor of Business Administration
The Darden School
University of Virginia
Charlottesville, Virginia, USA

Preface

The seed for this book was sown shortly before Andy and Dirk joined Jeremy at the International Centre for Corporate Social Responsibility (ICCSR), Nottingham University Business School. Between panels, meetings and socials at the 2002 Academy of Management Annual Meeting in Denver, we discovered a shared interest in the uses and abuses of the term 'corporate citizenship'. We then explored and extended this interest through several papers looking at how corporations and citizenship came together. At some point we recognized that in order to do justice to these ideas, and in order to respond to the numerous objections and refinements that had been suggested by others, a book length treatment was called for. Thus the book both synthesizes and expands upon the different papers we have also published in the area (see below).

Though the book has taken rather longer than intended we feel that it has benefited from the journey. Our papers on corporations and citizenship have been subjected to a variety of commentaries, challenges and criticisms at conferences and workshops, and through journal review and discussion. We are immensely grateful to all those too numerous to name, and some anonymous, who took the trouble to engage with our ideas.

We would also like to thank Ed Freeman, Stuart Hart and David Wheeler, the series editors, the Cambridge University Press staff and our research assistants Judy Muthuri (Nottingham), and Jesse Brodlieb (York) for all their support.

Finally, we would like to thank our students and colleagues at the ICCSR for providing such a fertile environment for our ideas to develop. We dedicate the book to you.

Andy Crane and Dirk Matten, Toronto
Jeremy Moon, Nottingham

Acknowledgements

Several of the core ideas presented in this book were first published in a substantially different form in the following publications:

Chapter 2 draws from material first published in Moon, J., Crane, A. and Matten, D. (2005). 'Can corporations be citizens? Corporate citizenship as a metaphor for business participation in society', *Business Ethics Quarterly*, vol. 15 (3): 427–51.

Chapter 3 draws from material first published in Matten, D. and Crane, A. (2005a). 'Corporate citizenship: toward an extended theoretical conceptualization', *Academy of Management Review*, vol. 30 (1): 166–79. See also Crane, A., and Matten, D. (2005). 'Corporate citizenship: missing the point or missing the boat? – A response to van Oosterhout', *Academy of Management Review*, vol. 30 (3): 681–4.

Chapter 4 draws from material first published in Crane, A., Matten, D. and Moon, J. (2004). 'Stakeholders as citizens: rethinking rights, participation, and democracy', *Journal of Business Ethics*, vol. 53 (1/2): 107–22.

The synthesis of our three relationships in Part A was first suggested in Moon, J., Crane, A. and Matten, D. (2006). 'Corporations and citizenship', *Revue de l'Organisation Responsable*, vol. 1 (1): 82–92.

1 *Introducing corporations and citizenship*

As the world continues to integrate, reconciling the tensions between efficient global economics and local democratic politics will test everyone's imagination.

Financial Times, Leader comment, 13 June 2006

Introduction

The assumption that corporations have economic, legal and even social roles but, beyond these, no political role or significance, is becoming increasingly untenable. Although conventional economic theory continues to be based on a clear divide between economic and political domains, where the state sets the rules within which business must act, a blurring of boundaries between the two domains is clearly in evidence. Wittingly or otherwise, corporations are becoming much more part of politics. They are now more engaged in governmental and inter-governmental rule-making at one extreme, and in community level issue-resolution at the other. The social and economic fortunes of whole communities are subject to corporate discretion to invest or divest, and the power that corporations necessarily possess in these decisions has increasingly brought them into the political sphere. Indeed, global political debates about climate change, conflict, poverty, human rights, equality and social justice, among other things, rarely now take place without some consideration of, or input from, corporations or their representatives. They have even become embroiled in the expression or suppression of particular racial or cultural identities, not only among their workers and consumers, but also among other humans with no obvious interest in their products or services.

For some then, corporations should self-evidently be considered as political actors (see Scherer and Palazzo 2007 for a summary). In the language of politics, we mean by this that they are increasingly part of the authoritative allocation of values and resources. For example, if we look to one aspect of this – the design and enforcement of rules that enable societies to achieve certain preferred outcomes – corporations are political actors when they are involved in the design and enforcement of these rules, or when they impact in some way upon the values that determine what the preferred outcomes of the rules might be. The question then arises as to how to make sense of these roles, both in themselves, but also in the contexts of changing global governance and of the economic roles and responsibilities of business.

In this book, we turn to the concept of citizenship in order to make sense of these political aspects of corporations. Citizenship is widely regarded as one of the key features of Western political thought. With the spread of liberal democratic ideas, the movement of people across national borders and the emergence of various inter-governmental institutions such as the United Nations and the European Union, it has also assumed a global currency. Citizenship offers a way of thinking about roles and responsibilities among members of polities and between these members and their governing institutions. It therefore offers an opportunity to evaluate certain aspects of the political roles and significance of corporations, both in terms of their strategies towards governments and communities, as well as in their consequences for policies and political aspirations of people and societies.

Of course, there are various other frameworks through which the political role of the corporation could be examined. In this introductory chapter, we will therefore set out in a little more detail why we believe citizenship is a useful heuristic for examining the political role of corporations, and also identify some of the challenges and limitations that we face in bringing together what are, on the face of it, relatively disparate fields of inquiry. Perhaps just as importantly, we will also discuss why we believe a focus on corporations helps to enrich our understanding of citizenship.

Why corporations and citizenship?

Corporations are widely regarded as the most prominent organizations of contemporary capitalism. Colloquially, the word corporation is generally used to denote any form of large, private sector business, characterised by private ownership and devoted to profit-making. However, the term is specifically reserved to denote a company recognized by law as a single body with its own powers and liabilities, separate from those of the individual members[1]. It is this identification of the corporation as a body separate in identity from its members that forms the basis for an account of the corporation as a political actor. After all, corporate members are already denoted as political agents by dint of being citizens who participate in politics through voting and other activities. That the corporation itself can act politically relies on it being separate and distinct from its constituents.

Traditionally, political debates about corporations have tended to focus on their role in the 'inner circle' of power elites (Useem 1984), and on their involvement in pressure group activity through business associations, lobbying and political donations (Grant 1987; Lord 2000). Surprisingly perhaps, the corporation has more recently become much more central in social and political analysis. This is evident among social critics, who point to corporations' responsibility for social and political ills concerning the pathologies of mass consumption, disparities in economic and social development, and environmental degradation. But it is also true of those who look to corporations as part of the solution to these same problems. For sections of the political left, whereas in the 1960s and 1970s the culprits were *capitalism* and/or government, today they are more likely to be *corporations*. As such, corporations also now feature in the non-business sections of mainstream newspapers and in popular books and films about social and environmental problems such as Blood Diamond, The Constant Gardener, Fast Food Nation and Supersize Me.

This rise in prominence within social and political debates is in part a function of the employment, production, investment and wealth that corporations account for, and in part a reflection of their sheer size and domination of certain markets. However, although there are some features of contemporary business that are certainly distinctive, the history of corporations has always been characterised by shifting balances between the desire to bestow them the freedom necessary to achieve large-scale economic tasks efficiently on the one hand, and the fear of their power and the concomitant need for protection of the public interest on the other. Thus, there has been talk about the proper roles and responsibilities of corporations for at least three hundred years.

Why then do we choose now to enframe an analysis of the changing political role of the corporation by means of the concept of citizenship? There are, after all, other approaches to corporations which have addressed their roles and responsibilities based on stakeholder relations

(Freeman 1984) or social contract theory (Donaldson and Dunfee 1999), for example. Even within political science, there are other alternative frameworks that we could have utilized in place of citizenship, such as power, governance, or democracy. While our analysis does most certainly incorporate some of these other analytical frameworks, we choose that of citizenship for four particular reasons.

First, the very fact that corporations, consultants, academics and others use the term 'corporate citizenship' as one of several synonyms for the social or community initiatives of business warrants taking seriously. The prospect of corporations claiming, or being assigned, a political or legal status analogous to individual citizens is, quite rightly, a cause of concern for some (e.g. Jones and Haigh 2007; Palacios 2004; Thompson 2006; van Oosterhout 2005). In Chapter 2, we will investigate the appropriateness of this label and consider what implications it might have. Further on, we will also explore ways in which corporations might be considered to be citizens of cultural groups (Chapter 5), ecological places (Chapter 6), or global communities (Chapter 7). In this way, we can, at the very least, evaluate corporations in part on their own terms by examining them through the lens of citizenship. After all, when ideas of citizenship are applied to the corporation it is not as if the concept is meaningless. Citizenship is arguably one of the most longstanding and highly developed fields of scholarship to have emerged from the social sciences and thus provides a wealth of intellectual insight that can be brought to bear on our analysis of the corporation.

Secondly, citizenship is a concept which is expressly concerned with roles and responsibilities. More specifically, citizenship is an organising principle for aligning roles and responsibilities *among* members of political communities (i.e. on a horizontal dimension) and *between* them and other institutions wielding power and responsibility (i.e. on a vertical dimension). This is important because current debates about the roles and responsibilities of corporations are specifically animated by concerns about who the corporation should be responsible to, why, and in which ways that responsibility should be discharged. Citizenship offers us a way of working through these relational issues using a set of ideas and frameworks that have been well established in theory and practice for many years, as we will see in Part A of the book in particular.

Thirdly, and more broadly, the concept of citizenship is at the heart of wider debates about societal governance of which corporations form a key part. Thus, critiques of corporate power, for example, are often underpinned by a view that citizenship autonomy and choice are being directly structured by corporations and their agendas. Alternatively, there is the view that that these citizenship pre-requisites are being undermined because the key institutional representatives of citizens, democratic governments, are being undermined or even superseded by corporate power (Ikeda 2004). Yet more broadly, there is concern that the contemporary forces of globalization and the undermining of national governments are also inimical to effective citizenship (Isin and Turner 2007; Schneiderman 2004). Although this latter point does not necessarily directly relate to corporations, by virtue of their role as agents of globalization they are implicated in broader political debates about citizenship.

Fourthly, the uniting of corporations with citizenship in this book is not intended to be a one-way street where citizenship is simply used to help us understand certain facets of the corporation. Rather, the corporation is also to be used to examine the theory and practice of citizenship. At a time when our ideas of citizenship are in flux, and where scholars of political science and sociology have become increasingly interested in the role of markets, multinationals and other economic factors in the transformation of citizenship (Isin and Turner 2002; 2007; Kymlicka and Norman 1994), the time is ripe for a focused examination of the nature and impacts of corporate actors on citizenship. At present, the literature offers only glimpses of how corporations fit into the contemporary apparatus of citizenship. This book represents the first attempt to provide a systematic examination of the various ways in which corporations and citizenship come together. Of course, to even begin this endeavour, we need to identify at least some starting points for what we mean by citizenship in this context, as we now discuss.

What is citizenship?

Ideas of citizenship form the bedrock of our political identity, yet the very concept of citizenship is both fluid and open to question (Kymlicka 1995; Lister 2003; Parker 1998; Vogel and Moran 1991). Indeed, the meaning of citizenship within political debates has been transformed in the space of the twentieth century alone. This has been due to, for example, women's enfranchisement, growth in multiculturalism and changes in political boundaries and institutions. Thus, as Parry

(1991: 168) notes, '[A] totally uncontested and uncontestable concept of citizenship appears to be particularly problematic'.

Within the debate on citizenship there are, however, some underlying themes that provide some common ground on what the subject of citizenship is about – even if there is disagreement about the various manifestations of these themes. For the purposes of this book, we refer to these themes as *status*, *entitlements* and *process*. These, we contend, are the main issues around which debates about citizenship take place. In Part A of the book, we mainly concentrate on a relatively traditional examination of these themes as they relate to the corporation. That is, we assume that the location of citizenship is the nation state, and the main basis for citizenship status (and, in turn, entitlements and process) is legal membership of that state. In Part B, we explore various reconfigurations of citizenship that identify the location and basis of citizenship elsewhere – either in cultural identities, ecological spaces or global communities. We will discuss these two approaches in a little more detail shortly. Before we do, though, let us look at what exactly we mean by the three themes of status, entitlement and process.

Status is the basic defining characteristic of what it means to be a citizen. The matter of who is or is not a citizen, or what it takes to become a citizen, are essentially questions about how the status of citizenship is acquired and by whom. As Turner (2001: 192) argues, citizenship is both an 'inclusionary process' and an 'exclusionary process' that confers a privileged status on some and excludes others 'on the basis of a common or imagined solidarity'. In its traditional manifestation, citizenship is regarded as a formal legal status within a specified political community (historically the nation state) that in turn provides the basis for various rights for individuals, and presumes upon them appropriate civic duties. In its various contemporary reconfigurations, citizenship status may be based on other, often more informal, characteristics such as membership of a particular cultural group or ethnicity. However, status based on nationality is still very much the dominant mode, and is the touchstone around which alternative versions of citizenship are evaluated.

This brings us to the second main theme of citizenship, entitlements. The citizenship 'paradigm' that has been more or less dominant over the past half century (Turner 2001) – the Marshallian concept of citizenship – is essentially a citizenship of entitlements. These entitlements consist of three types – civil, political and social rights – which include among them freedom of speech, rights to vote and welfare entitlements respectively (Marshall 1964). The importance of entitlements to theories of citizenship is clear – they are the benefits we receive in lieu of our submission to a sovereign authority. However, entitlements are not just a matter for vertical arrangements between members of a political community and their governors: battles over the distribution of entitlements among members of the community – the haves and the have-nots – give rise to investigation of horizontal arrangements and allocations too. Indeed, even in contemporary theories of citizenship (which mainly emphasize horizontal relationships) entitlements remain to the fore, with Marshall's three types of rights augmented with additional rights such as cultural rights, human rights and ecological rights (Turner 2001).

The third theme through which we characterize citizenship is process – or more precisely, processes of political participation. This provides an active component to citizenship that is absent in the status and entitlement components. Acknowledging criticisms that the dominant, rights-based paradigm of citizenship puts too much emphasis on entitlements at the expense of duties, we include here some of the thicker elements of citizenship, including obligations to participate in democratic governance. By bringing in the Aristotelian assumption about duties of citizenship, to each other and to the polity as a whole, we understand the citizen's participation in politics not simply as a right to vote or hold office, but also as a contribution to personal development and to societal flourishing. Again, in Part A, this participation is primarily examined in the light of traditional ideas of participation in national politics, whereas in Part B, a looser framing is employed to take account of our three reconfigurations.

So these are the three themes of citizenship that we will use to orient our examination of how corporations and citizenship come together. But the coming together of corporations and citizenship is not, it would appear, a straightforward task. In this book we join the two in a variety of ways for a variety of purposes. Let us look, then, at ways in which we shall be connecting the two.

Connecting citizenship with corporations: the metaphorical, the material and the normative

In part, the introduction of 'citizenship' terminology from politics and its application to the notion of the economic form of the 'corporation' represents a move to the metaphorical. The very word corporation is metaphorical, referring to the idea of a body (from the Latin 'corpus').[2] Terms such as 'corporate citizen' are yet more metaphorical. Thus, when claims about corporations' roles and responsibilities are made in terms of citizenship, it does not necessarily mean that corporations literally *are* citizens or *have* citizenship. Rather it is implied that their identity or actions can or should be understood as being in some meaningful way *similar to* that of citizens. Like the term 'legal person', that of 'corporate citizen' is designed to draw our attention to thinking about corporations in other ways than simply as a nexus of contracts, intermediaries between demand and supply, and makers of profits and losses and so on.

In this book, we apply citizenship metaphors in a range of ways to the corporation. This is most evident in our analysis of the terms 'corporate citizenship' (Chapter 2) and 'global corporate citizenship' (Chapter 7). However, we also examine corporations as if they were governments (Chapter 3) and explore the corporation as though it were a political arena (Chapter 4). Again, this is not to suggest that corporations have become global citizens, governments or political arenas, but that they are appearing to undertake similar tasks and relationships.

This brings us to the material conceptions of citizenship. Although our study is in part concerned with the appropriateness and implications of metaphors of citizenship for corporations, it is also concerned with the material relationships between corporations and other actors, most notably human citizens and governments. Beyond the metaphorical, corporations have real impacts on citizens and governments that can be analysed and evaluated with reference to theories of citizenship.

In other ways our use of the term citizenship is normative. Clearly, most adult people do not enjoy basic political power and responsibility that would be envisaged in the conceptions of citizenship in any humanistic political treatise from Aristotle to Rawls, even in the more minimal conceptions of Bentham and Schumpeter. The reason is that most humans live in political systems that are variously unrepresentative, unresponsive, illiberal or centralized where there is no rule of law or independent judiciary. Authority, which citizens are conventionally assumed to possess in some shape or form, is exercised on the basis of power premised on family, religion or ideology, and is often backed up by the threat of force against humans who challenge this. Thus our attribution of the citizenship label to all people is normative: we assume that it ought to be the case. Although we do not assume that corporations are responsible for all people's citizenship deficits, our evaluation of the ways in which corporations deploy their power and responsibility assumes that all people affected *should* be treated as bearers of rights and responsibilities, or, *as if* they were citizens.

Corporations and citizenship relationships

As will already be apparent, the changing roles of corporations in business–society relations are complex and multi-faceted. Rather than cram all of these relationships into a single framework, we present three distinct ways in which the concept of citizenship illuminates business–society relations. In each of these conceptions, we distinguish different roles and relations for *corporations*, for *governments* and for *citizens*, the latter also including what others describe as the third sector, or societal non-governmental organizations (NGOs).[3]

The first relationship we explore focuses on corporations as citizens (Chapter 2). Here, we examine the ways in which corporations, like other citizens in democracies, are members of communities, claim entitlements based on their status, and participate with other members in political processes. Like other citizens, corporations periodically bring their interests and values to the formal governmental processes of law-making, implementation and adjudication within their political community. As Figure 1.1 indicates, in this conception corporations are on a similar horizontal relationship with other corporate citizens and human citizens. Like human citizens, corporate citizens are also in a vertical

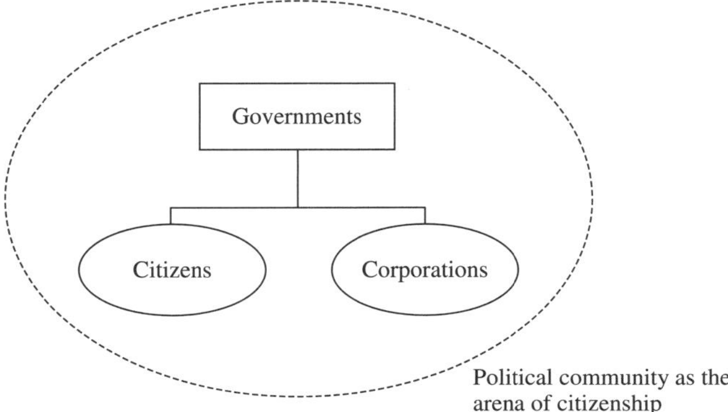

Figure 1.1 Corporations as citizens

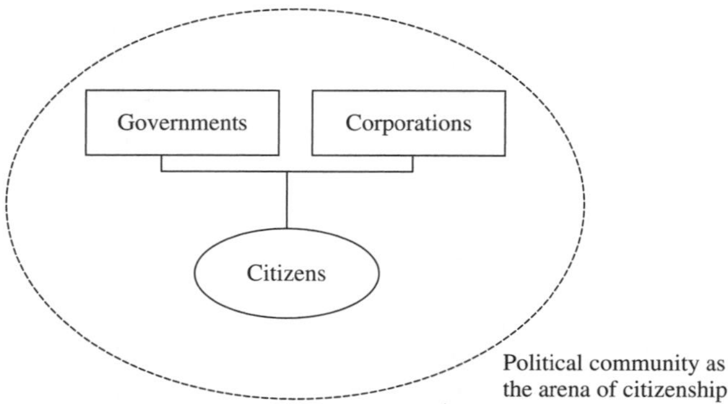

Figure 1.2 Corporations as governments

relationship of power with government in which the citizens 'author' the authority of government, most obviously through elections.

In our second relationship between corporations and citizenship, we consider the ways in which corporations are acting as if they were governments and are responsible for the delivery of public goods and for the allocation, definition and administration of rights (Chapter 3). This could either be in the absence of government, in substitution for government or to complement government. As Figure 1.2 indicates, in such a conception the corporation shares a horizontal dimension with government and is vertically aligned with human citizens within a political community. The focus here, then, is how corporations inform the status, processes and entitlements of people as citizens.

Our third relationship between corporations and citizenship introduces a rather different perspective upon corporations as it envisages circumstances whereby corporate activity itself can shape opportunities for corporations' stakeholders to act as if they were citizens in relation to the corporation (Chapter 4). Thus Figure 1.3 presents vertical relations within the context not of governing the political community (as in Figures 1.1 and 1.2) but of the corporation. The focus here, then, is on how corporations constitute an arena in which people can engage in citizenship processes, which may include engagement concerning the definitions of their status and entitlements.

It could be argued that our threefold distinctions are rather artificial. We would concede that, from the perspective of Aristotle they might seem otiose. Aristotle would regard these as mutually reinforcing facets of citizenship. However, for the purposes of evaluating corporations

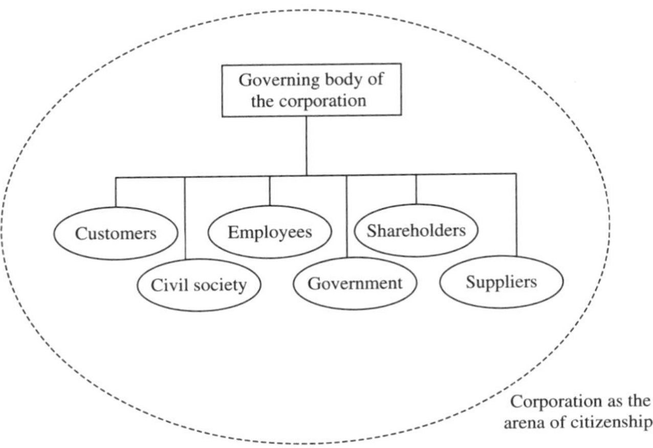

Figure 1.3 Stakeholders as citizens

this approach brings the advantages of general conceptual clarity in a field where this is sometimes lacking, and of underlining the political significance of our dimensions of citizenship when applied to corporations. By distinguishing the different roles and responsibilities that corporations adopt, we are better able to identify the dynamic qualities of corporations in context. As a result, our findings can be addressed to wider questions of the roles of corporations in democratic governance. Chapters 2, 3 and 4 develop each of these relationships between corporations and citizenship in greater detail.

Corporations and citizenship reconfigurations

As we have already indicated, citizenship is a dynamic concept (Joppke 2007). Our purpose in Part B of the book is to identify ways in which citizenship is being reconfigured and explore the role and responsibilities of corporations within these reconfigurations. The three chapters respectively focus on three such ways, through citizenship identities (Chapter 5), through ecological citizenship (Chapter 6) and through a globalized 'cosmopolitan' citizenship (Chapter 7).

In Chapter 5 we consider the relationship of corporations to citizen identities. Changing and contested identities have proved a potent source of dynamism in the history of citizenship and we find that this is also true of their relationships to corporations. We examine how corporations reflect, enable and inhibit citizen identities particularly through branding, marketing, employing or not employing, opening or not opening business opportunities, and providing products and services conducive or inimical to citizenship of various social and political identities. We conclude that, wittingly or not, corporations can play key roles particularly in informing citizenship entitlements and processes.

In Chapter 6 we explore the relationship of corporations to ecological ideas of citizenship and thereby to the status, entitlements and processes of participation that citizens enjoy in relation to the natural environment. It outlines the relevance of citizenship as a connection to place(s), and possibilities for citizenship to be applied to ecological communities, suggesting that ecological citizenship can be both about a reterritorialization or deterritorialization of citizenship. Applying these perspectives to corporations, we explore the impacts of corporations on indigenous peoples' notions of place, identity, knowledge and property, and the implications of ecological citizenship for expanding the stakeholder set to include non-humans and future generations.

Chapter 7 examines the effects of globalization on the reconfiguration of citizenship towards a more cosmopolitan model, and the role of corporations in influencing, and being influenced by, this process. The concept of cosmopolitan citizenship is applied to corporations in four main ways: through the role of corporations in driving globalization; through the role of corporations in contributing to global governance systems and processes; through global resistance to corporations in the emergence of more global notions of citizenship and civil society; and through companies' engagement in 'global corporate citizenship'.

Corporations and citizenship in question

It might be asked why we distinguish these three relationships and three reconfigurations. In the first place, it is because many contemporary accounts of corporations, whether academic, polemical or practical, whether pro- or anti-business, tend to adopt a rather uni-dimensional perspective. One view states that business is too powerful and has exceeded or usurped the power of states. Another view proposes that business has become too concerned with government and societal agendas and that this has proved a distraction from its main responsibility, that of making profits and all the social good that goes with it. Yet another view suggests that business is now being hounded by, often unaccountable, special interests.

Our purpose is to bring to light the different dynamics that lie behind these contrasting business roles and responsibilities and to indicate that they can simultaneously be true. The concept of citizenship provides one such vehicle for this and for consideration of the implications for business, government and society. As we shall see in the conclusion (Chapter 8), this approach improves our understanding of corporations, and particularly their political roles. We find that corporations combine roles which might in other contexts appear incompatible. In diverse metaphorical, material and normative ways they are citizens, governments and arenas for citizenship. They are also significant actors in the construction of citizenship and the meaning and values applied to it. We therefore improve the understanding of corporations, but without attempting to assign them to any easily applicable political category. This is because they combine roles and responsibilities without obvious comparators in terms of the sorts of power resources they command and the types of relationships they engage in.

Conclusion

In this chapter we have identified the main issues and problems that have animated our exploration of corporations and citizenship; we have set out our perspective on the core concept of citizenship; and have elaborated on the approach taken in the chapters that follow. It may already be clear that our intention in this book is not to present a single unified picture of how corporations and citizenship do, or should, come together. Rather, we seek to develop a rich and multi-faceted picture that does justice to the complexity of the political role and status of corporations. As such, each of the substantive chapters can be easily read as a stand-alone analysis of a certain relationship or reconfiguration, and do not necessarily have to be read in sequential order (though there is some logic to the sequencing). When we bring the insights that we glean from the next six chapters together, however, a number of key conclusions emerge. We could summarize these along two major lines.

First and foremost, analyzing corporations through the lens of citizenship theory(ies) exposes the political nature of many of the social and economic relationships of corporations within their wider environment. Ultimately our analysis suggests that contemporary notions and models of the corporation, in particular in management and economics, are simply outdated, or at least too limited to capture this new corporate role including adjacent rights, responsibilities and patterns of interaction with other civic actors.

Second, and directly flowing from the first conclusion, our analysis in this book amounts to a strong argument in favour of an explicit inclusion of corporations into contemporary ways of analyzing and theorizing citizenship. However desirable, problematic or otherwise this conclusion might be, corporations have become deeply involved in the citizenship arena, and any meaningful understanding of citizenship can no longer afford to ignore their role – as is currently still the case in much of the debate on citizenship in political science and in the citizenship literature in particular. Corporations, we suggest, are transformative of the very institution of citizenship.

Notes

1. In practice, the precise legal status and commercial activities of corporations will be regulated by governments, reflecting the public interest considerations of specific environments. Moreover, they are also subject to an internal governance regime, again reflecting specific rules and norms of a given business system, as well as industry requirements and company-specific factors. The various dimensions of this definition of the corporation (i.e. ownership, legal status, regulation and governance) have varied significantly over time and across national business systems. Thus, the concept of a corporation is not a given but is contingent, particularly upon its regulatory and cultural context.
2. This usage is not to suggest that the corporation is the same as the human body any more than does the phrase 'body politic'. The word initially captured a distinctive organizational feature of late medieval English government: the collective entity empowered to rule towns. It was also applied to early modern business enterprises to capture their collective nature and their public purpose, either when a plurality of businesses established a guild or when a plurality of owners established a company.
3. Our assumption here is that such NGOs are broadly reflective of and mediate citizens' interests and values.

PART A

Corporations and citizenship relationships

2 Corporations as citizens

Since its inception Diageo has been committed to building and sustaining its reputation as a good corporate citizen. Supporting this objective is our success in the public policy arena where we work with key government and industry stakeholders on issues that influence, protect, and promote our business strategy or impact our stakeholders.

Diageo (2005), *3rd Corporate Citizenship Report*, 29[1]

Introduction

As we have discussed in the previous introductory chapter, three types of relationship are relevant for our analysis of corporations and citizenship. In this chapter, we turn to examining the first of these relationships, namely the possibilities and potential for, and limitations of, understanding corporations as citizens.

We start with this aspect not least because the idea of 'corporate citizenship' has received so much attention in management theory and practice. As such, claims that corporations can be citizens or even 'good citizens' deserves serious examination. For many corporations, as our opening quote in this chapter suggests, it is quite natural, and indeed, reasonable to speak of themselves as good citizens. But for many commentators there are profound dangers in identifying corporations as citizens and especially in extending the entitlements of individual citizenship to such non-human, or even 'pathological' entities (Bakan 2004). In this chapter, we therefore ask whether we can seriously consider corporate citizens as in some way analogous to human citizens, and what the implications might be of doing so. In order to accomplish this, we will first provide a flavour of the current ways in which corporations are spoken about as if they were citizens. And then, based on this overview, we turn to key arguments as to why it might be warranted to apply the metaphor of citizenship to corporations. Thus, we examine whether corporations can enjoy either the status of human citizens in the polity, their entitlements, or their opportunities/ duties to participate in processes of governance.

Corporations enjoy great and, arguably, growing economic status. The question from our perspective is their role in political terms of membership of the polity. This involves analysis of the legal status and entitlements of corporations, as well as more philosophical analysis of the nature of the corporation. Perhaps most crucially, though, we draw on the political theory literature on citizenship to develop a framework by which the corporate participation in politics can be evaluated. Themes running through this chapter are how power and responsibility are played out through citizenship roles; the ways in which these are in balance or in contradiction; and how self-interest and social interest can be balanced. Some of the advantages and dangers of corporations being considered as citizens are reviewed.

Extant uses of corporate citizenship

Talking of corporations as if they were citizens has emerged as a prominent terminology in the management literature dealing with the social role of business. This has chiefly been manifested in the language of 'corporate citizenship' (CC). Although this terminology has been around for quite a while (e.g. Gossett 1957) we can clearly witness a substantial rise in its usage during the last two decades. This initially occurred in the realm of management practice. Having originated in US businesses in the 1980s (Altman and Vidaver-Cohen 2000), the CC label has since entered the language of the global business community. For example in 2006, major global companies such as Citigroup, Diageo, ExxonMobil, Hewlett-Packard, Microsoft, Panasonic, Pfizer and Xerox all labelled their annual non-financial reporting document as a 'citizenship report', a 'global citizenship report' or similar versions of the terminology.

Table 2.1 provides a flavour of the usage of CC terminology by corporations. First, it is interesting to note that 'citizenship' is often referred to by a number of attributes, of which 'good corporate citizenship' and 'global citizenship'[2] are by far the most popular ones. Furthermore, the overwhelming emphasis of these statements focuses on the embedding of the corporation into its direct local community and evokes notions of being a good neighbour (BHP Billiton) with mutually beneficial relations between companies and their stakeholders

Table 2.1. *Examples of corporate usage of CC terminology (emphasis added)*

Company	Industry and country of origin	CC statement	Source
BHP Billiton	Mining, Australia	As stated in the BHP Billiton Charter, one of the indicators of success is that 'the communities in which we operate value ***our citizenship***'. Sustainable community development ensures communities benefit throughout all phases of the life of an operation – through development, operation and closure.	Sustainability Report 2006
Manulife	Insurance and Financial Services, Canada	To Manulife, being a ***good corporate citizen*** is part of our corporate culture. We are proud to participate in various education initiatives and hope to help Vietnamese children have a better life and a brighter future.	2006 Public Accountability Statement
Microsoft	Software, US	Microsoft's ongoing work in the area of ***global citizenship*** is focused on mobilizing our resources across the company to create opportunities in communities around the world, to foster economic growth, and to serve the public good through innovative technologies and partnerships with government, industry, and community organizations.	Citizenship Report 2005
Total	Oil and Gas, France	As a ***responsible corporate citizen*** with specialized expertise and an obligation to explain the realities and constraints of our businesses, Total has a stake in certain public debates being conducted in France, Europe and worldwide.	Corporate Social Responsibility Report 2005
Toyota	Automobiles, Japan	Toyota's aim is to become a ***trusted corporate citizen*** in international society through open and fair business activities that honor the language and spirit of the law of every nation.	Sustainability Report 2006

(Microsoft). This includes compliance with local laws (Toyota) and contributions to the flourishing of local communities, most notably in developing countries (Manulife).

Citizenship seems to be a desired metaphor in the corporate world to counter notions of impersonal, bureaucratic and inhumane power-players and to replace these with the image of the 'good guy' next door who cares for you and looks after the interests of those with whom, as it were, s/he rubs shoulders. In some cases, however, as the example of Total shows, citizenship is also used to describe the corporate role in key debates in society and in influencing public decision-making on contested political issues, such as in this case global warming. These political references, however, are relatively scarce and the key orientation seems to be the local community. Toyota, for instance, prides itself on an eighty-person 'Corporate Citizenship Division', whose primary focus is to coordinate corporate contributions to local communities in the worldwide operations of the company (Toyota 2007: 66).

The proliferation of the term 'corporate citizenship' has not been confined to the corporate sphere. There has been an escalating body of academic work specifically dedicated to CC issues (see Andriof and McIntosh 2001b for an overview); there is now a dedicated Journal of Corporate Citizenship; and a number of research centres framed explicitly around CC have emerged, including those at Boston College in the US, Warwick University in the UK, Deakin University in Australia and Eichstätt University in Germany. Likewise, many consultants and business publications have adopted the terminology of CC in reference to the firm's social and environmental policies (Miller 1998; Roberts *et al.* 2002; Wagner 2001). This 'cozy consensus' around CC (Norman and Néron 2008) is also manifest in a growing number of government units, consultancies and think-tanks specifically dedicated to CC, such as the US Chamber of Commerce Center for Corporate Citizenship, the African Institute for Corporate Citizenship, The Copenhagen Center and the London-based Corporate Citizenship Company. In a similar vein, the influential US magazine 'Corporate Responsibility Officer'[3] – previously titled 'Business Ethics' – conspicuously labels its annual ranking of the 100 most socially responsible companies as the list of the '100 Best Corporate Citizens'.

What does all this mean? Are companies, consultants and academics really saying anything significant about the political role of the corporation when they invoke the label of CC? Indeed, are they really saying anything at all or is it just a new label to say the same old things? In our view, the usage of CC has been far from consistent and rarely very clear. In the following sections, we shall therefore briefly examine current usage of the term, and in so doing, delineate three different perspectives on CC evident in the extant management literature.

Limited view of corporate citizenship[4]

Initially, CC was, and in many respects still is, used to identify the philanthropic role and responsibilities the firm voluntarily undertakes in the local community, such as charitable donations. Carroll (1991) for example identifies 'being a good corporate citizen' with a specific element of corporate social responsibility (CSR), philanthropic responsibilities, his fourth level of CSR. We term this the limited view because it equates citizenship behaviours with a specific aspect or slice of social responsibility. CC in this sense is essentially a re-labelling of philanthropy or community action.

Accordingly, Carroll (1991) places CC at the top level of his CSR pyramid, suggesting that it is a discretionary activity beyond that which is expected of business. CC in this respect is regarded as a choice to 'put something back' into the community, but since it is merely 'desired' by the community it is, according to Carroll (1991: 42), 'less important than the other three categories', namely economic, legal and ethical responsibilities.

Many present CC's contribution to the debate on corporate philanthropy as one that brings a *strategic* focus. As opposed to corporations engaging in charity simply for the sake of it, CC presents a case for strategic philanthropy. For the firm, CC is generally seen therefore as fuelled by issues of self-interest – including the insight that a stable social, environmental and political environment ensures profitable business (Windsor 2001; Wood and Logsdon 2001). This understanding is close to the majority of the corporate examples given in Table 2.1 which is typical for the limited view of CC insofar as it focuses mainly on the direct physical environment of the company, resulting in a strong focus on local communities (Altman 1998).

Equivalent view of corporate citizenship

The second common understanding of CC is more general in scope, and is essentially a conflation of CC with existing conceptions of CSR, stakeholder management, or corporate sustainability, without attempting to define any new role for the corporation. The most striking example of this use of CC in the academic literature is probably Carroll (1998) himself who, in a paper entitled 'The four faces of corporate citizenship', defines CC in exactly the same way as he initially defined CSR two decades ago.

This approach has been taken up by numerous authors, although in some cases by using slightly different phrasing. For instance, Andriof and McIntosh (2001a) talk of CC as corporate 'societal' responsibility but use it synonymously with CSR. Similarly, in a number of papers, Maignan and colleagues (Maignan and Ferrell 2000; Maignan *et al.* 1999) define CC as 'the extent to which businesses meet the economic, legal, ethical and discretionary responsibilities imposed on them by their stakeholders' (Maignan and Ferrell 2000: 284). This is largely synonymous with the Carroll (1991) definition of CSR. Much of the CC literature currently uses the concept in this sense, stressing various aspects of CSR, such as sustainability (Marsden 2000), the stewardship role of business (Reilly and Kyj 1994) or drawing conceptual lines towards the stakeholder approach (Davenport 2000). In the corporate world, too, we can see that many companies have switched from having a sustainability or CSR report to a CC report with little evidence of any change in emphasis or content.

What we see in both the limited and equivalent views, then, is an attempt to use the CC label simply to rebrand existing ideas about business and society, probably to make them more accessible and attractive to various audiences. There is little evidence of conceptual development or genuine engagement with the political dimensions of citizenship. Furthermore, although in our interpretation those referring to CC in this way appear to be conflating CC with philanthropy, CSR or other concepts, few ever appear to acknowledge that this is the case. As such, we should recognise that for the large majority of academics or corporations using this language, CC has no particular political significance or meaning. As Norman and Néron (2008: 11) argue, 'corporate citizenship seems to have arisen primarily within corporate circles as a way of describing and praising businesses that "did a little more", that "gave back to community", or that "recognized the interdependence of businesses and the communities in which they operate"'.

Extended view of corporate citizenship

There is, however, a small but growing stream of the management literature that has approached the CC debate by taking the political nature of the 'citizenship' concept seriously. These contributions have in common an attempt to extend or enrich our existing understanding of business–society relations with recourse to political theory, even though they may or may not end up suggesting an actually extended set of responsibilities for corporations (i.e. they may still focus on philanthropy or CSR). Among the first to develop such an extended view of CC were Donna Wood and Jeanne Logsdon (e.g. Wood and Logsdon 2001), who subsequently directed their idea towards a richer understanding of the multiple roles and responsibilities of companies in the context of what they coin 'global business citizenship' (Logsdon and Wood 2002; Wood *et al.* 2006). Others have examined the potential, conditions and limits of the political notion of citizenship for corporations, with so far mixed results. While some authors share some optimism for the usefulness of talking about corporations as citizens, especially in terms of their involvement in politics (e.g. Jeurissen 2004; Moon *et al.* 2005; Norman and Néron 2008) others point to the limits of this venture and question the possibility of corporations as citizens (e.g. Thompson 2006).[5] There are also some recent attempts to scrutinize the language and concept of CC from within the political science field (e.g. Gerencser 2005; Moon 1995), and from citizenship studies specifically (e.g. Palacios 2004). Needless to add, then, this chapter attempts to analyze the citizen-like qualities of corporations from this 'extended' perspective – namely, we wish to examine the status, entitlements and participation of the corporation in terms of their political significance beyond the economic and social roles of the firm.

Can corporations be citizens with regard to status and entitlements?

We have seen so far that the label of citizenship is widely used for corporations. While much of this usage really has little political significance there is still considerable unease from among various quarters of the academic and activist communities regarding the dangers of extending the political status of citizenship in this way, even if only rhetorically. Moreover, it is clear that there is some potential for understanding dimensions of the political role of the corporation by considering them as citizens. In this section we therefore examine the degree to which such an extension might be warranted. Concurrent with our introductory remarks in Chapter 1, we will analyze this link chiefly from a

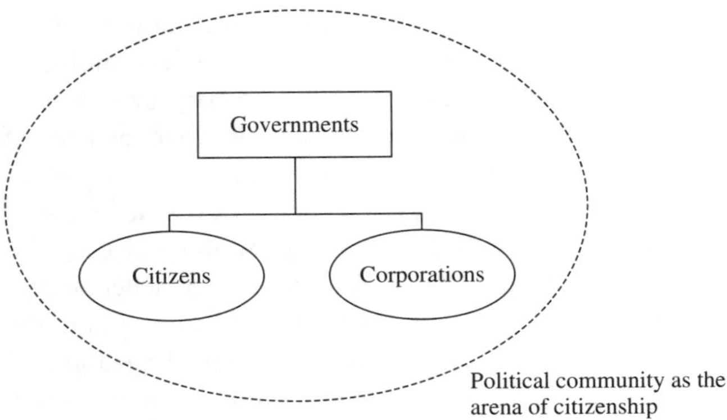

Figure 2.1 Corporations as citizens

metaphorical and material perspective and evaluate a number of arguments that might allow us to conceptualize corporations as citizens. Again, as we discussed in Chapter 1, the assumption here is that corporations are in horizontal relations of community with human citizens (and presumably other 'corporate citizens'), and in vertical relations of power with governments. This is graphically illustrated in Figure 2.1.

The key obstacle to following this route, however, seems to be the contestation that the citizenship literature seems to share the consensus that the 'subject of citizenship' (Yeatman 2007) is an individual human being. Typically, the political science literature, such as for instance in liberal minimalist theories, sees citizens as being in need of protection from arbitrary rule and oppression by government (Stokes 2002: 27–31). These theories are either rights- or utilitarian-based. Rights-based conceptions of citizenship owe most to John Locke (1690), who assumed that citizens have natural rights to life, liberty and property, and that these are the duty of government to secure and the basis for citizen protection from government. When government fails to uphold these, the citizens have the right to withdraw their consent. The utilitarian view is premised on similar expectations of government but in the absence of rights as normative guides.

Schumpeter (1976) developed a minimalist (and utilitarian) theory of citizenship for the democratic age (i.e. in which there is political as well as legal equality). He prized systems of representation in which citizens participate merely by selecting among elites who contend for office. The elites perform the basic functions of governing. He assumed that the very desire of the elites to secure and retain office would make them responsive to citizens' preferences as expressed by their choice of representatives at periodic elections (or, by extension, through opinion polls in-between elections). Although Marshall's (1964) version for the age of welfare accorded a wider set of rights to citizens, his model was still premised on the primacy of individual rights and the political division of labour between citizens and government which are both central to the liberal minimalist model.

From the aspect of citizenship status there is, therefore, little reminiscent of the corporation in this liberal conceptualization of citizenship. One way of dealing with this conclusion would be to just accept that 'it is analytically incorrect [...] to apply the legal term 'citizenship' to anything other than a natural person (it would be like asking whether a dog or a fish, or even a mushroom, can be a citizen)' (Thompson 2006: 12). While acknowledging that the concept initially was devised for humans there are still material ways in which corporations have some of the status and entitlements of citizens, albeit in a somewhat more limited scope – as we will analyze in the next section.

Corporations as 'de facto citizens'

Our first argument for admitting corporations as citizens is that their legal identity allows us to identify a status which essentially makes them de facto citizens. A strong but contentious basis for business both to claim and to be attributed a political role is their legal status. Clearly this varies from country to country and even among sub-national jurisdictions, and varies among types of business (particularly between corporations, partnerships and sole proprietorships). In essence, the point is that in law, businesses are recognised as being capable of acting il/legally and as having duties and rights of legal protection and compensation. Businesses can enter into legal agreements, own property, employ workers, sue and be sued. As a result businesses can be treated in the eyes of the law as if they were people and a company is therefore described in law as being an 'artificial person'. This enables corporations to be subject to the law notwithstanding the identity of any particular owners or managers by virtue of the principal of 'perpetual succession'. Although this status is in contradistinction to 'natural persons' who have other legal attributes, the point is that in law, a major medium for norm-building and dispute resolution among natural persons, companies are for some purposes treated as if they were humans.

In particular in the US, but to similar degrees also in other democracies, the debate on corporate personhood is long and contested. Gerencser (2005: 634), tracing the varied interpretations in numerous court rulings in the US regarding corporate personhood, concludes:

> The history of a 'person' and 'citizen' reveal that their content is on the one hand subject to change from political and legal contest, and yet at any given moment, often direct and clear – if sometimes outrageous.

Among the similarities between corporations and individual citizens are, for instance, that both can claim equality of protection and treatment before the law, trial by jury, protection from unreasonable governmental or political interference and harassment, protection from takings without compensation, the exercise of due process and non-discrimination. On the other hand, corporations cannot command a political vote or claim protection against self-incrimination (Norman and Néron 2008; Thompson 2006). Other issues have been hotly contested. There has been criticism that corporations have sought the protection of the law under the Fourteenth Amendment of the US Constitution, the entitlement to due process and equal protection of the law, which was designed to apply to freed slaves. Likewise, the First Amendment, the right to free speech, has been extended to allow corporations to contribute, as individual citizens, to election campaign funding which has been criticised as corrupting the wider American political system (Bakan 2004). In both these cases the critics of business judge that the power and interest of corporations makes them inappropriate bearers of rights that were designed for human persons.

While acknowledging that corporations, with regard to their 'de jure' status, are clearly different from individual citizens, we would argue that the status and entitlements of corporations gives us ground for a metaphorical use of citizenship. First, significant elements of their rights are similar to those of 'normal' citizens, which often provides them 'de facto' a similar status. Second, and closely related, looking at the duties flowing from such a status, corporations have to obey the letter and spirit of the law and are subject to sanctions rather similar to those individual citizens in breach of their civic duties would face, which again puts them in a similar status of membership as individual citizens. With regard to the latter aspect it is therefore no surprise to see that some legal scholars have shown much less inhibition to refer to corporations as citizens in the context of compliance and avoidance of illegal behaviour (e.g. Simons 2002).

As we will discuss in more detail in Chapter 5, it is significant to see that corporations, as citizens, also have a national identity. This can, first, be part of their explicit branding, as we see in the case of multinational companies such as American Apparel, British Telecom, Deutsche Bank or Electricité De France (EDF). Often, governments undertake significant efforts to prevent takeover of corporations by foreign companies and thus, as it were, protect their national identity (Norman and Néron 2008: 17).

Second, corporations actively choose which country or state they want to be a 'citizen' of. The fact that many corporations in the US are listed in Delaware is a reflection of the fact that companies prefer the legal status (in terms of tax and other legal obligations) this provides them; similar arguments could be made for companies locating their headquarters in the Virgin Islands, Luxemburg or Singapore.

Finally, we would like to add that to dismiss corporate citizenship just on grounds of legal status becomes even more problematic in a world where citizenship based on legal status within the political community of the nation state becomes more and more eroded, even for humans. If we accept that modern conceptions of citizenship have captured alternative bases for membership in political communities, to exclude corporations from being regarded as citizens just because some legal aspects of their status differ from natural citizens becomes somewhat less convincing. We will discuss these aspects in more detail in Part B of the book where we relate modern reconfigurations of citizenship to the corporation.

Corporations as 'quasi citizens'

Up to now we have discussed the potential of corporations being considered as citizens based on their legal status and some adjacent entitlements. While this mainly entailed us examining the vertical dimension in the relationship of citizens to governments, these aspects also have an implication at the horizontal level, with regard to relations between citizens. In the following section we will discuss several arguments that might lead us to understand corporations as 'quasi citizens' in this respect. What unites these arguments is that they portray corporations' human or social characteristics.

Corporations are made up of individual humans

From some perspectives, the idea of businesses being equated with human citizens makes a lot of sense. Indeed, when representative politics was emerging in the late eighteenth and early nineteenth centuries, principally in Great Britain and the US, the property requirements of the franchise tended to admit business owners along with other landowners.[6] First, in some highly commercialised jurisdictions, such as the City of London in the UK, there is still a 'business vote' which enables corporations to nominate non-resident voters from among their members – which can provide certain citizenship entitlements to a greater number of corporate employees than it does to local residents.

Second, since medieval times, many European business people had the experience of engaging in citizenship-like ways through their membership of and participation in their guilds. Such guilds provided systems of governance within individual trades as well as forms of mutual support. Although their significance began to diminish with the industrial revolution – in part because of the new forms of business organization, ownership, regulation and governance which the corporation heralded – their legacy is still apparent, particularly in the Rhenish model of capitalism (Albert 1991). Thus, the history of European business included participation in addressing the common concerns of those sharing a common trade and their economic and social dependents (Whitley 1992).

Third, and by extension, it could be considered a commonplace that corporations are part of society in that their members, be they owners, managers or employees, are also human members of societies. Indeed, it was on this sort of assumption that its early enthusiasts saw capitalism as a concomitant of political liberalism and a precursor to a greater level of human flourishing. This was because the free movement of capital and the operation of demand and supply principles would liberate business activity from the irresponsible exercise of power associated first with feudal, monarchic and aristocratic regimes and later with mercantilism (Hirschman 1977).

To conclude, then, we would argue that a business that is run and made up of individual human citizens can only partly be disassociated from these individuals in its responsibilities and interactions with society. While this characteristic gets somewhat blurred with regard to large corporations,we would still argue that many of the recent CSR practices in the area of community involvement (Brammer and Pavelin 2005) actually focus on the re-invigoration of this aspect of corporations. For instance, employee volunteering schemes target exactly this feature of a citizen-like face of the corporations, where individual employee–citizens become involved on behalf of the corporations in various activities to the benefit of local communities and the individual citizens therein (e.g. Muthuri *et al.* 2008).

Corporations can have a civic identity

Whereas many accounts of business organizations of the nineteenth century present Marx's images of industrial misery and Dickens' tales of sharp practice, there was also a tradition of industrial paternalism or industrial philanthropy. In some cases, industrial paternalism was underpinned by religious convictions of the company owners and in others this was expressly linked with the interests of the company (Cannon 1994). Industrial philanthropy was both built upon the genuine social roots of the business and as a compensation for the apparent lack of big business' community orientation.

In other cases, the projection of a human face of business reflected a fear of loss of community connection. As Bakan (2004: 16) comments, '[a]s the corporation's size and power grew, so did the need to assuage people's fear of it' in the wake of what he calls 'its first full-blown legitimacy crisis in the wake of the early-twentieth-century merger movement'. He illustrates this with respect to the way in which AT&T decided to present itself as a 'friend and neighbor' by using real people from the organization, including shareholders and employees (particularly telephone operators and linesmen) in its advertising (2004: 17). This is a recurring trend in the presentation of business as illustrated by the branding of companies and products with human beings.[7]

A further argument in favour of this citizen-like feature of the corporations arises if we turn around this – hitherto somewhat benign – perspective on the civic identity of corporations: corporations actually can also have a very 'un-civilized' face. Marx drew attention to the incentive structures in capitalism which set the interests of those owning great concentrations of wealth against those of the rest of society. This arises from the paradoxes of markets and market behaviours, unanticipated by Smith and the market enthusiasts. He argued that these led wealth holders, the capitalist class, to regard society, and workers in particular, as mere instruments in the competitive wealth-acquiring strategies. Therefore capitalism was regarded as inimical to the socially constructive engagement of corporations in political arenas. In contrast, the citizenship we are considering here would be engaged with social institutions and with wider societal values.

Our argument applies specifically to corporations technically defined, and follows Dahl's claim that 'every large corporation should be thought of as a *social enterprise*; that is, as an entity whose existence and decisions can be justified only insofar as they serve public or social purposes' (1972: 17). As several commentators and critics (Bakan 2004; Gerencser 2005) have pointed out, corporations in the UK and the US initially had to prove public interest if they were to be granted a corporate charter in the first place. The key point here is that making profits is based on the fact that corporations, through their goods and services and beyond, cater to certain needs of society and thus ideally are conducive to public good (Parkinson 1993: 24).

Whether beneficial to society or not, whether part of rather instrumental marketing and branding considerations or part of good intentions – corporations have a social face and a civic identity. Similar to other citizens, they use this identity to integrate themselves as members of the political community. As Norman and Néron (2008: 18) argue, citizenship can also be interpreted as a 'locus of solidarity' and it is exactly here, where the civic identity of corporations, for better or for worse, becomes a feature of similarity with individual citizens. We will also examine this line of reasoning in more detail in Chapter 5.

Corporations have a distinct functional identity

Earlier in this section we discussed the legal identity of corporations and concluded that companies can be regarded as de facto citizens in the way that they are treated as legal persons. Closely linked to this legal aspect, then, we can also see that corporations, like many organizations, are often treated as a person in that they are praised or blamed, they make deals, enter into contracts etc. This is because, notwithstanding the multiplicity of their human members, they are often regarded as separate from the people who invest in them or work in them. There is, after all, continuity of organization notwithstanding the coming and going of owners, managers, employees and customers. Moreover, the purpose and values of corporations can outlive individual stakeholders, suggesting that the company has a life of its own.

Extending this logic, French (1979) points to the fact that corporations possess an internal decision-making system and structures which are entirely independent of the people within the company. He argues that the corporation, and not just the people within it, are moral actors and thus the proper subject of ethical evaluation (French 1979). He illustrates this with reference to the evidence that corporations have intentions and thus undertake moral responsibility; that they have the ability to rationally evaluate their intentions and make rational decisions about them; and that they have the facility to respond to events and criticism by altering intentions and action. Corporations thus share certain characteristics with humans which require us to consider them as social actors (Coleman 1990). Given the relative scale of their social impacts this is clearly significant in the context of questions of citizenship.

While we can see that for legal and ethical reasons the assumption of a functional identity for corporations might be warranted, we might still question whether this translates into a civic or political identity in this context. If, however, we consider political activities such as lobbying, party funding or participation in legislative debates, we see that corporations indeed enact this functional identity in political terms. The internal decision-making structure enables corporations to pursue these political roles strategically.

Summarizing corporation's citizenship status and entitlements

The discussion on the citizenship qualities of the corporation thus far appears to provide us with a somewhat mixed result. If we consider potential similarities between individual citizens and corporations we have to conclude that corporations lack the formal legal status and share only a limited number of entitlements with citizens. On the material level therefore, admitting corporations into the citizenship arena would raise some well-grounded anxieties. However, as we have argued in this section, there are also distinct material commonalities with regard to the legal status of the corporation, often amounting to a treatment as de facto citizens by the law. Next to these vertical aspects we have also seen that – in a metaphorical sense – corporations are quasi citizens with regard to key features on the horizontal level of relations between citizens.

One of the key features of the citizenship concept is to exclude some persons and strategically include others in order to provide those included with an equal status and equal set of rights. This is where the fit of 'corporate citizens' appears problematic. While from the material aspect of citizenship, there is some similarity in the vertical relation of citizens to government, the desired feature of equality with citizens on the horizontal level leaves much to be desired. We will revisit these aspects in the concluding section where we address specific normative aspects of corporations as citizens. Before that, though, we examine whether corporations can be seen as citizens with regard to citizenship processes.

Can corporations be citizens with regard to participation?

As we have discussed in Chapter 1, to be a citizen does not only include status and entitlements (what a citizen 'is' or 'has'), but most notably also focuses on processes of participation within the political community (what a citizen 'does'). In this section, therefore, we turn to the potential of corporations being involved in political participation in society. We use Stokes' (2002) taxonomy of citizenship and democracy as it takes a broad view of citizenship, recognising that it is not only about status but also about 'accountability, legitimacy and participation' (2002: 44). Stokes also locates his analysis of citizenship in the context of democracy, which is appropriate to much contemporary analysis of corporations' involvement in politics. In the following, we draw from, and build upon, three of his main models of democratic citizenship – 'civic republicanism', 'developmental democracy' and 'deliberative democracy' – to elucidate different modes of societal participation, and to provide a more developed theorization of citizenship processes as they might apply to corporations.[8] Table 2.2 provides a summary of our discussion in the following section.

Civic Republicanism

Civic republicanism (Stokes 2002: 31–4) shares the assumptions of equal legal rights and political equality with liberal minimalism but it also prizes the public or civic good, rather than assuming that the public

Table 2.2. *Corporations participating in governance as citizens*

	Civic republicanism	Developmental democracy	Deliberative democracy
Nature of citizenship	Citizenship as participation in a community, involving obligations towards the public (or 'civic') good	Citizenship as a dense network of interpersonal relations in society for individual and social flourishing	Citizenship as free deliberation over public decisions in a community
Basis for citizenship	▪ Legal and administrative status ▪ Process of participation	▪ Legal and administrative status ▪ Process of participation	▪ Legal and administrative status ▪ Process of participation
Nature of participation by citizens	Obligation to governments and sharing governance with elites ▪ Pressure group activity ▪ Direct participation in governing	Fulfilment of obligations to society (rather than just to government) and enactment of direct relations to fellow citizens	Direct involvement in collective problem-solving on basis of equality and plural values to address complex problems
Potential as metaphor for 'corporate' citizenship	▪ Corporate lobbying of government ▪ 'New governance': business as partner of civil society actors ▪ Governance through everyday economic activities	▪ Corporate involvement with all stakeholders beyond the bottom line rationale for social flourishing	▪ Corporations assume deliberative role in society ▪ Corporations enable/open up to processes of deliberation by societal members; development towards 'stakeholder democracy'
Normative basis for corporate citizenship	Corporations *should* participate in societal governance	Corporations *should* align self-interest with social flourishing	Corporations *should* participate in civic deliberation as equals
Conditions for applying citizenship metaphor to corporations	▪ Corporations represent aggregates of human interest ▪ Corporations discharge accountability analogous to other surrogate citizens	▪ Corporations represent aggregates of human interest ▪ Corporations discharge accountability analogous to other surrogate citizens ▪ Reciprocal ties between corporations and civil society	▪ Corporations represent aggregates of human interest ▪ Corporations discharge accountability analogous to other surrogate citizens ▪ Reciprocal ties between corporations and civil society ▪ Corporations exercise self-restraint ▪ Arenas for free and fair deliberation

good is simply an aggregation of individual goods. Civic republicanism is often underpinned by a set of communitarian ties (e.g. McIntyre 1984; Taylor 1992; Waltzer 1983) or 'moral bonds' (Oldfield 1990: 148) that provide a motivational basis for civic virtue. Accordingly, it prizes obligations such as obeying the law, paying taxes, performing jury and even military service. Valuing the civic good and meeting one's obligations is described as 'civic virtue'. In contrast to the political division of labour of more minimalist conceptions, in this model citizenship is a political activity which both forms and expresses the will of the people and which expresses one's commitment to the community (Stokes 2002: 32).

Although corporations cannot share the entire set of civic duties, obedience to the law and paying taxes are clearly criteria of citizenship that they can fulfil. While tax payments would normally be a question of compliance – and thus a given – the framework of civic republicanism provides a more compelling normative lens on the ascription of citizenship to corporations. As one example among many, research on the oil companies Chevron and Texaco identified that they managed to avoid the payment of more than $8.6 billion US income tax between 1964 and 2002 by setting up a complex system of transfer pricing with their Indonesian subsidiaries (Gramlich and Wheeler 2003). Although perfectly legal, a perspective of civic republicanism would expose such practices as largely incompatible with good corporate citizenship since tax payment would be one of the criteria against which such claims could be measured (SustainAbility 2006). Indeed, the Director General of the Confederation of British Industry, Richard Lambert, articulated this very point in a recent commentary on tax avoidance by members of the finance industry working in London and claiming non-domicile status. He called for the laws to be reviewed in the interests of equity and reminded business of the social pre-requisites of business success: 'We need to be sure that there is a social consensus behind pro-growth policies' (Buckley 2007).

In broader terms, there is evidence that corporations are capable not only of recognizing public goods but also that business success is critically dependent on this and that corporations can contribute to their maintenance and revival. Moon (1995; 2002) argues that this recognition informs a shift from concerns with *internal* social pre-requisites of business captured in the managerialism of Coase (1937) and Williamson (1967), to a concern with the *external* social pre-requisites of business.

This recognition of mutual dependency is precisely the sort of sentiment that underpins Stokes' civic republicanism, which not only presumes the recognition of public goods but also expects the citizen to pursue these through civic participation. This raises the thorny question of whether and, if so, how any form of participation beyond the minimalist version of periodic voting can be achieved in modern mass societies, be it by individuals or corporations. A great deal of political science has been devoted to unpacking the concept of participation and, in particular, to thinking about its possibilities in modern, mass societies in which many liberals have thought direct participation either impossible or, in the case of Schumpeter (1976), undesirable.[9]

In the business ethics literature, however, there seems to be some optimism for corporations participating in governing, not only on a descriptive level, but also on a normative level. In particular the work of Fort (1996; 1997; Fort and Noone 1999) highlights the role of business as a 'mediating institution' in society which, next to, for instance, the family or the church, serves as the institutionalized social link between individual citizens on the one side and society and the public good on the other. As a mediating institution, business provides an environment where many, previously otherwise allocated, needs are met. Consequently, Fort (1997: 156) argues that one of the key responsibilities of business is to provide a non-discriminatory internal working environment. In a citizenship context, Fort's argument then would spell out the role of the firm as one of the key arenas where civic participation takes place. As the history of affirmative action policies or the example of the Sullivan Principles (Sethi and Williams 2001) shows, by providing space as mediating institutions, corporations can directly participate in societal governance, not only initially within their own boundaries, but indirectly reaching out to wider society in general.[10]

In our further discussion of the civic republican model of citizenship we distinguish two levels of participation for individuals and corporations: in the form of pressure group activity; and in sharing in governing.

Participation through pressure group activity[11]

Famously, Dahl (1956) extended the liberal minimalist model of citizenship by arguing that through membership of interest groups – or in Fort's terminology 'mediating institutions' – citizens can participate in policy debate and decision-making in a far richer way than through periodic voting in elections for representatives or even in periodic referendums on policy alternatives. Dahl assumes that since citizens form and join interest groups that reflect their interests and values, the groups become engaged in policy debates in order to represent their members and, thereby, become effectively surrogate citizens. Whilst Dahl still assumed the political division of labour, he argued that policy-making was enriched as it reflected much wider forms of political participation than that of the elected representatives and permanent bureaucracies alone. Interest groups enable a wide range of perspectives to be brought to bear on policy debates and allow continual political engagement between elections. Participation through pressure groups is therefore seen as a good in its own right.

This raises the question as to whether corporations, severally or collectively (through business associations) can, by extension, constitute part of the interest group world that Dahl presents as acting as a surrogate citizenry. If they were compared with, say environmental or other campaigning groups (usually referred to as 'promotional groups' in the pressure group literature (Smith 1990)) the answer to this question might be in the negative. This is because members of promotional groups are composed mainly of those who have no functional dependency on the groups concerned, but join because of their shared values. In contrast, corporations individually represent the functional interests of, variously, their employees, managers, owners, customers and suppliers. If, however, corporations were compared with the second main form of pressure group, 'sectoral groups' (Smith 1990) such as trade unions or professional associations, then the answer might be in the affirmative. Sectoral groups clearly exist only because their members have collective functional interests yet might nevertheless be considered as surrogate citizens in Dahl's original terms. Certainly some large corporations have embraced this view, sometimes even in their interpretation of CC. So, for instance, for a company like ExxonMobil it is part of their commitment to CC 'to engage in public policy debates and discussions with governments around the world' as well as to provide 'support to political candidates' (ExxonMobil 2003: 31). For other firms, such practices may be more an element of non-market strategy (Baron 2003). The key point is that we can consider and evaluate such practices against the criteria for citizenship.

There is certainly an extensive literature on corporations, individually (e.g. Grant 1984; Useem 1984) and collectively (e.g. Coleman

1988) participating in politics in which, like other interests, they combine expression of private interests with engagement in collective processes of decision-making (Getz 1997; Lord 2000; Vogel 1986; Wilts and Quittkat 2004; Wilts and Skippari 2007). There is also evidence that corporations individually and collectively have acted as pressure groups when governments have been reviewing the role of regulation in matters pertaining to the social and environmental responsibilities of business. A recent example is the Global Climate Coalition (GCC), which was built by about forty US companies and industry associations of the fossil fuel industry in order to fend off potential tighter legislation based on global treaties, such as the Kyoto Protocol (Levy and Egan 2003; Levy and Newell 2005). To illustrate that lobbying need not only be about opposing regulation, there is the case of a coalition of UK corporations, the Corporate Leaders Group on Climate Change, which lobbied Prime Minister Blair to introduce clearer policies for carbon emissions (Harrabin 2005).

While a framework of corporations as citizens based on civic republicanism would assign these roles to corporations, it would, however, also accommodate these roles in a context that establishes certain conditions and duties to such a citizen-like role of corporations. Certainly, the attitude towards tax payment of major oil multinational corporations (MNCs), as discussed above, sits uneasily with their role as 'corporate citizens' in this political framework. Furthermore, such a role for corporations raises some further evaluative issues, which we discuss later in the chapter.

Participation in governing

Whereas Dahl identified political participation through and by pressure groups as constituting a modern equivalence of classical direct participation, more recent debates in democratic theory have led to the identification and valorization of more direct forms of political participation in governing itself. Ironically perhaps, some of these arguments initially drew on experiences of participation in industry (e.g. Pateman 1970). However, there have also been more thorough attempts to retrieve for modern times the classical assumption that citizens rule as well as being ruled. Often these attempts have been associated with an increased individual level of participation in local politics and in national politics through the increased use of referendums or participation in public hearings on environmental matters, for example. In these cases, the political division of labour between government and citizens is maintained but the citizens avail themselves of increased opportunities to inform agendas and the definition of issues.

There is also an interest in collectivist opportunities for increased participation that do not assume a political division of labour. Hirst, for example, argues for associationalism, contending that:

> . . . human welfare and liberty are best served where as many of the affairs of society as possible are managed by voluntary and democratically self-governing associations (1993: 112).

Once again, we find evidence that corporations are participating in this more direct form of citizenship. We identify two broad ways in which corporations can participate in governing: (i) sharing in new governance in developed *political* systems; (ii) assuming neo-governmental roles within the corporation's usual *economic* activities.

The first form is in the complex relationships that arise in 'new governance' in developed political systems. Moon (2002) argues that this is in the context of governments seeking to share responsibilities and to develop new modes of operation, whether as a result of overload or of a view that they do not have a monopoly of solutions for society. This is often in the form of 'social' partnerships with non-profit and for-profit organizations (Moon and Sochacki 1998; Waddock 1988). Though some of these are premised on market and contractual relations (Cashore 2002; Earles and Moon 2000), others (which fit into citizenship models) are based on reciprocity and consensus-building (Moon and Willoughby 1990; Orts 1995; Renn *et al.* 1995; Ronit 2001; Seitanidi and Ryan 2007). These have brought non-profit organizations such as non-governmental organizations (NGOs), pressure groups or societal associations into governance roles (e.g. in the delivery of social services for which governments retain legislative and fiscal responsibility). They have also brought corporations into aspects of the delivery of programmes in such areas as economic development, environmental improvement or education.

Secondly, corporations participate in governing by sharing in the administration of individual citizens' rights, both within companies and, more broadly, within the boundaries of companies' external economic relations. We will discuss this further in Chapter 4. However, a citizenship lens also points to new ways in which corporations' citizen-like roles have become institutionalised internally (e.g. in the allocation of resources, in decision-making systems and by internalisation within corporate culture) and externally (e.g. in continuing partnerships with social and political organizations, in membership of business coalitions for business citizenship). Evidence of institution-building is taken as concomitant of serious engagement within the polity and thus points to corporate engagement in governing clearly beyond traditional philanthropy (Moon 1995).

The particular benefits of applying this conceptual framework of citizenship to corporations are that it accommodates a full range of social and political participation, and by predicating participation on obligations towards the common or 'civic' good, provides a means to examine the legitimacy of ostensibly citizen-like behaviour. While corporations normally are willing to participate in governing when it is in their self-interest – as the example of the GCC shows – a republican perspective would ground the normative basis of citizenship in participation that is enacted for the common good, even if it is not in their immediate self-interest. Indeed, under this model, a 'corporate citizen' would be expected to readily and actively participate in lobbying and governance for the civic good across a reasonable span of its operations and influence. However, there are numerous instances of supposedly 'good corporate citizens' desisting from such participation. For example, the current debate on the corporate responsibility for attending to escalating rates of obesity illustrates a common pattern. Corporations such as Coca Cola (which has enthusiastically embraced the notion of CC), have been seen to be extremely reluctant to readily accept a role in participating for the civic good when the political solutions are unlikely to be in their favour. Although many commentators have observed that 'the [American] sugar industry has its hands wrapped around the political system' (Revill and Harris 2004), the normative basis of the civic republican framework would demand that such political involvement was harnessed for achieving social good, rather than simply fending off legislation.

Developmental democracy

Thus far we have seen that civic republicanism envisages wider opportunities for citizen involvement in informing or even participating in policy-making and in governing beyond simply voting for those that govern. We have seen how corporations can be drawn into such forms of participation. Conceptions of citizenship within developmental democracy (Stokes 2002: 34–9) offer the view that to flourish, democratic polities require citizens who are highly participatory and who have very close bonds with one another. This is because advocates of developmental democracy, such as Alexis de Tocqueville, J.S. Mill and G.D.H. Cole, see participation as the principal means of personal and intellectual development as well as for societal flourishing (another illustration of the possibility of individual benefit being consistent with social benefit). Indeed Cole sees such increased societal capacity as an alternative to state administration (Hirst 1989). Thus, participation is not merely a manifestation of citizen obligation, or a pre-requisite of good government, but also a basis for individual human and societal improvement.

Interestingly, Stokes expressly identifies this developmental model of citizenship with corporate citizenship because it entails fulfilling obligations to society rather than just to government (2002: 38). There is much in the use of the term sustainability by corporations which gestures in this direction. In particular, we suggest that 'triple bottom line' thinking, with its commitments to social justice, environmental responsibility and economic development, is predicated on an assumption that business can and should provide a major contribution to society through a long-term commitment to social participation (Warner and Sullivan 2004). This is illustrated in Hewlett-Packard's conceptualization of itself as an organization which 'is helping people overcome barriers to social and economic progress' and is 'learning to compete better in the region [South Asia] and around the world' (Dunn and Yamashita 2003: 46) as a result of its engagement in the Kuppam region of India. This is not only described as the company's responsibility to the Aids-infected area but also in terms of the value that the Kuppam community will contribute to Hewlett-Packard.

The developmental perspective on citizenship contrasts to extant views of citizenship as applied to corporations, particularly in terms of the breadth of roles and commitments that a citizenship role would entail for the corporation. It allows a critical assessment of the relations between corporations and governments in that the notion of developmental democracy suggests that rather than delegating the responsibility for the governance of contested societal issues to governments, corporations as citizens can be rightly expected to become active protagonists in governance processes.

A number of examples of corporations living up to a citizen role in a developmental democratic setting can be found in the UK grocery retail industry, which has been under pressure from civil society for a number of years now. A landmark decision certainly was the voluntary initiative of UK supermarkets to ban genetically modified (GM) food from their shelves in the late nineties. This occurred in response to public anxieties about this technology even though the UK government still had not established any regulatory framework for the issue (Kolk 2000: 96–7). More recently, following campaigning by Greenpeace among others, Wal-Mart's UK subsidiary, Asda, has committed itself to sourcing only sustainably caught fish. As a result it has worked with civil society groups including fishermen's associations and the Marine Stewardship Council and has publicly promoted policies of withdrawal from the European Union Common Fisheries Policies to the UK government. Therefore, as well as working to advance it own commercial interests, it has sought to promote community interests and has engaged in wider political processes.

We will return to the question of whether the assumption of human flourishing within the developmental model offers a metaphor for corporations, and the compatibility of this with wider assumptions about societal flourishing.

Deliberative democracy

Deliberative democracy (Stokes 2002: 39–44) not only emphasizes citizen participation in public affairs but also assumes that they participate in a deliberative fashion, enabling them to better address issues of complexity, pluralism and inequality in decision-making. Reference to the reality of pluralism encourages scepticism about a single moral view uniting the polity, which civic republicanism tends to assume. Cohen (1997: 73) suggests that the outcomes of deliberative democracy are only legitimate 'if and only if they could be the object of free and reasoned argument among equals'. This is in greatest contrast to the representative model of politics, which is incapable of involving the citizen in the resolution of the complexities of decision-making. Adherents argue that deliberative participation constrains the articulation and pursuit of self-interest as well as contributing to individual flourishing. The citizen would become used to and good at listening to and understanding other perspectives (see Bohman 1996; Dryzek 1990;

Fishkin 1991). This model emphasizes equality, which raises the issue discussed above of the significance of corporation-specific resources in political processes. The model of deliberative democracy has recently met growing interest by scholars interested in the social and political role of the firm (Scherer and Palazzo 2007).

The model of deliberative democratic citizenship specifies a style of engagement which emphasizes a problem-solving approach rather than one based on a show of hands or a meeting of wills. The emphasis is less on the resolution of competing interests and more upon the identification of solutions through deliberative participation. In the literature on business and society relations, such a concept has been discussed for some time, though under different labels and assumptions. For example, in application of Habermas' (1983) concept of discourse ethics, Steinmann and Löhr (1994) have proposed corporate dialogues, mediation processes and other forums, to both involve citizens in corporate decisions as well as making corporations active and accountable members of their respective communities. As befits a deliberative democracy model, discourse ethics prescribes rules for a process of participation in governance. As such, the main criteria for those taking part in participative discourses are impartiality, non-persuasiveness, non-coercion and expertise, thereby underscoring the appreciation for individual freedom and autonomy in the deliberative model.

The idea of discourse participation has been used quite widely especially in environmental disputes, for example by the US Environmental Protection Agency (EPA) in regulatory negotiations (Fiorino 1995). One major challenge for such discourses, though, is in overcoming conflicts about values. On the positive side, they have the potential to enable collective decisions which are informed by the expertise and values of all those who are affected by a decision. The proximity of deliberative citizenship and discourse ethics from a business perspective lies in the fact that both specifically envisage the direct involvement of citizens in the governance of public affairs.

Ultimately, deliberative democracy also comes close to ideals developed in stakeholder theory, especially in relation to the term 'stakeholder democracy' (Matten and Crane 2005b). The actual extent to which corporations engage in the various participatory forms of governance in a deliberative way is an empirical question. Interestingly, the model does have a strong resonance with the call for increased stakeholder participation and dialogue. Even though this is advocated for strategic as well as ethical reasons, Freeman's expectation is that stakeholder relations should be on the basis of voluntary negotiation of corporations with multiple stakeholders on critical issues to secure voluntary agreements and, more broadly, that corporations should serve stakeholder needs (Freeman 1984: 78–80).

Corporations as citizens: evaluative issues

A number of evaluative issues remain for corporations to be recognized as acting in citizenly ways, participating in debates, sharing in decision-making and sharing the responsibilities of governing. The first evaluative issue concerns the significance of citizenship as processes versus citizenship as a legal status and entitlement. We showed earlier that the status and entitlement elements of citizenship only partially applied to corporations and thus it could be argued that admitting corporations into the political process is inappropriate for those without the requisite legal and administrative attributes. The problem with this move is that in order to accommodate the notion of increased participation in modern liberal polities, other organizations have been recognized as conforming to citizenship processes and thus acknowledged as surrogate citizens. This is true of pressure groups, societal associations and new social movements. The question therefore arises as to the basis for excluding corporations (which as we have shown do exhibit de facto and quasi citizen features) but not other collectivities. It is an empirical question as to the closeness of the bonds that develop among corporations and between them and other participants, which the developmental view of democracy would presume. There are, however, other theoretical questions which follow.

One argument for admitting other collective organizations to citizenship processes but excluding corporations could go that the former are essentially composed of aggregates of citizens and that the latter are composed of special resources and interests. If we come back to the example of an MNC such as ExxonMobil and its efforts to participate in the governance of environmental issues such as the reduction of greenhouse gas emissions, this problem becomes rather visible: an oil MNC has some very specific interests which could be regarded as opposed to those of other societal actors. However, the problem is also that many societal organizations whose engagement in governance is valorized by participatory models of citizenship do not reflect participation either in their own operations or, moreover, represent interests which transcend aggregates of individual citizens (e.g. the environment, religious norms or rights claims). Moreover, corporations also represent aggregates of human interests (e.g. of shareholders, consumers, employees, business customers and suppliers). One could argue, then, that corporations actually are participating in governance anyway in the same way as other surrogate citizens. ExxonMobil donates to political actors and parties, builds pressure groups such as the GCC or tries to influence public opinion through massive communication efforts (Livesey 2002). The key strength of framing these activities in a framework of citizenship as proposed here is that it not only conceptualizes these different functions and furthers our theoretical understanding of the corporate role in society but – even more importantly – provides a normative basis for evaluating corporate responsibility which the assumption of a citizen-like role implies, i.e. that corporations should participate in governance.

This leads to a second evaluative question, that of corporations' accountability to the constituencies or stakeholders who represent those aggregates of human interests. The issue of corporate accountability to a broader constituency than shareholders alone has been a strong theme in recent business ethics research (Cumming 2001; Gray *et al.* 1997). To return to our example, it is common currency that ExxonMobil was the biggest single sponsor of George W. Bush's presidential campaign, in 2000, but the fact that the public is still left to guess the strength of their influence on subsequent political or even military decisions in the White House exposes the accountability problem.

However, in order to exclude corporations from citizenship processes, one would have to show that other participants, such as governmental and non-governmental organizations, are necessarily more (or more able to be) accountable to individual citizens whose interests they ultimately might be said to represent. Given that corporate accountability mechanisms and tools are currently underdeveloped, there might be some basis for making this claim. Nonetheless, it is evident that many other interest and pressure groups, which might be expected to claim to be appropriate participants in policy-making, also face considerable deficits in accountability (Bendell 2000; Unerman and O'Dwyer 2006).

It should be noted though that these issues of corporate accountability exist regardless of corporate attempts to assume the metaphor of citizenship for their role in society. However, the notion of citizenship not only identifies and exposes these problems but would also provide a basis for assigning modes, forms and institutional arrangements of corporate accountability (Scherer and Palazzo 2007). If corporations participate in governance in the respective frameworks their accountability should be analogous to those other actors with whom they share in governance. Returning to our earlier example, ExxonMobil as a corporate citizen in turn would be obliged to account for the ways in which it lives up to its obligations to the public good. The fact that we know about their donations is due to the fact that these standards of accountability exist for political parties. Understanding corporations as citizens would suggest the application of those standards to corporations as well, with the result of disclosure of a far broader range of activities, such as lobbying or influences on regulatory processes.

A third issue emerging from the above is that of the private interests that corporations bring with them. Clearly, there is a business proclivity for engaging directly in the political process in order to press their case on public policy questions (Reich 1998). But it is unclear that this uniquely applies to corporations. In political theory, as in debates about business, there is an acceptance that participation entails tolerating some overlap between private and public interest (Phillips 2000). Again, the example of the oil MNCs in the GCC illustrates the point. The European corporations such as BP and Shell, which pulled out of the GCC in 1996, did not do so only because they suddenly changed their views on the issues. One could rather argue that, as the developmental view of democratic citizenship suggests, because they work in a dense network of interpersonal relations in society, they perceived that they could not act against seemingly well-established societal preferences (Pulver 2007).

Admitting them into the role of citizens then ultimately leads to a situation where corporations align their self-interests in a controlled and accountable way with interests of society. One result, as seen in the cases of BP and Shell, is processes of self-regulation, which allow corporations to pursue societal demands in a fashion that is still compatible with their own corporate interests and goals. An awareness of these conflicts of interests is reflected by the fact that many large MNCs, such as Vodafone or Shell, increasingly set up separate foundations which then have a higher degree of independence and some looser alignment to the immediate interests of the corporations.[12] While these foundations participate in the governance of key political issues, most notably in the developing world, being a foundation helps them to operate more as a surrogate citizen than just a representative of narrow corporate interests.

A fourth criterion for excluding corporations from the category of citizenship entirely could be their relative power premised, for example, on wealth, on the structural dependencies that they create (e.g. for work, income), or on their access to other key decision-makers (e.g. in government). ExxonMobil Canada as one of the self-declared 'largest corporate donors' to Canadian Air Rescue Services (ExxonMobil 2003: 31) shapes the administration of the public good in a manner that might even exceed the influence of local or regional governmental authorities in Canadian healthcare. Indeed, Dahl himself (1985) recognized problems with his own earlier arguments as he came to the view that businesses possessed such economic power that they could not be equated with surrogate citizens. Rather, in the same way as governments need to be constrained for liberals, Dahl argued that firms needed to be subject to democratic processes. It is not clear that Dahl's argument is conclusive. As indicated in his earlier work (1956; 1961), different political resources are efficacious in different contexts. In other words, corporate power does not always trump the mobilization of ideas; popular majorities, other coalitions and, moreover, corporations are often aligned against each other in policy debates (Vogel 1986; 1983).

Certainly on a global level, the example of the GCC is quite a good example of corporations finding themselves restricted and controlled by other corporations, if we think particularly of the transatlantic divide in the corporate take on global warming. Therefore, the issue of power differentials in civic republicanism may not be as straightforward as first thought. However, as indicated by the deliberative view of citizenship, it may nonetheless be appropriate to consider either the extent to which the powerful, be they corporations or otherwise, have incentives to exercise self-restraint, or whether arenas for free and fair deliberation are institutionalized. Again, we would argue that citizenship theory – though not prescribing immediate answers to these anxieties – nevertheless provides a conceptual framework for discussing these issues in a systematic and consistent manner.

Ultimately, these evaluative issues associated with granting corporations the role of citizens as discussed in this section refer to problems around the contemporary role of corporations in society – regardless of whether they are framed as corporate citizens or not. A framework of citizenship as discussed here, however, opens up the possibility of assessing this role in a way that systematically conceptualizes the potential benefits as well as the constraints of that role: it also ultimately provides an opportunity to apply duties and obligations analogous to those of individual citizens to corporate actors.

Conclusion

Our examination of whether corporations can be citizens, then, ends on a somewhat ambiguous note. We have examined themes and questions regarding the application of the term citizen to the corporation which we believe have been underplayed both by corporations and academics who refer to the linkage rather uncritically. In this chapter, therefore, we have tried to bring some clarity to the question of whether the extension of citizenship to corporations is justified and to examine the anxieties often voiced towards this approach.

If we think of citizenship status, and also about some of the key entitlements of citizens, there are material differences and reasonable grounds to exclude corporations from the purview of citizenship. In particular the classic, more minimalist, notions of citizenship would suggest that corporations are just too unequal to citizens to grant them similar status and entitlements.

We have, however, discovered that corporations as artificial persons are often granted some status and some entitlement which, on the material level, puts them in the position of de facto citizens. The fact that governments, in the vertical dimension of citizenship relations, grant them some rights and protection weakens the case for excluding them from the purview of citizenship.

The case for excluding them becomes even more brittle if we examine how corporations interact with other citizens on the horizontal level of citizenship relations. Metaphorically, many of the features of individual citizens apply to them and we tried to capture this by alluding to them as 'quasi citizens'. The civic nature of the corporation becomes even more pronounced if we acknowledge notions of citizenship which prize participation as a dominant feature of what a citizen is or does. Our analysis has not only raised a rich array of issues, tasks and roles corporations are involved in while participating in political governance in society; it has at the same time raised the potential of citizenship thinking to apply a clearer normative agenda to a host of activities corporations currently consider as part of their voluntary public policy of CSR activities.

Admittedly, in evaluating corporations in the role of citizens we have found a number of problems and limitations. However, many of these also apply to other civic actors participating in governance. Furthermore, we argue that citizenship thinking also provides a solid basis of addressing these issues and devising institutional innovation. On top of that, as we will particularly see in Part B of the book, some of the material differences between individual citizens and corporations are eroded in contemporary reconfigurations of citizenship theory anyway. We have seen in this chapter and will continue to discover throughout the book that the material arguments for excluding corporations from being seen as citizens become even less convincing the richer the notions of citizenship become. This is not to suggest that corporations should therefore be extended the status of legal citizens – in fact quite the opposite. The case for citizenship to be exclusively about formal legal status becomes weaker as our ideas of citizenship become richer.

In this chapter we have shown how one element of this enrichment of citizenship – participation in governance – offers considerable scope for accommodating corporations. In fact, in the final analysis perhaps this admits too much scope for the corporation in that it can become more involved in governance than any other aspect of citizenship. At some point, then, it may begin to look more like a quasi government actor rather than a quasi citizen. It is to this argument that we turn in the following chapter.

Notes

1. Diageo is a British drinks conglomerate, owning major brands including Smirnoff, Johnnie Walker, Guinness and Baileys.
2. We will discuss the usage of the terminology of 'global corporate citizenship' by corporations in more detail in Chapter 7.
3. http://www.thecro.com/.
4. While our terminology of 'limited, 'equivalent' and 'extended' views on CC, initially suggested in Matten *et al.* (2003), has been widely accepted we acknowledge other approaches. Recently, for instance, Norman and Néron (2007) have suggested a 'minimalist' and 'expansionist conception'

of CC, which substantially amounts to a differentiation similar to the one suggested here.

5. In our own first attempts at an 'extended view' (Matten *et al.* 2003; Matten and Crane 2005) we even concluded by arguing that corporations, on the whole, more resemble governments than citizens when seen from this specific conceptual angle. In this book, this rather radical extension of CC is dealt with as a separate topic – corporations as governments – which is the subject of Chapter 3.
6. In some jurisdictions this sometimes enabled business owners to have two votes: one where they lived and another where their business was registered.
7. Examples are: Ronald McDonald for McDonald's, Colonel Sanders for Kentucky Fried Chicken (US); Mother's Pride bread, Sara Lee Corporation, the Little Chef chain of restaurants, the Meister Proper brand (Germany) and the Michelin Man (France).
8. Stoke's fourth model of 'liberal minimalism', predicated on the legal status of citizenship, was discussed in the previous sections.
9. The literature here is voluminous. The work of Dahl (e.g. 1961; 1985; 1989) provides a good primer.
10. The Sullivan Principles were designed to assist American companies working in apartheid South Africa treat their black employees equally.
11. Whereas Stokes places this in the liberal minimalist model we place it under civic republicanism due to its stress on participation and engagement.
12. http://www.vodafonefoundation.org; http://www.shellfoundation.org.

3 Corporations as governments

Parliament is no longer sovereign in its decisions. It depends on powerful pressure groups – the banks and multinationals – which are not subject to any democratic control . . . Democracy has become a pawn to the dictates of globally volatile capital. So can we really be surprised when more and more citizens turn away from such blatant scams . . . and decline to vote?

Günter Grass, Essay on VE Day, *The Guardian*, May 7, 2005

Introduction

In this chapter, we take up one of the most hotly debated topics in many societies around the globe, namely the role of corporations in the governance of citizenship. The suggestion that governments have ceded authority and that now 'corporations rule the world', as the title of a popular book suggests (Korten 2001: 354), is by now fairly commonplace. However, it is important to question the veracity of this claim and, indeed, to explore its implications for citizens and for citizenship more generally.

The idea that corporations have taken over from governments is fuelled by a number of phenomena and at different levels. Recent invigoration of the debate, for instance, came from questions about the role of private security organizations in fuelling the abuse of prisoners in Iraq. In Europe, in a similar vein, corporations are increasingly perceived as being more powerful than national governments in tackling the most salient social issues for their citizens, most notably persistently high levels of structural unemployment (Grahl and Teague 1997). For instance, in the context of the 2005 French referendum on the new European Constitution, many critics of the constitution were concerned that it provided too much power to corporations through further liberalization of markets for labour, goods and services. Similarly, in many developing countries, multinationals are often considered to be more powerful than governments in upholding (or infringing) human rights, protecting (or harming) the environment, or accelerating (or impeding) economic, social and political development. Corporations, it would seem, are governing citizenship where once we would have expected this to be the preserve only of governmental actors.

On the following pages, we will take a closer look at this alleged takeover of governmental roles and responsibilities by corporations. In doing so, we will extend the discussion of some of the questions we raised at the end of the previous chapter. When exploring the potential of the citizenship metaphor for corporations we argued that under certain well-defined conditions, corporations could indeed act as citizens. However, while admitting corporations into the sphere of societal governance we also raised some evaluative issues, one of which particularly addressed the problem of power differentials between corporations and other citizens. It is one thing if citizen groups take part in the provision of certain social services, for instance, by setting up a bus service for disabled or otherwise needy people. It is, however, a completely different issue if a large corporation dominates the delivery of such projects. In the latter case, the financial and organizational resources of corporations bestow upon them a far more dominant role in shaping the way in which the processes of citizenship are carried out, and in defining the criteria under which such services should be provided.

Ultimately, by admitting corporations into the sphere of citizenship and having them participate in societal governance, the lines between those 'corporate' citizens on the one hand, and corporations as governments with ultimate authority over these governance processes on the other, get blurred. A social actor with the resources and power of a large multinational that *participates* in governance becomes increasingly indiscernible from the government as the ultimate and sovereign *authority* over these governance processes. In this chapter, we will examine in detail this aspect of corporate involvement in citizenship by asking, first of all, what exactly could be meant by talking of corporations as governments. This will entail an analysis of tasks, roles, intensities, scope and specific ways in which corporations have become involved in the governance of citizenship. We will then analyze the reasons for these shifts and identify ways in which corporations assume governmental roles in the arena of citizenship. Finally, we will discuss the implications of corporations taking up a governmental role, first for corporations themselves, but then also for the citizens whom they govern and ultimately for the governments whom they (at least partially) replace.

Our main emphasis is on the new obligations and responsibilities that the governance of citizenship might impose on corporations – and whether they have the mandate and capacity to perform these. Although we acknowledge that citizenship is about a symmetrical relation of rights and responsibilities, one issue that we do not directly address is the question of the rights that corporations might have if they act 'like' governments. It is not that this issue is entirely unimportant, but it is at present little more than a footnote to the major debate on the responsibilities of corporations towards citizens. As such, we will restrict our discussion of this to the concluding chapter of the book.

A citizenship perspective on the corporate 'takeover' of governmental functions

In Chapter 2 we discussed the participation of corporations alongside that of human citizens, in a vertical relationship of power with governments. In this chapter, we move from this distinction and analyze the idea that corporations can be on a horizontal relationship of power with governments, and a vertical relationship with citizens. Thus, rather than being 'like' citizens, corporations are regarded as 'like' governments, as shown in Figure 3.1. This, of course, raises the question of what governance role corporations are actually adopting over citizens if they supplement or even replace governments.

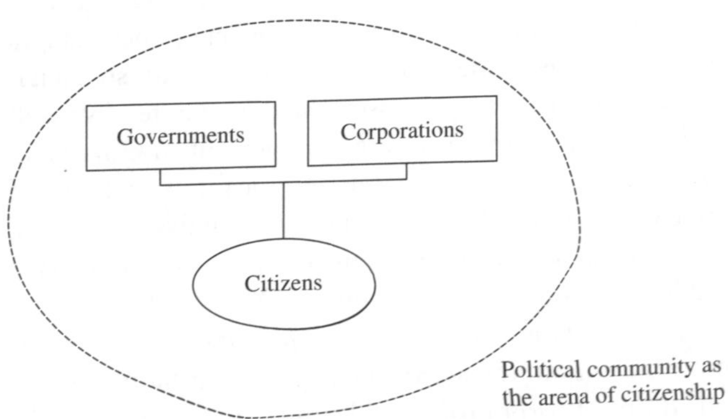

Figure 3.1 *Corporations as governments*

Corporations and the governance of citizenship

If the contention is that corporations can or have taken on the same role as governments as the counterparts of citizenship then, in order to examine the usefulness or plausibility of this contention, we would need to specify what exactly this might entail. As we have explained in Chapter 1, citizenship is essentially about three things: status, entitlements and processes of participation. Therefore, the governance of citizenship is basically concerned with how these elements are governed, by which we mean three main things: the definition, administration and guarantee of citizenship. When we refer to government we refer to government as a system involving law and policy-making, the administration of the law and policy, and the adjudication of disputes either about the conformance of any single policy with a higher law or about the proper administration of legislation. Different polities have different institutional arrangements to fulfil these function; that these have different merits is not our present concern.

First, governments, in their legislative function, *define* citizenship. This is basically established when constitutions define civil rights (and duties). Although in some systems constitutional change requires approval by citizens, governments formulate the alternatives and authorize successive definitions of citizenship in broad terms. Further down the line, and in the case of democracies through the legislatures, governments also make specific laws that define at which level and in which intensity certain entitlements and processes of participation should be guaranteed. For example, the government will issue legislation defining the status of asylum seekers, or on entitlements to unemployment benefits.

Second, the executive of a government *administers* citizenship. This function includes the executive in the narrow sense of the cabinet or ministers, but also includes wider governmental bureaucracies for the provision of healthcare, welfare, education, the military and the police force. For instance, the government will provide passport, immigration and visa processing services to administer the status elements of citizenship, just as it will operate a national health service to provide for certain welfare entitlements.

Third, the judicial function of the government *guarantees* aspects of citizenship, in that it allows citizens (and other arms of government) to address an independent body in scrutinizing the definition as well as the administration of various aspects of citizen status, entitlement and process. Perhaps the best example of courts informing citizenship is through the US Supreme Court and the European Court of Justice. The judiciary normally consists of a hierarchical system of courts, and may include institutions such as employment tribunals and small claims courts, all the way up to state, national and supreme courts.

The functions of government here are perhaps most visible in the arena of entitlements to what is often referred to by commentators as 'social citizenship', most notably in the operation of a welfare state. The notion of the welfare state, or welfare capitalism, rests to a large extent on the assumption that governments are responsible for ensuring that their citizens are provided with basic social services, such as education and health. As Kymlicka and Norman argue, in T.H. Marshall's thinking, 'the fullest expression of citizenship requires a democratic welfare state' (1994: 354; White 2003). There are different levels and distributions of welfare state provision if we compare, say, the United States with some European countries such as Sweden or Switzerland, which have provided more comprehensive coverage (McCraw 1984). These contrasts are even more dramatic when we compare North American and West European welfare states with countries in the non-democratic and/or non-capitalistic world, such as China, Cuba, Iran or Nigeria. Still, though, the notion that governments are responsible for a basic provision of healthcare, education or security is a fundamental trait of most developed countries around the globe (Hacker and Pierson 2002; Swank and Martin 2001). The existence of a welfare state in most modern democracies is critical to mention in this context, because its fate in most countries since the late 1980s suggests some fundamental changes in the way citizenship is enacted and governed throughout the world. These changes, we would argue, have a direct implication for the way corporations are located within the citizenship arena, as we shall now discuss.

Shifts in the governing of citizenship

In the modern era, and most notably in the nineteenth and twentieth centuries, governments gradually became the dominant actor in governing (i.e. defining, administering and guaranteeing) citizenship. This was as much true for western democracies, such as the UK or US, as it was for communist regimes, such as the USSR, and many developing world countries such as India and Brazil. In general, the relative importance of other actors involved in the governance of citizenship, such as the church, charities or landowners, declined, while that of the state increased. Corporations, too, which might once have had some significant if rather irregular role to play – such as the model village experiments of Cadbury and Lever Brothers that we alluded to in Chapter 2 – became less important than governments in providing for the social welfare and political participation of citizens. However, the starting point for suggesting that corporations are now more 'like' governments is the contention that this model characterizing the modern era is being fundamentally overturned.

The supposed decline of the governmental responsibility for certain aspects of citizenship can be traced through a number of indicators (White 2003: 3–9). One such indicator of the declining effect of the welfare state is the growing levels of inequality between citizens in many liberal democracies such as the US, but also in developing and transition economies. Given that the avowed or tacit goals of welfare states are greater equality this is a sure sign of a problem. Yet, the United Nations has identified growing disparities in income and wealth within many countries, including much of Latin America, Eastern Europe and almost two thirds of OECD countries (see for example United Nations 2001). The UN has also identified general under-provision and widespread deterioration of basic services in many countries, coupled with an inability to keep pace with even the most basic needs of citizens. Probably the most compelling evidence in a European context seems to be persistently high levels of unemployment, which serve to exclude a significant number of citizens (e.g. as high as 20 per cent in some parts of Germany) from enjoying certain basic status and entitlements. Beyond the goal of equality, then, the failure of welfare systems to generate such a major concomitant of citizenship, employment, serves as a further blow to the claims of state efficacy.

As one of the main engines of economic development, the role of corporations in contributing to, benefiting from and addressing these new circumstances are increasingly widely questioned. Moreover, the explanations for the decline of the traditional welfare state approach are undoubtedly too complex for a full rehearsal here. Thus, we shall therefore confine our analysis to three factors that have a direct implication for corporations and their changing roles as major actors in the citizenship arena.

The first of these is the *institutional failure* of governmental institutions to provide the level of welfare provision they initially built up (at least in developed countries) after the second world war, encouraged by Keynesian economic policies. However, in the 1980s most industrialized democracies in the West not only faced severe budget problems and excessive demands for social provision, but also developed arguments for choice and efficiency that favoured a more marketized (rather than status-based) approach to provision. These developments subsequently led to a gradual cutback in the level and scope of straightforward governmental provision of public services.

Beyond these economic shifts and constraints there have also been arguments from an institutional perspective of a more fundamental failure of modern democracy (e.g. Beck 1997b; 1994; 1996; Giddens 1990). These commentators suggest that while, among other things, the welfare state was a key element of the 'modernization' process of Western society over the last two centuries, we have entered a phase where governments are increasingly faced with the – mostly unintended – 'consequences of modernity' (Giddens 1990). While governmental institutions have been able to implement the logic of wealth distribution, they are intrinsically unable to serve as institutions that 'manage' the side effects of industrial modernity. In the age of reflexive modernity, as it is referred to, societies are governed by a form of 'organized irresponsibility', which leaves major ecological, economic and social risks unaddressed. As such, certain fundamental citizen entitlements, such as security and clean air, have been threatened, while citizenship status has been reshaped by technological incursions into privacy, reproduction and consumption, for example. As a consequence, we witness the emergence of a shift in the process of political participation to that which takes place in an arena below the institutions of traditional political actors. In this sphere of 'subpolitics' (Beck 1997c) such issues are tackled by a plethora of actors, including civil society groups and, of course, corporations. For instance, concerns over organizations supplying genetically modified products in the UK led to pressure group campaigns, consumer activism and corporate decisions to ban their sale, even though the national government hesitated to act.

A second reason for this decline in the traditional role of government in governing citizenship is of a more political or even *ideological* nature (White 2003: 8–15). Partly informed by the institutional failure of the classic welfare state, but also as phenomenon in its own right, there have been significant shifts in political thinking and practice since the 1980s regarding the necessity for 'big' government. This proved to be influential first in the US and the UK but increasingly so also in most liberal democracies and, yet more dramatically, in the former communist world. Though these views are held most intensively on the right of the political spectrum, there has been increasing suspicion of the idea of a welfare state and a government that is in charge of so many aspects of its citizens' lives. At the core of the libertarian model are private property, a free market economy and a limited state. In particular, the 'New Right', as this political movement is often referred to, is suspicious of taxation as the basis of any decent welfare state provision and considers taxation to be directly impinging on the individual's freedom and property. Consequently, beginning with the Reagan and Thatcher governments of the 1980s, we have witnessed a radical restructuring of liberal welfare states, thereby leaving significant areas of former governmental involvement in administering citizenship delegated to private actors, be they charities or companies.

Though not to the same extent, and arguably more due to practical constraints, the new centre-left governments in Europe in the late 1990s, most notably in the UK, have followed a similar approach. The thinking here, often informed and underpinned by communitarian arguments, is that the state is still responsible for guaranteeing basic citizenship entitlements, but that it does not necessarily have to actually run the services themselves. The role of the state here is to ensure that everybody enjoys sufficient access, but actually enables the provision of appropriate services by private actors. This approach has often been discussed and implemented under the label of the 'enabling state' (Cope *et al.* 1997; Deakin and Walsh 1996; Gilbert and Gilbert 1989).

Regardless of whether these shifts are informed by libertarian or communitarian thinking we have witnessed a fairly common trend: a substantial part of the welfare state provision and, in some cases even the guarantee of basic citizenship entitlements, has been delegated into the hands of private actors and governed by markets and contracts. It is at this point where corporations enter the picture: they are increasingly delivering goods and services which in the modern view of citizenship were clearly a responsibility of governments. And what is more, if markets fail to deliver these goods, citizens tend to regard corporations rather than governments to be responsible for those failures.

The third factor we see as contributing to the decline in the governmental role in citizenship and the emergence of corporations in vertical relations of power with citizens is the increased internationalization of economic, social and political processes, often termed *globalization* (Turner 2000). As we will explore in more detail in Chapter 7, various commentators have identified a decline in importance of the nation state due to globalization, leading to a reshaping of citizenship (Falk 2000). The status and entitlements embodied in the traditional concept of citizenship are linked to a state that is sovereign in its own territory. The central characteristic of globalization, however, is the progressive *deterritorialization* of social, political and economic interaction (Scholte 2003). This means that a growing number of social activities are now taking place beyond the power and influence of the nation state. In part, this development is closely linked to the rise of new libertarian political thinking that, in particular, encouraged liberalization of world trade, reduction of regulation for foreign direct investment, and increased economic freedom for corporate actors. But this is also due in part to technological change, particularly in the sphere of new communications, which have transformed the ability of information, financial capital, labour, and goods and services to be moved around the world at speed (Castells 1998; 1989; 2000).

The disempowerment of states through globalization is nonetheless a rather subtle process (Beck 1998: 19–25). Nation states still have governments with full sovereignty in their own territories and they retain considerable power to make and administer rules, extract and deploy fiscal resources, and exercise force. There have even been various attempts at re-empowerment of government, such as the EU project to 'lever up' government authority. Nonetheless, the crucial changes effected by globalization are that: (a) nation states are exposed to economic, social and political forces beyond their own control; and (b) actors within their own territories face increasingly lower obstacles to relocating activities into territories beyond the control of their original government. While the first aspect puts governments under pressure to provide more freedom to economic actors in order to secure employment and attract investment, the latter exposes government to the constant threat by corporations to relocate their activities where governments threaten to impose 'unacceptable' levels of regulation, taxation and control. Thus globalization provides an incentive to governments to refrain from costly and heavily regulatory action to sustain a welfare state or any other intensive form of governance of citizenship.

All three of these developments – institutional failure, new political ideologies and globalization – have common implications for the governing of citizenship, namely that governments reduce direct delivery of citizenship entitlements and that shifts in the modes of governance open up spaces for other actors, such as civil society organizations and corporations to fill. Since our concern is primarily with corporations, we will desist from discussing at length the role of civil society here. However, it is important to note that the changing role of corporations in this respect is part of a broader shift in institutional boundaries and responsibilities between the actors and what had become their conventional modes of operation (Moon 2002). Let us then look at the ways in which the governance of citizenship is distributed among corporate and governmental actors.

The division of labour between corporations and governments

There is a broad and inconclusive debate about this new societal role for corporations. While some contend that the takeover of governmental functions is a deliberate process by corporations (Monbiot 2000) others would suggest that we face a 'silent takeover' where corporations enter this arena reluctantly, often even without precisely knowing what new functions they implicitly assume by entering new fields of business activities (e.g. Hertz 2001b).

The first point we would like to make is that this process of governmental retraction from governing citizenship is a gradual process rather than a clear-cut shift (see Figure 3.2). Clearly, in certain functions, such as core elements of policing, the military and key political functions of governing, governments still generally remain the central, and often the sole, actor. The exceptions here are where corporations find themselves unable to rely on governmental sources of security and are obliged to provide their own security systems for their operations and personnel as is the case for Shell in Nigeria. In other cases of core governmental responsibilities, issues such as immigration, climate change, or the perceived threat of global terrorism, there is evidence that the roles of governments have even become more pronounced.

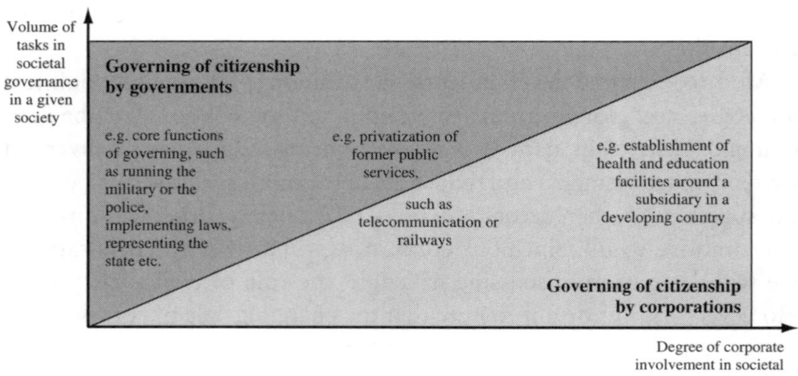

Figure 3.2 Division of labour between business and governments in governing citizenship

In other areas, though, such as the privatization of key welfare state elements, we see a gradual shift towards growing corporate involvement. In this case, corporations tend to focus on the administration of citizenship while governments still set targets and supervise the process. Again, in many respects, governmental roles here have become more pronounced because, while outsourcing the delivery function of governing citizenship, governments in many areas tightly regulate these privatized services. Thus, where telecommunications have been privatized such that governments no longer deliver such services, governments have also introduced a great deal of new legislation to govern the new telecommunication markets (Majone 1997). Likewise where new markets for social care have been introduced, governments have introduced new rules to govern these and maintained fiscal outlays to sustain them (Earles and Moon 2000). In other cases, governments have even re-regulated areas where deregulation did not provide the desired outcomes. An example for this is the approach the British government has taken to private rail transportation in the UK over the last decade.

The examples of corporations replacing governments entirely are, however, a fairly rare phenomenon. The closest examples we would suggest at this stage are 'company towns' or situations where corporations establish systems of health and education provision in developing countries. More generally, though, although governments have maintained or even increased regulation and fiscal outlays in many developed countries, they have transferred delivery responsibilities to other actors, including corporations, who at least take an increased share in the governance of the respective policy areas.

The transition of governing citizenship from governments to corporations thus can be thought of in terms of a continuum where different modes of sharing in governing between the two parties occur (see again Figure 3.2). Such transitions are often rather country, sector and even firm specific. If a company, such as Nike in Thailand, seeks to protect labour rights (e.g. by limiting working hours, paying living wages, preventing discrimination, enabling freedom of association) it is clearly involved in the administration function of governance. In the absence of governmental regulation (or the enforcement of it), such a role, however, could also entail the definition and the guaranteeing functions of governance, for example by designing a code that sets out basic entitlements (i.e. definition), and by implementing auditing, verifying and ensuring other compliance measures to prevent violations of the code (guaranteeing). We would posit, however, that in most cases corporations will become involved mostly in administering citizenship while defining and guaranteeing citizenship still largely remains in the hands of the government, particularly in more developed systems. Finally, there are only a limited number of cases imaginable where corporations become involved only in the definition and guarantee of citizenship, such as in cases of extreme state capture.

Modes and mechanisms of corporate involvement in governance

The shifts in the division of labour in governance identified above are part and parcel of the continual reshaping of citizenship relations through history. Governments have not always been the main counterpart to citizens, but clearly became so in the past two centuries or so. It is important, therefore, to identify how the current transition in the governing of citizenship has taken place and what its implications are for corporations. In the following, then, we will examine the modes and mechanisms by which this change is, or could be, occurring and posit three different ways in which governmental and corporate roles in governing citizenship are changing.

First, corporations might become involved in governing citizenship where *government ceases to do so*. This situation mostly occurs as a result of institutional failure and new political ideology in liberal

Table 3.1. *Modes and mechanisms of corporations becoming actively involved in governing citizenship*

Mechanisms of corporations becoming actively involved in governing citizenship	Key situations in which corporations are confronted with the governing of citizenship		
	Entitlements	Status	Process
1. Governments cease to govern citizenship	• Privatization of public services • Providing elements of a former welfare system by outsourcing of services or direct investment • Corporate philanthropy in areas such as healthcare, education, public services	• Violation of civil rights by governments in developing countries* • Cut down on regulation and/or subsidies for 'old' industries in developed countries (e.g. coal, steel, agriculture, manufacturing) faces corporations with redundancy decisions • Privatization of public services (e.g. prison management, policing)	• Influence of political decision-makers through, e.g. lobbying, party funding • Boycotts and other forms of civil protest targeted at corporations
2. Citizenship has not been governed as yet	• Working conditions in developing countries • Provision of basic social services in developing countries	• Civil rights infringements in developing countries • Use of new technology such as information technology or biotechnology which have an impact on basic protections	• Lobbying by civil society in the home country to take political action in host countries • Creation and sustaining of background institutions in developing countries

3. Governing of citizenship on a transnational level is beyond reach for nation state governments	• Negotiations on conditions for foreign direct investment with competing host countries ('race to the bottom') • Regulation by global bodies, e.g. WTO, GATT etc which have a direct impact on social entitlements	• Direct governing of basic protections, e.g. in global financial markets • Regulation by global bodies, e.g. WTO, GATT etc which have a direct impact on civil rights	• Private regulation by global bodies • Regulation by global bodies, e.g. WTO, GATT etc which have a direct impact on political participation

* By the term 'developing country' we do not necessarily confine ourselves to third world countries but all countries which do not dispose of a political system of a longstanding liberal democracy.

democracies, and in the shift from communist to capitalist systems in transitional economies. For example, in some Eastern bloc countries, a whole host of social and economic entitlements that were once provided and guaranteed by the state have fallen into an 'institutional void' that in many instances is only sustained by foreign direct investment from overseas corporations.

Second, corporations become active in the citizenship arena where *government has not as yet assumed the task of governing*. Historically, this was the situation that gave rise to paternalistic employee welfare programs by wealthy industrialists in the nineteenth century. More recently, exposure to this situation for multinationals is particularly a result of globalization, where lack of local governance in developing countries presents corporations with a choice as to whether to step in as 'surrogate' governments.

Third, corporations become involved where the governing of citizenship is *beyond the reach of the nation state government*. These situations are a result of the globalization of business activities, increasing liberalization and deregulation of global economic processes, and escalations in trans-border activity by corporations.

As we shall now see, each of these contexts brings forth a range of mechanisms through which corporations might take over the governing of citizenship, most notably in terms of entitlements, but also in the context of civil rights (status) and processes of political participation (process). An overview can be found in Table 3.1, and more detailed discussion follows below.

Where governments cease to govern citizenship

Where governments cease to govern citizenship, this leaves open space for corporations to enter (or not enter) the arena of citizenship. This may happen in two ways: (a) either corporations have the opportunity (or are encouraged) to step in where once only governments acted or (b) corporations are already active in the territory concerned, and therefore their role becomes more pronounced as governments retreat.

In the area of *entitlements*, we see corporations increasingly active in the takeover of formerly public services, such as energy, water, transport, postal services, healthcare or education (Crouch 2003; Moon 1999). With the UK and New Zealand taking the leading role, this development has meanwhile spread throughout most liberal democracies of the West including European countries with a strong traditional emphasis on the welfare state (Grahl and Teague 1997; Green-Pedersen 2002). This can either be the case in terms of a total privatization, as with telecommunications in most countries, or mixed forms of public–private partnerships up to partial privatization, where the government still sets the policies and goals while the operative implementation of the policies is sourced out to private companies (Wettenhall 2001). Furthermore, in an increasing number of instances in local communities, corporations have been encouraged to step in to attend to those 'positive' rights that governmental actors have retreated from, either through the mechanism of privatisation or welfare reform (Harding *et al.* 2000). In fact, many so-called 'corporate citizenship' initiatives are fundamentally equivalent to corporate philanthropy and targeted at reinvigorating (or replacing) the welfare state, such as improving deprived schools and neighbourhoods (see David 2000), sponsoring university education or the arts, or setting up foundations for health research.

In the area of *status*, most developed countries arguably provide their citizens with reasonable protection of their status and civil rights. Governmental failure, however, might become visible in developing or transforming countries (e.g. Kline 2005: 44–85). In Nigeria, for example, Shell was implicated in the failure of the state to maintain the protection of the civil rights of the Ogoni people (see Wheeler *et al.* 2002). Suggestions that corporations should 'step in' when the status of citizens is threatened indicates that, where corporations are already active in some way in a territory, government retraction of protection might conceivably be partially offset by corporate action.

Other common areas, particularly in the developed world, where corporations might be directly involved in defining the degree to which citizens can claim citizenship status, result from the downsizing of traditional industries, such as coal mining, steel production or certain areas of manufacturing. As a result, say, of owning property, or taking part in labour and product markets, even though governments may conventionally have taken responsibility for protecting employment through regional economic policy, corporations also assume new responsibilities (Dawkins 2002; Moon 1991; Moon and Sochacki 1996; Moore *et al.* 1985).

In these situations, rather than governments retaining responsibility, decisions may be effectively made by corporations (through their investment or divestment decisions) that determine the economic fate of local suppliers, the local economy, even the level of house prices, and more generally, the economic prosperity of entire regions (Hopkins and Hopkins 1999).

Another particularly delicate area of corporate involvement in civil rights is the growing number of attempts in the US and Europe to privatize parts of their correctional and security services, such as prisons (Chang and Thompkins 2002) and traffic regulation (Cope *et al.* 1997). We will come back to this area later in the chapter since corporate involvement in issues such as freedom of movement, speech, information etc. epitomizes many of the anxieties that this corporate takeover of governance raises.

In the area of *processes* of political participation, the corporate role is actually rather more indirect. Corporations might help to facilitate, enable, or block certain political processes in society, rather than directly taking over formerly governmental prerogatives (Jacobs *et al.* 1991; Sethi 1982). At one level, as we saw in the previous chapter, corporate influence through lobbying and party funding has established corporations as more or less officially accepted players in the arena of political participation (Lord 2000). More significantly, we can see that voter apathy in national elections in many industrialized countries has increasingly weakened the government's role as the sole conduit through which political choices and demands have been channelled. In contrast, there appears to be a growing willingness on the part of individuals to participate in political action *aimed at corporations rather than at governments* (Hertz 2001a; 2004). Whether through anti-corporate protests, consumer boycotts, or other forms of action outside of the usual political arena, individual citizens have increasingly sought to effect political participation by leveraging the power (or vulnerability) of corporations (see for example, Micheletti *et al.*, 2004). Hence, rather than replacing governments, corporations here could be said to have provided an additional conduit (or another node in an existing conduit) through which citizens could engage in the process of participation. This theme will be taken up more comprehensively in our analysis of the third relationship of corporations to citizenship in Chapter 4.

Where citizenship has not yet been governed

The second way in which corporations can enter the arena of citizenship in a way that is similar to government is where government has not as yet assumed the governance of citizenship. Historically, this was obviously the situation that many early corporations might have found themselves in prior to the twentieth century. Thus, through the welfare state governments assumed responsibilities which some companies had assumed for their workers, customers and communities through, for example, housing, recreational facilities, or education. More recently, this has particularly been a situation in developing countries. Globalization raises awareness of these 'vacuums' and exposes Western multinational corporations (MNCs), in particular, to charges that they are 'responsible' in some way for governing aspects of citizenship in such situations. This is because in the absence of a viable governmental role, corporations become a kind of 'default option' for governing citizenship. More recently, Chinese companies in Africa have been held responsible for failures regarding health and safety at work and wages much to the surprise of Chinese policy-makers (Kurlantzick 2007).

In the area of *entitlements* we have already seen that improving working conditions in sweatshops, ensuring employees a living wage, and financing the schooling of child labourers, are all activities in which corporations such as Nike, Adidas, Levi Strauss and others have engaged. Here, involvement in citizenship arises from MNCs outsourcing policies or foreign direct investment decisions. There is also an increasing number of examples where corporations are considered to be responsible for providing basic social services beyond their immediate stakeholders in these countries (Hippert 2002). This is mirrored by the debate on the TRIPS agreement and whether large pharmaceutical companies have an obligation to provide drugs for free (or at an affordable price level) to developing countries just because they are the only actors who can immediately address these issues because of government inability or reluctance to do so (Dunfee 2005; Werhane and Gorman 2005).[1]

In the area of *status*, corporations might play a crucial role in either encouraging (or discouraging) oppressive regimes to offer genuine citizenship status to their people, perhaps because the corporation's very presence in the country already assumes some form of enabling relationship with the government. Questions about the presence of multinationals in South Africa during the apartheid era illustrated that arguments could be made both for and against corporations having a more positive role in promoting civil rights, for example through accordance with the Sullivan Principles (Donaldson 1989). Similar discussions have since arisen over the presence of multinationals in Burma, Chad, Uganda and Sudan (Kline 2005).

Another growing area where civil rights and other status issues are touched upon (in particular, issues of privacy and the protection of basic freedoms), is the emergence of new technologies, such as information technology or biotechnology. The protections that might be involved here for citizens have not been undertaken to any major extent by governments simply because the issues are new, the consequences yet unknown, and they involve complex ethical debates. Nevertheless, in areas such as genetic engineering or stem cell research, which can have massive implications on life choices of citizens, we find that corporations are increasingly in the situation to make critical decisions of governance long before governments have developed appropriate regulatory interventions. American information technology (IT) companies have found that as a condition of operating in China, they have become implicated in policing free expression as they have had to share information on the identity of dissidents with the government (Crane and Matten 2007: 484–5).

Similarly, in *processes* of political participation, corporations can potentially be seen as a default option in the face of governmental inability (or unwillingness) to protect basic civil rights. For instance, in the case of Aboriginal land rights in Australia, it was corporations, long before the Australian government, that tried to involve Aborigines in complex deliberations about their claims to sacred places and to address contestations on land ownership. The Ogoni people in Nigeria, largely disenfranchised and marginalized by the Nigerian government, used the Western MNC Royal Dutch Shell as a conduit to alert the wider public to the infringement of their minority rights. We will discuss this aspect of corporate involvement in political participation in more detail in Chapter 5.

Where governing of citizenship may be beyond the reach of the nation state government

A third scenario that may emerge on the global level is where the governance of citizenship may be beyond the reach of the nation state government. This is because relevant status, entitlements and process are associated with supranational or *deterritorialized* entities such as global markets or the ozone layer. Here, corporations may (or may not) take on a role in reforming or creating transnational institutions that play a role in governing citizenship where national governments cannot act effectively. The political role of the multinational has been an object of concern from the very beginning of its emergence and the very nature of transnational operations has fuelled a debate on the political influence of the corporation at a global level and its power to foster or impede the power of nation states (Bock and Fuccillo 1975; Osterberg and Ajami 1971).

In the area of *entitlements*, for instance, the global market for foreign direct investment can put considerable pressure on state regulation of economic, social and environmental standards. It has been argued that only if governments can offer 'favourable' conditions to MNCs in terms of special taxation allowances, low social standards, depressed wages and limited regulation of working conditions can they survive the 'race to the bottom' and attract much desired foreign investment (Scherer and Smid 2000). Accordingly, it can become incumbent upon the actions of MNCs rather than governments to protect (or not protect) social rights, such as through the introduction of global standards and codes of conduct.

It is instructive that, as a result of their frustrations with the failure of governments to address various cross-border issues, prominent non-governmental organizations (NGOs) turned their attention to corporations and international institutions to seek redress (Moon and Vogel 2008). As Newell remarks for social movements, 'targeting companies directly offers the prospect of higher "returns" given that the investment decisions of major TNCs now dwarf those of many states' (Newell 2000: 120). One example of this is the creation of the Forest Certification Council on the instigation of NGOs following 'the failure of international organizations that ought to have had the remit to enforce, to implement and develop good forestry standards' (Bartley 2003: 452). Similarly, given that the World Trade Organization limits national governments from requiring product labelling that describes how a product was produced outside its borders, many NGOs regard private product labelling and certification as a way to provide consumers and firms with information about labour, human rights and environmental standards in supply chains (Moon and Vogel 2008).

In terms of *status*, we might suggest that in a world that is economically interlinked by global financial markets, nation states have only limited ability to protect certain aspects of their citizens' property (one of their civil rights). With pension funds and life insurance being linked to international capital markets, US or French pensioners rely on these markets to protect their property, yet they are beyond the full control of the US or French governments. Again, since corporations are the main global organizations active in world financial markets, they might be said to be one of the few actors able to reform them to improve protection of property rights.

Thirdly, concerning *processes* of political participation, the aforementioned arguments already seem to suggest that corporations themselves *assume* some indirect political role if they adopt such a pivotal place in granting and facilitating major rights linked to citizenship. This becomes especially evident if one analyses current changes in global governance. With increasing privatization of regulation, through programmes such as the Chemical Industry's Responsible Care or the Apparel Industry Partnership, corporations have stepped in and taken an increasingly active role in the global political arena (Ronit and Schneider 1999; Schneidewind 1998).

An increasing number of commentators also highlight the powerful role of corporations in regulations by global bodies such as the WTO, GATT or the OECD. Though often indirect and via the conduit of their national governments, corporations and their associations have quite a significant influence on the way transnational regulation is made (e.g. Bakan 2004: 22–5; Dahan *et al.* 2006). Such regulation, however, has significant impacts on the way governments all over the world govern their relations with their citizens.

Corporate roles in governing of citizenship

If we draw together the analysis so far, we can see that corporations could be said to become involved in the governing of citizenship in a rather varied and complex fashion. With regard to entitlements, the corporation mainly either supplies (or does not supply) individuals with social services and other entitlement-based services, such as health, education and security. Hence, we might suggest that corporations here are mainly governing by taking on a *providing or ignoring role*. In the case of status, corporations either provide capacity for or constrain people's status as citizens. Therefore, they can be viewed as governing through more of an *enabling or hindering role*. Finally, in the realm of participation processes, the corporation is essentially an

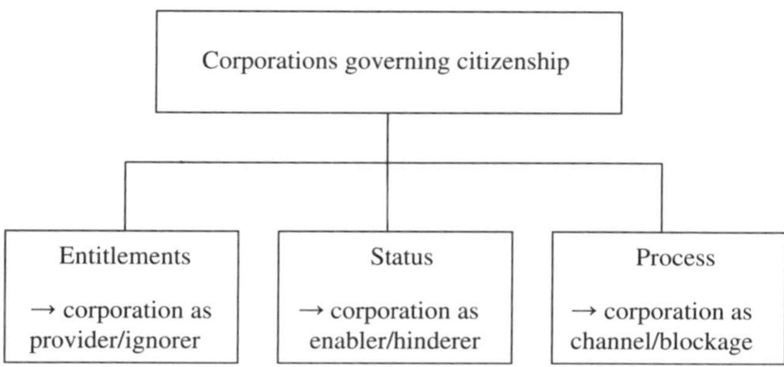

Figure 3.3 The corporate role in governing citizenship

additional conduit for the exercise of individuals' political participation. Hence the corporation primarily governs citizenship through a *channelling or blocking role*. These three roles are presented in Figure 3.3.

Linking this analysis back to our discussion of basic governing functions – defining, administering and guaranteeing – we can offer some interesting insights. In the area of entitlements the providing (or ignoring) role chiefly involves corporations in administering citizenship, or in the executive-like functions of government. In the area of enabling (or hindering) status and channelling (or blocking) political processes, the corporation defines, administers and guarantees citizenship, with a greater emphasis on the guaranteeing function in the absence of governments fulfilling those roles.

Having now clarified what it could mean to say that corporations are like governments in the governance of citizenship and having elaborated our case for suggesting that corporations are indeed practising some, if not all, of the roles and functions usually associated with governments, we come to the question of whether or not they are equipped to take on such a role and to address various related evaluative issues.

Evaluating the corporate governance of citizenship

In the following, we highlight some of the key implications and indeed problems associated with any potential uptake of responsibility for governing citizenship by corporations. Our discussion first raises issues around the capacity of corporations to discharge the governance of citizenship in an effective manner. Do they even have the basic apparatus to successfully achieve the task? Second, and relatedly, do, and should, corporations have appropriate power to participate in the governance of citizenship? Third, the change in roles and responsibilities implied by such shifts also suggests significant changes in the nature of citizenship. What are these changes likely to be, and what are their consequences? Finally, what new obligations should corporations assume if they adopt such government-like roles? We address each of these four questions in turn.

Corporations and the capacity to govern

When corporations join governments in governing citizenship, whether fully or partially, a first evaluative issue is the question of the extent to which corporations have the capacity to live up to this task. Liberal democracies have been equipped with what some call 'the machinery' of government, which equips government to adequately govern relations of citizenship. It may be useful, then, to assess corporate capacity to replicate the typical institutional elements of liberal democratic governments, such as a constitution, law, judiciary, legislature, executive, bureaucracy and military and police forces. By extending the government metaphor to corporations we can show that this perspective, on the one hand, helps to conceptualize a plethora of recent changes and innovations in the corporate toolbox. On the other hand, this comparison exposes significant deficits in the corporate infrastructure and capacity to replace government in the governance of citizenship.

Among the key functions of a *constitution* counts the establishment of unifying values and goals, a framework for stability, protection of freedom, and the legitimating of a regime. Equivalents of this in the corporate sphere include mission and values statements, as well as the burgeoning practice of issuing codes of conduct. Corporations, in particular multinationals, adopt these codes for similar reasons: to define and establish goals for their global operations. In the majority of cases, corporations adopt these codes initially to ensure that public criticism about their approach to various issues, such as labour rights, can be fended off. In this, codes have a legitimating function for the firm. From the perspective of citizenship though, the adoption of a code – for instance one that commits the corporation to refrain from dealing with corrupt officials – suggests that to some extent the corporation has already acknowledged a responsibility for governing aspects of citizenship, even if the language of citizenship is not typically employed in this context. In fact, the existence of codes in so many corporations is probably one of the most powerful empirical indicators that corporations are involved in the citizenship arena. The crucial deficit with codes, however, is that in many cases they are developed or adopted without substantial input from those citizens whose rights they are supposed to be protecting and governing. In the democratic governmental realm, often constitutions emerge from, and are amended by, a democratic, or at least representative, process. In the corporate sphere, most of these codes are simply the result of executive decisions.[2] In addition to that, there are only weak mechanisms to hold corporations to account in the event of shortfalls, none of which, outside the governmental judiciary, have the power of enforcement. The strongest sanctions appear to remain opprobrium.

In the context of privatized public services, the contract with the respective governmental body in charge of the particular policy area would be as close a surrogate as possible to a constitution. Though this would be on a much more operational level, the contract or franchise that governments provide to the companies that are selected to run a particular public service provides the basic goals and values of the business. For instance, in the area of public transport this would stipulate the exact terms of service with regard to punctuality or fare pricing. The reason why this is not just left over to market forces is that – aside from the necessity to govern natural monopolies – the corporations in charge are not just running any transport business but are implicated in the public necessity to provide citizens with access to essential and affordable transportation. Where corporations sign contracts there is, of course, scope for judicial review and sanction.

The *law* as a set of binding public and enforceable rules basically breaks down the abstract norms and values of the code to specific and concrete areas in which citizens' rights need upholding and protecting. In the corporate sphere, with the increasing spread of codes and other corporate commitments, there is a growing attention to different forms of monitoring and control of these commitments, for instance through industry self-regulation or 'civil regulation' (Zadek 2007). This typically revolves around compliance to industry or third party codes, such as the chemical industry's 'Responsible Care' programme or the UN Global Compact. As voluntary commitments, the correspondence of such initiatives with 'laws' remains rather loose, especially given that most initiatives do not impose penalties for non-compliance.

The analogy with government machinery becomes even more stretched if we look at the way these equivalents of basic elements of governments could be mirrored in the corporation in the area of *legislatures*. The general function of assemblies is to represent citizens in the making of laws. There is quite a vigorous debate about whether corporations can and should allow citizens to participate in their governance, which we will discuss in more detail in Chapter 4. We will restrict our comments here to the consideration of some equivalents of assemblies in corporations, the most obvious one being the Annual General Meeting of shareholders. Though the initial function of this meeting is to control the board with regard to financial issues, there are an increasing number of examples where shareholders have used this platform to express their will with regard to the way corporations have dealt with key citizenship issues, such as the entitlements of indigenous people or human rights issues, commonly referred to as shareholder activism. Some corporations have created stakeholder forums or focus groups that, it could be argued, serve as another surrogate of the functions of legislatures in the context of governments. However, while legislatures are components of *the* government, the fact that there are multiple corporations within single political spaces means that stakeholder forums are only representative for *a single* corporation, affording them rather less significance as forums for the exercise of citizenship. Moreover, as we will discuss in Chapter 4, these mechanisms of corporate democracy are all somewhat deficient. The ongoing debate on stakeholder democracy (Matten and Crane 2005b) suggests that while corporations have succeeded in providing voice and representation to some direct stakeholder groups, most notably employees, there is only limited democratic control of corporations by constituencies beyond this, such as in the case of citizens in democratic polities.

The *executive* and the *bureaucracy* in a governmental context serve to implement the democratic consensus on how citizenship should be guaranteed and implemented. In principle, the equivalent of these parts in the corporate context, namely the (executive) board and the management of business operations, could serve the same purpose. However, in practice these elements of the corporate structure only deal with citizenship explicitly as an exception. As Friedman (1970) in his critique of corporate social responsibility (CSR) noted that is not their express purpose and thus they are neither accountable nor trained for such purposes. Furthermore, the control of the executive by bodies representing citizens is fairly limited, which again exposes significant deficits in the governing of citizenship by corporations.

As elements of control, an important facet of government is the *judiciary*, which independently provides citizens with an opportunity to enforce their status and entitlements, and which controls the government's administration of these entitlements. The judiciary is therefore part of the government but, crucially, in liberal democracies, an independent one. The latter criterion poses something of an obstacle to drawing analogies with corporations. Although there are ethics committees, compliance departments and such like in many business organizations, they are mostly part of the internal hierarchy and, therefore, not independent. Even if external stakeholders or civil society actors are involved, the funding of these committees might pose conflicts of interest (Grimshaw *et al.* 2002). The closest equivalent to a judiciary in many Western European countries, then, might be the role of works councils since they have a legal framework for acting as an independent body in scrutinizing the company's treatment of employees and their rights. On a broader, but somewhat looser, level, we might also see the public, and especially the media, in the function of an independent scrutinizer of the corporation, although the nature of the influence, in particular the legal status of the 'judgements' are less binding and restrictive compared with the judiciary in the governmental context.

In order to enforce their policies governments rely on inspectorates and, most crucially, the *police* and in special circumstances, the *military* (which is otherwise mainly deployed in defence). This is probably the most striking contrast of governmental with corporate capacity for governing citizenship. After all, companies do not typically have the right or ability to enforce their policies in a fashion similar to government. There are a limited number of features of policing within the corporate governance infrastructure, such as internal investigating or the employment of security personnel. But these elements are more derived from the fact that managers are entrusted with protecting the corporation's assets, rather than a result of corporations having the authority to protect the interests of citizens more generally. Where corporations do resort to the use of violence in the democratic context, this is generally regarded as illegitimate and a usurpation of a uniquely governmental role, even though historically corporations have been ceded these roles (e.g. East India Company).

The issue of the right to deploy violence in order to secure policy perhaps most clearly reveals that corporations are generally established for different purposes than government and, consequently, have a very limited and underdeveloped capacity to govern compared with governments. There are certain elements of governmental machinery that can be found in corporations which are or could be used to support their role in the governance of citizenship. However, on the whole, there are clear deficits in the corporate infrastructure for the purpose of governing citizenship which, in turn, raise serious concerns about the ability of corporations to act like governments, as we will discuss in more detail in the following sections.

Corporate power and citizenship

When talking about the mechanisms by which corporations enter the citizenship arena we argued that in certain situations, corporations, rather than governing citizenship themselves, exert substantial influence on the way governments define, guarantee and administer citizenship. Key examples could be seen in cases such as the withdrawal of American companies from South Africa under the apartheid regime, which contributed significantly to the collapse of apartheid in this country. Other examples, more on the negative side, though, include the failure of big corporations in developing countries to exert pressure on governments to uphold citizenship rights, such as the case of Shell in Nigeria.

The crucial question in this context, then, is the extent to which corporations are able to exert power on governments either to uphold and honour or to infringe and neglect the rights of their citizens. We briefly touched upon this issue in the last chapter when we problematized the existence of power differentials between corporate and other societal actors in participating in governance. In this section, though, we take a slightly different angle: rather than looking at corporations as participating in governance (Chapter 2), we argue here that corporations may in fact be powerful enough to, as it were, 'use' governments as a tool of upholding or infringing certain citizenship rights. This ultimately leads us to the question of corporate political power or the power of corporations over the political process.

There are those obvious cases of state capture, often observed in developing and transitional economies (Hellman *et al.* 2000; Hellman and Schankerman 2000), where corporations directly shape the administration of regulation by payments to public officials and politicians or simply by the threat of exit. However, in most cases, and in the context of most Western democracies, there is much contestation about the claim that corporations actually influence political actors in a direct way. Certainly, the broad literature here paints a somewhat inconclusive picture (Akard 1992; Epstein 1973; 1974; Parkinson 1993). While there seems to be consensus that corporations *do* have some degree of influence on the political process, there is debate about the strength and legitimacy of this influence. The crucial problem here lies in the very nature and definition of power. Following the Weberian definition, power could be defined as the capacity of an actor to force other actors to behave in a certain fashion, even if this behaviour is against the will of these actors. In the context of corporate influence on political decision-making, the crucial problem seems to be that the political process in democracies is often far too complex to (a) trace the actual influence of corporations on political actors and (b) clearly identify whether a certain decision is solely or at least largely a result of corporate influence.

In this context we would like to highlight aspects of corporate power that are particularly conducive to providing business with influence over the way governments govern citizenship. Interestingly, the bulk of the literature on corporate power is more than thirty years old. In particular, in the US there was quite an intense debate on these issues during the 1960s and early 1970s (see the discussion in Epstein 1973; 1974). In the following, we draw on two key elements from Epstein's typology of 'Elements in Assessing Corporate Power', which, despite being somewhat dated, still seem to capture the relevant aspects for our discussion in this context – namely, bases of power and means of power.

A first factor is the *base of power*, the most important elements of which are the wealth of the organization, the access it has to government decision-makers, its degree of patronage and its influence over mass media. While most elements are fairly obvious as a base of power, two particular aspects are worth highlighting. First, the element of patronage, meaning the dependence of other social groups, employees and governmental units upon the corporation, seems particularly important in areas where a corporation or an industry is the sole employer. In these cases, be it locally or beyond, governments appear to be rather open to corporate pressure since they depend heavily on their investment decisions and the commitment of corporations to maintain their operations in a certain region or country. Notorious in this context is the influence of the oil industry in the US or the role of the car industry on political decision-making in Europe (Orsato *et al.* 2002) and the US (Luger 2005). Even if this base of power is not constantly put forward by corporations, the very fact that it is there, and that companies can exert the threat of withdrawal, is argued to be a major leverage for corporations on governments (Matten 2004). A second aspect is the media: apart from the rather obvious case of the overlap of governmental leadership and media ownership in Berlusconi's Italy, there is a general tendency in most liberal democracies towards growing corporate control of the media. This might be a direct result of liberalization and privatization efforts in the past but also indirectly through the fact that with growing competition from the internet, print and visual media increasingly rely on funding through advertising. This provides corporations not only with increased influence over the way citizenship is framed, but makes government far more responsive to corporations because they have influence over how policies are represented in the media. Thus, it has been argued that UK governments have been unusually attentive to the view of media owned by Rupert Murdoch (e.g. The Sun, The Times, Sky Television) and thus to Murdoch himself.

Furthermore, corporations also have various *means of power* on the political process, which can be grouped as governmental and electoral politics. The most common and obvious element of governmental politics is lobbying, be it by a single corporation or by industry associations. While this is a long-established practice in the US (Akard 1992; Lord 2000) there is growing evidence that corporate influence on legislation processes is growing in the EU as well (Coen 1999; Dahan 2005; Dahan *et al.* 2006). In a similar vein, the exchange of staff between corporations and government is a powerful way of securing corporate influence on governing. Though originating in the US, this practice has more recently spread throughout the UK and Europe as well.[3] While some of these means are transparent to the public, transparency is often lacking. If a former corporate representative stands as a candidate for political office in an election, or if corporations contribute to funding electoral campaigns, the influence of corporations is far more long term and covert. It is here where the biggest conflict from a citizenship perspective lies: the means by which corporations influence environmental or social legislation – all of which directly impinge on citizens' entitlements – are only partially transparent and therefore are a significant source of controversy about whether or not corporations actually have power over the governance of citizenship through governments (Coen and Grant 2001).

The changing nature of citizenship

If we are to take the involvement of corporations in the governance of citizenship seriously, we also need to ask if the very construct of 'citizenship' has changed. Granted, the concept of citizenship and its application have been in continual flux, but it does bear asking whether citizenship, when governed by corporations, is still characterized by a bundle of rights about status, entitlement and participation in the political process. Or, does the nature of corporate involvement transform these and, if so, how and why?

The answer to this question depends on the degree to which corporations take over governmental functions. Arguably, the nature of citizenship changes only marginally if corporations take merely a share in the executive functions of government. If governments still define and guarantee aspects of citizenship while the actual provision, for instance, of healthcare or prison management, is executed by private corporations, we could reasonably expect that citizens' entitlements should not change very much. In this case, only the responsibility for the delivery of the entitlement has changed from a governmental actor to another, a corporate one. The government retains responsibility for the guarantee of these entitlements by controlling the conditions under which corporations deliver the services. In this case, the nature of citizenship changes only in the way it is executed and this could even be regarded as offering a positive as citizens may obtain, inter alia, choices about the way their entitlements are delivered.

The problem, though, seems to reside in the fear that the involvement of private actors even in only the delivery of citizenship would change the very nature of the citizen's status and entitlement themselves. Arguably, the quality and price of many privatized public services do not remain constant but may vary significantly. If the provision of the services improves, such as in most cases of privatized telecommunication services over the last two decades, the creation of a market for these services has led to the fact that citizens make use of these services less as a citizen and more as a consumer. This has implications for the status held by the citizen/consumer, and furthermore transforms an entitlement to a public service into a market transaction for a commodity. This therefore raises the thorny question as to whether all public services need be a concomitant of citizenship and many would regard telecommunications as simply a service best delivered by competitive markets. Conversely, there is evidence that access to cheap telecommunications has not only enhanced economic development but also social and political development in developing countries. So, for instance, research has shown that a developing country with an extra ten telephones per 100 people between 1996 and 2003 would have had gross domestic product (GDP) growth 0.59 per cent higher than an otherwise identical country (Coyle 2005). Mobile telephones also significantly improve healthcare and access to other amenities for rural populations in the developing world.

There is also, however, ample evidence that in a large number of instances, corporate involvement in the governance of citizenship through privatized public services does *not* improve the quality of the services, and can even exclude certain citizens from the service. This is because access becomes regulated by markets rather than by governmental bureaucracies according to legislated criteria (Grimshaw *et al.* 2002; Nelson 1992; Wettenhall 2001). In this case, corporate involvement reflects what we referred to above as ideological shifts in many governments in liberal democracies. These shifts, often referred to as 'neo-liberal' thinking, in fact suggest a far more minimalist view of citizenship, confining basic rights of citizens to 'life, liberty and property' (John Locke, in Schuck 2002). The notion here, then, is a much thinner view of citizenship in that it confines the government to a very limited role of, as it were, a 'referee' over a process which is fundamentally in the hands of private actors and controlled by markets.

The result of this process, however, is not only that citizenship is enacted in a different fashion, but also that the actual scope of entitlements and processes of participation may become smaller. One of the reasons for this is that the public goods associated with citizenship are often delivered in imperfect markets, or even, as in the case of public transport, in natural monopolies. The key problem, however, seems to be that the relation between governments as 'referees' and corporations as 'players' often lacks the requisite power and authority relations that would enable adequate refereeing to take place. Either because governments are too weak, corporations too powerful, or simply because the interconnections between the two parties are too strong, the delineations between executing and defining/guaranteeing may often be difficult to make (Sellers 2003; Wettenhall 2001). Thus, in the case of water privatisation in many developing countries, the rules of the game that are ostensibly intended to protect citizen interests in the new market context, are not made by governments alone, but after intensive lobbying by, and in dialogue with, private corporations and industry bodies.

The more corporations become involved in the definition and guarantee of citizenship, we would contend, the more the nature of citizenship changes. The most interesting example is the role of companies who provide healthcare or education for their workers and their families in the developing world. While these services ostensibly put the recipients in a similar position as de facto citizens of a liberal welfare democracy, the provision of such services is not the result of entitlements of citizens but the result of a voluntary decision by the company.

In some respect, this way of governing citizenship could be referred to in the Habermasian terms of a 'refeudalization' of society (Habermas 1989). In the current state of welfare capitalism and mass democracy, he argues, political debate and consensus in the public sphere has increasingly been dominated by political, economic and media elites that control public opinion and political will formation. From a citizenship perspective, we would argue that entitlements and rights granted by independent governments are increasingly transformed into either philanthropic acts from the goodwill of private actors, or commodities that can be accessed through markets. The actual service an Aids-infected employee of the mining company Anglo-American in South Africa receives might not look too different from what s/he might also receive from the government – apart from the fact that the government might not even be able to provide these services at all or in a similar quality. The legal status, though, of this service is rather different. While s/he could claim these services as an entitlement of a South African citizen, receiving them from a private company, in fact, makes her dependent on the goodwill of her employer. This leaves the employee without any way of knowing or ensuring that the service is maintained over time, or continued in another organization should s/he wish to seek a new job. Similar to a dependent subject in a feudal context, her situation would not be a result of a secure legal status but a result of a decision of private actors, which might or might not choose to bestow a certain benefit upon her.

While the situation of corporations acting as governments in assuming all three functions of defining, guaranteeing and executing citizenship makes this shift in civic status fairly obvious, the picture becomes more blurred in situations where corporations exert power on existing governments to define and guarantee citizenship. The corporate governance of citizenship through governments is rather difficult to assess by objective criteria, but there are certainly some clear indications that citizens in many Western democracies feel more and more disenfranchised and regard the power and influence of governmental institutions as increasingly on the wane. In Chapter 4 we will consider the ways in which corporations have opened up more opportunities for citizenship-type engagement by their stakeholders.

Arguably the strongest indicator of this changed perception of citizenship is the growing voter apathy in many developed democracies where often up to half of the electorate is not making use of its right to vote, a core feature of democratic citizenship. Though we would not put this down to corporate influence on governments alone (government remoteness and untrustworthiness are other variables), citizens also appear to see the democratic process in their countries as being increasingly dominated by the economic interests of corporations (as represented in the quote at the start of this chapter). The implication, then, for citizenship is not so much that these citizens have a changed perception of what their specific status as citizens should be, but rather that they do not see governments as entirely able (or willing) to govern citizenship alone. If this is the case on a descriptive level, then what, if any, are the normative implications of a shift towards corporate involvement in the governing of citizenship?

Obligations of corporations in governmental roles

We have hitherto argued that the governmental role of corporations is increasingly a civic reality occurring in different fashions, modes and forms all over the globe. We have said little, though, about the normative implications of this shift in the political landscape. There are three main problems that we want to discuss here: that of commitment, transparency and accountability.

A first problem from a normative perspective focuses on the *commitment* of corporations to their role as government-like entities. Corporations enter the arena as actors which have a particular economic self-interest. This self-interest may or may not be the motive for their assumption of governmental roles but it will certainly affect the way they govern citizenship. If a company assumes responsibility for healthcare in a village in a developing country or if it gets involved in public–private partnerships in public transport they become involved in delivering basic entitlements of citizens. As these are linked to specific rights (rights to life, health, education etc.) the question immediately arises in how far a company is able and willing to guarantee these rights in a fashion similar to government. If corporations donate free medication to developing countries or engage in other forms of philanthropy, what happens if these philanthropic activities cease to be in the company's self-interest? If companies take over the provision of former governmental services in education, how can citizens still claim these rights and be assured that they can rely on these services and that their citizenship rights are still guaranteed given that the corporation may move its operations to another country entirely?

There are examples of charities who have refused corporate donations of pharmaceutical products on these grounds and preferred to rely on – albeit insufficient and limited – governmental provision of these goods. The key problem with a corporate commitment to providing these services as rights of citizens lies in the fact that in many cases they enter the citizenship arena inadvertently. A company taking over the provision of water services may simply be in the water business, rather than seeing itself in the delivery of basic citizenship entitlements. As a consequence, companies are highly unlikely to assume their role with the same commitment as governments – it may not necessarily be *less* commitment, but it is almost certain to be different.

The other deficit with regard to the corporate commitment to citizenship lies in the legal framework of corporate activities. As this development towards corporations as governments has happened largely unacknowledged over the last couple of decades, there is hardly any legal framework that actually commits companies to the governance of citizenship, leaving large swathes of regulatory responsibility to the market.

One response to the concerns on corporate commitment to the governance of citizenship is simply that the countries in which these anxieties are most acute are precisely where either governments have consistently failed to provide the services or lack the regulatory and judicial teeth to hold corporations to their commitments. Something is better than nothing. However, this observation should both qualify the claims made by the corporations about their contributions, and focus critiques and international government policy on the deficiencies of the respective governance systems rather than on the corporations.

This problem is closely linked to the issue of *transparency* in the governance of citizenship. Because governments govern the exercise of rights of citizens, there are extensive demands for transparency of governmental activity, to ensure that fairness and, increasingly, effectiveness are maintained. The mechanisms for transparency in most liberal democracies are numerous, including government reports and inquiries, budget reports and announcements, 'league tables' of public sector performance and other features of the 'audit society' (Power 1999). If corporations become involved in similar activities, then a similar degree of transparency to citizens might be expected. To some extent, corporations have begun to address this through non-financial reporting and other communication vehicles. However, transparency is particularly a problem in situations where corporations exert their power on existing governments and shape the way these governments govern citizenship. We addressed these issues in the last chapter when we argued that the participation of corporations in governing demands a degree of transparency – this is even more the case if corporations exert influence on governments as institutions on the same horizontal plane. Arguably, the distrust in governments and the feeling of disenfranchisement of many citizens in liberal democracies derives not so much from the fact that certain corporate interests have played a role in decision-making, but that the modes, channels and results of corporate influence are not transparent.

Closely related to the claim for more transparency is the claim for more *accountability* of corporations as governors of citizenship. We have discussed the claim for accountability in the last chapter in the context of corporations participating in societal governance. There is a wealth of literature in management looking at forms of increased corporate accountability to stakeholders (Logsdon and Lewellyn 2000; Owen and O'Dwyer 2008), most of which looks at innovative forms of reporting and interaction patterns with stakeholders – and in some cases governments could also learn from these. In the context of corporations acting as if they were governments, however, accountability would require mechanisms similar to those which ensure that governments discharge accountability, most notably through the electoral process. This would in particular be the case in situations where corporations administer citizenship *as* governments. What, for instance, are the mechanisms through which citizens of developing countries can hold pharmaceutical companies to account for their effectiveness or otherwise in providing affordable drugs? In cases where corporations govern citizenship on the administering level, there are normally governmental bodies who hold the companies accountable by setting them targets and goals. However, the reality often seems to be that these mechanisms of accountability are only working to a very limited degree (Grimsey and Lewis 2002) and, crucially, do not provide direct channels of discharging accountability to citizens.

This whole issue of how corporations can be opened up to processes of participation and democratic control by citizens is indeed a crucial one, and it is to this that we direct our attention in the next chapter. In order to do so, we turn the metaphor of citizenship to the specific realm of the corporation, and focus on corporate governance rather than societal governance. We do this in order to explore whether the metaphor of citizenship is useful for examining the status, entitlements and processes of participation open for specific stakeholders in the governance of the corporation.

Conclusion

In this chapter, we have explored in some depth the contention that corporations play a similar role to governments in vertical relations of power towards citizens, and have examined the applicability of the government metaphor for assigning responsibilities to corporations. We have seen that the notion of citizenship offers a powerful lens for examining the power and responsibility of corporations towards citizens, and it would appear to be particularly useful for examining the *entitlement* dimensions of citizenship, especially in relation to basic social and human rights, such as rights to health, education, security and decent working conditions. This contrasts with the previous chapter, where we saw that the idea of corporations being like citizens was particularly useful for examining *process* dimensions of citizenship.

What is clear from our discussion is that governments have indeed reduced direct delivery of certain citizenship entitlements, and that there are shifts in the mode of governance that open up spaces for other actors notably, but not only, corporations, to fill. The point is not, in general, that corporations replace governments completely, but that they take on some of the roles and responsibilities previously assigned to governments – or where governments have yet to, or cannot, take up responsibility. Indeed, by breaking down the functions of governing into defining, administering and guaranteeing citizenship, we can see that claims for government-like roles of corporations are actually strongest in the area of administering citizenship (where corporations take on a providing role), although aspects of defining and guaranteeing citizenship can also come under the influence of corporations, particularly when their power is exercised through governments. In general, though, the metaphor of corporations as governments begins to break down when we explore the capacity of corporations to organize the governance of citizenship in the same way as governments. While there are echoes of constitutions, laws, judiciaries and the like in the corporate realm, their correspondence with governmental forms is rather limited. Thus, whilst corporations have significant roles to play in the delivery of entitlements, their ability to guarantee, enforce and enable democratic participation of citizens is substantially compromised.

Finally, the main limitation of the metaphor of governments for corporations is the fact that corporations essentially compete with other corporations in political spaces, while governments generally do not (at least not in relation to citizenship issues).[4] Citizens participate in relations of power and responsibility with *the* government, but with *a*, or *many*, corporations. Citizens' relations with corporations are therefore more transient, shifting and polygamous. What is particularly interesting here is that citizens in fact may take up varying relations with corporations depending on the type of interaction and expectations they have, whether as employees, consumers or local communities. In the next chapter, we will explore this in more depth by examining the contribution of the citizenship metaphor for understanding stakeholder relations with the corporation – i.e. the notion of stakeholders as citizens.

Notes

1. The agreement on Trade Related Aspects of International Property Rights (TRIPS) is administered by the World Trade Organization (WTO) and was a result of the 1994 round of negotiations of the General Agreement on Tariffs and Trade (GATT). It was strongly advocated by the developed world, but many critics see it as a way to limit access to medication and generic drugs in the developing world (Sule 2007).

2. There are of course exceptions to this, especially in the case of third party codes. For example, the base code of the Ethical Trade Initiative, which is a coalition of employers, trade unions and NGOs, is based on the ILO labour conventions and draws on deliberations between the member organizations.
3. We acknowledge, however, that in Europe, and in similar shapes also in Japan or South Korea, close relations between business and governments historically have not been uncommon. However, in societies with strong corporatist traditions, phenomena such as the 'pantouflage' system in 1950s France are more an expression of strong institutional links between and amalgamation of both societal sectors (in particular with a high level of state ownership of businesses), than the deliberate effort of private business interests to influence and shape governmental actors and to manipulate the democratic process as such.
4. Although governments in federal systems could be seen as in competition for political support, this rarely extends to citizenship type issues. (An exception could be the Canadian system of asymmetrical federalism, which grants Quebec a role in citizenship status alongside that of the federal government by virtue of its unique powers over immigration.)

4 *Stakeholders as citizens*

The provenance of the 'corporate democracy' oxymoron has long been understood. The idea results from the inappropriate conflation of political ideals with market institutions. Its persistence can only be attributed to the intelligentsia's far greater comfort and familiarity with political models and events than with knowledge and appreciation of how markets function.

Henry G. Manne, The 'Corporate Democracy' Oxymoron,
The Wall Street Journal, 2 January 2007

Introduction

In the previous chapter, we saw how our conception of corporations as acting like governments prompted us to consider an expanded and reconfigured constituency for corporate decision-making. Rather than thinking simply in terms of traditional stakeholder groups and relationships, a view of corporations as governments suggested a focus on citizens more broadly. This idea, that relevant corporate constituencies are not only stakeholders but can also be conceptualized as citizens, is not entirely new, nor is it relevant only for a view that assumes that corporations have adopted governmental responsibilities. Indeed, there has been a whole collection of work that has examined stakeholder groups as though they were citizens, but in the main this literature has not been concerned with the political role of the corporation as such, but rather with using the political metaphor of citizenship in some way to examine the specific rights and responsibilities that employees, consumers and other stakeholders might have in their relations with the firm.

As we will show, there have been numerous such conceptualizations of stakeholders that have adopted a citizenship framework, or that have incorporated elements of citizenship terminology and theory in order to explore stakeholder relations. For instance, there has long been a strain of stakeholder theory valorizing democratic forms of governance and accountability in the corporation (Stoney and Winstanley 2001), which in turn has given rise to a growing, but surprisingly limited, literature on 'stakeholder democracy' (e.g. Matten and Crane 2005b) and 'corporate democracy' (Engelen 2002; Freeman 1984: 196). However, citizenship thinking has been most widely adopted in the specific context of employees. Hence, various authors over the years have integrated citizen thinking into models of industrial organization and employee relations. This has ranged from exploring notions of workplace democracy and employee participation (e.g. Collins 1997; Collins 1995) to more direct applications of citizenship, where the idea of employees exhibiting 'citizenship behaviours' within the organization has sustained a vigorous stream of research across a number of domains and disciplines (Podsakoff *et al.* 2000).

In contrast to employees, other stakeholder relations have probably been subject rather less, or at least much less explicitly, to citizenship thinking. Nonetheless, notions of, for example, shareholder democracy (Parkinson 1993), and political consumerism (Micheletti *et al.* 2004) suggest that our understanding of shareholders and consumers has also been shaped in some way by ideas from citizenship. Moreover, other groups typically conceived as stakeholders of the corporation, such as governments and civil society organizations, are by their nature already substantially grounded in notions of citizenship, irrespective of their relation to the corporation. Thus, governments and civil society groups can be thought of as *representing* citizens' interests when they interact with a corporation.

What we have, then, is a fairly heterogeneous set of quite disparate literatures that have offered a perspective on stakeholders as citizens, usually from the very narrow perspective of a single stakeholder (such as employees), or a particular aspect (such as democracy). This has left us without any real understanding of what it means to conceive of stakeholders as citizens in a general sense, or of the challenges and possibilities of integrating insights from one area of theorising to another. Our intention in this chapter is therefore to provide a critical evaluation of these literatures, and to try and make sense of them within an overarching framework that makes possible a thorough assessment of the overall potential for conceptualizing stakeholders as citizens.

In the first section, we will therefore start by exploring the underlying metaphorical basis for representing stakeholders as citizens, and in so doing, determine what exactly stakeholders are thought to be citizens *of*, and what role the corporation takes within this particular deployment of citizenship. We will then seek to establish the key criteria and dimensions of citizenship that are relevant to conceptualising stakeholders as citizens, and then use these to develop an overarching comparative framework. In particular, we focus on issues of rights, representation, participation and democracy. These, we contend, are at the heart of any substantial theorizing about stakeholders as citizens and, just as importantly, are the key issues informing debates about corporate power and responsibility.

Once these initial foundations are in place, we will go on to look at the literature concerned with each of the main stakeholders of the corporation. In this way, we will show that current conceptions of stakeholders as citizens are largely fragmented, often sketchy, and rather narrowly situated, both practically and theoretically. At the same time, we will also show that there is considerable potential for further development, and for generating important new insight into how corporate responsibilities to their stakeholders can be institutionalised and governed.

Understanding stakeholders as citizens

The notion of a 'stakeholder' is, on the surface, very simple, but at heart, deceptively complex. There are a multitude of definitions of stakeholders (see for example Mitchell *et al.* 1997), and these rest on a variety of assumptions about what constitutes a legitimate stake, and how different stakes should be evaluated. At a basic level, though, a stakeholder can simply be regarded as a constituency that has some sort of relationship with an organization that confers it with a set of obligations and/or claims or entitlements of one kind or another. This can range from the type of ownership relation that shareholders have, to the market relations that customers or suppliers have, to the political relations that governments have.

For the sake of simplicity, in this chapter we are mainly going to focus on five stakeholder groups – shareholders, employees, customers, suppliers and civil society. This is not to suggest that these are the only stakeholders, nor the only way of grouping stakeholder constituencies. But this designation does capture a fairly broad range of potential stakeholder relations that might be evaluated from a citizenship perspective. The issue is actually not so much about whether a particular group is a legitimate stakeholder or not, but whether the constituency's relation with the corporation can (or should) be explored in the context of citizenship. The key point here is that when issues of governance, democracy, participation and sovereignty are brought to bear on our understanding of various stakeholder relations, we can be said to be witnessing the import of at least some elements of the discourse of citizenship. This might be in relation to a specific constituency, such as shareholders, or to the range of stakeholders more generally.

The import of citizenship terminology and concepts into various stakeholder relations may or may not be a conscious decision on the part of those that are writing about them. Where it is conscious, the reasoning is typically of the kind, 'If stakeholders are thought of as citizens of the corporation, then this would mean that they should have particular rights and responsibilities commensurate with the status of citizens'. As such, a set of appropriate expectations for stakeholder relations could be devised. Similarly, authors might think along the following lines, 'A suitable model of workplace democracy can be found in models of political democracy'. Hence, the citizenship literature might be used as a source of inspiration for devising forms and norms of employee participation.

This type of deliberate incorporation of citizenship concepts and models has started to feature in the burgeoning literature on corporate social responsibility and stakeholder management, not least because of greater attention in recent years to the problem of making corporations more democratic through stakeholder engagement and participation. As we saw in Chapter 1, this has been fuelled by anti-capitalist protests and a swathe of popular books, films and articles in the late 1990s and early 2000s that were critical of the disenfranchisement of citizens in a global economy dominated by 'unaccountable' multinational corporations. The response in the academic management literature has included developments such as Harrison and Freeman's (2004) special topic forum on 'democracy in and around organizations' in *The Academy of Management Executive*, (which was also the theme of the Academy of Management conference the same year), and Matten and Crane's (2005) special issue on 'stakeholder democracy' in *Business Ethics: A European Review*. There have also been ongoing attempts to develop and evaluate auditing and reporting practices according to their correspondence with the political participation of citizens. For instance,

Cumming (2001) has sought to assess stakeholder involvement in social accounting using Arnstein's 'ladder of citizen participation'.

This conscious and deliberate appropriation of models of citizenship and democracy is also evident in numerous treatments of *employees*, though rarely so for other constituencies. For example, Collins (1997) compares the roles of sovereigns and subjects in political, economic and organization theories to argue for the 'ethical superiority and inevitability' of participatory employee relations over autocratic management. In so doing, he acknowledges that, 'the first key assumption is that organizational systems are analogous to political and economic systems' (1997: 491). More recently, Manville and Ober (2003) have attempted to develop a new model of employee involvement from the Athenian model of citizenship, and Boatright (2004: 4) has drawn on Dahl's (1985) conception of the corporation as a political system to argue that 'employees have a right, similar to that of citizens, to participate in decisions that affect them'.

What we see here, then, is an explicit attempt to articulate and appraise employee relations according to the touchstone of political models of citizenship. However, not all authors are as sanguine about the correspondence of political frameworks to organizational analysis. As Kerr (2004) points out in his examination of organizational democracy, 'The fact is, no matter how appealing it may be as a political and intellectual construct, organizations are not societies in the political sense, and managements are not governments'. He quite rightly points to potential disjunctures in equating the individual role of 'employee' with that of 'citizen', as well as different bases of legitimate power (ownership versus elected government), differences in decision-making processes, and significant differences in the very nature of an organization as a collective compared with a social polity. Nonetheless, even here, it is necessary for Kerr to exhume the underlying elements of political democracy and compare them with organizational theory in order to come to such a conclusion.

Outside of the literature dealing with employee participation, the explicit and conscious use of citizenship concepts to discuss other stakeholder relations is rarer. This does not mean it is not in evidence, but it does show that these other relations are more readily accommodated within other discourses, and the application of citizenship thinking may be more problematic than for employees. For instance, although notions of consumer sovereignty are at the heart of economic theories of market exchange, contemporary marketing theory rarely, if ever, makes any explicit comparison between models of citizen–sovereign and producer–consumer. Even for employees, citizenship thinking is more often implicit rather than explicit. This is not exactly surprising. As we have already seen in the previous chapters, much of the attention to notions of citizenship in the realm of the corporation has been metaphorical in nature. The suggestion is not usually that corporations are literally citizens (Chapter 2), or that they are literally governments (Chapter 3), but that there are certain aspects of the relationships that are like, or can be seen in terms of, relations of citizenship. The same goes for the notion of stakeholders as citizens. In the main, the issue is not that stakeholders really *are* citizens, but that stakeholders are *like* citizens, at least in some non-trivial ways. This is why stakeholder relations with corporations can be, and have been, conceptualized using metaphors of citizenship, although such usage may be unintentional and unexamined.

Citizenship as a metaphor for stakeholder relations

Given the preceding discussion, it should be fairly clear by now why employee relations have witnessed by far the most attention to citizenship – they are the most like citizens in their relation with the corporation. After all, alone among stakeholders, employees are actually a part of the corporation – they physically and legally represent it, and are members of it in much the same way that citizens are part of society, or the polity. In some corporations employees are even known as associates. Consumers or civil society, on the other hand, are not usually members of the corporation (except in the case of consumer co-operatives), and so the same level of equivalence is not in evidence. Also, employees like citizens are individuals rather than organizations (unlike say, suppliers or governments), which again suggests they have a greater degree of congruence with citizens than do some other stakeholders. Finally, simply because they work within its boundaries, employees are at least able to participate in certain decisions made by the corporation (albeit with rather less influence in some sorts of decisions than shareholders), which is an aspect of citizen-like status and participation not open to other stakeholders such as consumers.

Although the metaphor of citizenship is most readily applicable to employees, the key issue is that stakeholders *in general* can be considered as like citizens, even if the analogy is less convincing for some stakeholders than others. In fact, it is not only the case that some stakeholder–citizen analogies are stronger than others, but that their underlying basis varies. As Fitchett (2005: 15) argues, 'stakeholder groups vary in terms of, for example, allegiance to core organizational interests, degree of consolidation or fragmentation, the presence of visible power structures and means of representation, as well as their ability to effect change'.

The analogy of employees and citizens, as we have shown, is based on similarities in membership status, unit of analysis and participation in organizational decision-making. The analogy of other stakeholders, however, differs in certain important respects. Civil society, for example, is mainly analogous to citizens because they represent individual citizens' interests. Consumers are mainly 'like' citizens because although they are a 'body without organization' (Fitchett 2005: 24) they can bring their 'real' citizen identities into their market relations with corporations in order to express their political will through 'purchase votes' (Smith 1990). Shareholders are like citizens because, in voting at the Annual General Meeting, they get to exercise their sovereignty through similar mechanisms of participation. So, while sharing a basic similarity in form, the application of the citizenship metaphor to describe stakeholder relations relies on various different facets.

In order to develop an overarching framework for understanding stakeholders as citizens – i.e. one that encompasses the range of possible analogies – we must, therefore, uncover an underlying metaphorical basis. One way of addressing this might be to articulate what stakeholders are actually supposed to be citizens of. In a sense, this is quite evidently the corporation, which means that the metaphorical equivalent of the corporation would be the nation state. However, on deeper analysis, a few problems arise here. For a start, while employees might easily be conceived as (metaphorical) citizens of the corporation, this does not sit so easily with non-members of the corporation, such as consumers and civil society. Moreover, the (metaphorical) citizen relation of these constituencies with the corporation is simultaneously informed by a (non-metaphorical) citizenship relation within broader society (depending on their polity).

Consequently, it might make more sense to move away from a straightforward description of corporations as the object of citizenship (i.e. 'stakeholders are citizens of the corporation') towards understanding the corporation more as an *arena* in which a particular set of citizenship-like relationships can be examined (i.e. 'stakeholders are citizens within the context of the corporation'). This more nuanced, though admittedly looser, conception allows a more sophisticated reading of stakeholder relations, as will become evident as the chapter progresses. It also mirrors certain currents in contemporary thinking about citizenship, which have emphasized the multiple relations of citizenship that people are embedded in – for example, the intersecting of ethnic, national and global citizenship identities. We will look at these in more detail in the second part of the book.

Returning to our metaphorical puzzle – if the corporation is an arena of citizenship, who or what are the metaphorical citizens and government? Well, clearly, we are equating stakeholder groups with citizens, which means that the government-like organ ultimately responsible for administering various stakeholder relations is the governing body of the corporation – usually the board of directors, and/or any form of supervisory board. In this scenario, the board has government-like properties because it makes the key decisions about the corporation, it has the facility to protect the status and the entitlements of stakeholders (at least within the realm of the corporation), and degrees of stakeholder democracy can be assessed according to the extent to which stakeholders can participate in, or have their interests represented in, the board and its executive. It is, after all, no coincidence that the concept of corporate governance, which deals with the workings of the governing body of the corporation, is itself a metaphor of governmental activity drawn from the realms of politics.

Figure 4.1 represents the basic metaphorical model outlined above. It is based on, but deviates from in certain key respects, the conventional stakeholder model devised by Freeman (1984) that has subsequently made its way into many mainstream treatments of stakeholder theory (see Figure 4.2).

Freeman's model is basically a representation of a management approach that takes into consideration the interests of multiple organizational constituencies rather than just one (shareholders). For this reason, Freeman deliberately centred the corporation to emphasize that the organization is the locus of these multiple interests (or the nexus of these relationships) from the point of view of management. While this clearly privileges the organization, it does not explicitly denote a formal hierarchy between the organization and its stakeholders. The principal

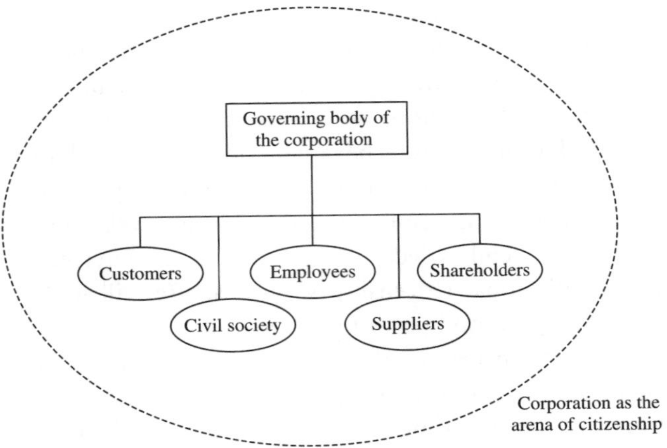

Figure 4.1 Stakeholders as citizens

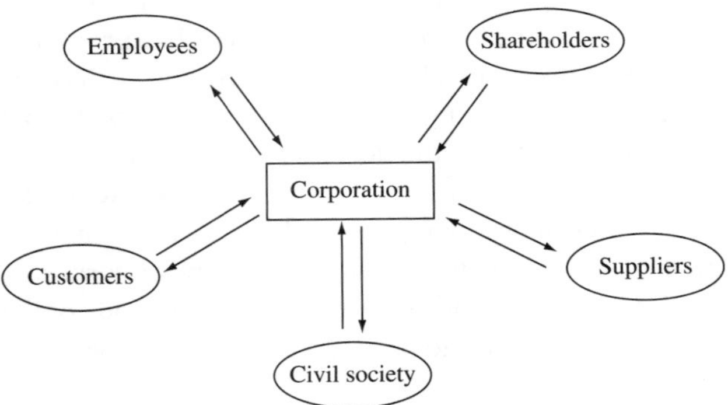

Figure 4.2 Freeman's stakeholder model (adapted)

point of departure for our model is obviously its hierarchical structure. This is because thinking about stakeholders as citizens attunes us to the relations of power and responsibility between stakeholders and the governing body of the corporation. Thus, in contradistinction to Freeman,[1] the central rectangle represents the governing body of the corporation, not the corporation itself; and crucially, the central rectangle has been placed in a position of power over, and responsibility for, stakeholders. In our model, the corporation is actually depicted as the outer oval (identified by the dotted line) since this organizational community is to be regarded as the arena of citizenship in this context.

Key themes in stakeholder relations from a citizenship perspective

The model presented in Figure 4.1 encapsulates a whole range of citizen-like relations between the governing body of the corporation and different stakeholders. Again, it should be emphasized that the role of the corporation here is in providing an arena for citizenship-type relations of its stakeholders. Within these relations, a number of themes and issues are raised by adopting a citizenship perspective, namely: stakeholder rights; mode of representation; mechanisms for participation; and degrees of democracy.

In Chapter 1, we identified status, entitlements and process as the key constituting elements of citizenship. In the remaining part of the chapter, we will discuss the potential, relevance and implication of this perspective for firm–stakeholder relations. When thinking about what could constitute the context in which we could grant stakeholders the *status* of citizens we think of the fundamental basis on which corporations could accept citizen-like claims or demand corresponding duties from their stakeholders. These vary considerably from rather tangible elements such as ownership on the part of shareholders, or membership on the part of employees, up to softer forms of attachment, such as in the case of consumers. In all groups discussed, then, we have different mechanisms and institutions that would bring stakeholders in a specific and distinct relation to the corporation with the consequence that the latter would be obliged to respect and facilitate certain entitlements.

Turning to *entitlements* of citizens, we would argue that in stakeholder relations, issues of rights are clearly a central aspect, and indeed some of the most influential treatments of stakeholder theory have located the normative core of the theory in aspects of rights (Donaldson and Preston 1995). Indeed, one of Freeman's (1997) most well-known elucidations of the case for management obligations to stakeholders was largely based on the argument that stakeholders had specific rights and other claims that had to be respected. What is clear then is that in contradistinction to citizenship rights, the types of rights claimed by stakeholders tend to vary depending on the type of relation concerned. The rights of shareholders, for instance, are quite unlike the rights of suppliers with respect to the governing body of the corporation. One of the tasks of this chapter is therefore to identify these different rights and to identify any potential for an underlying basis for rights based on notions of citizenship.

With regard to the third element of the citizenship *process*, we again can distinguish quite a variety of different modes for various stakeholders. Certainly the mode of *representation* is a factor that varies according to stakeholder, and this has a considerable bearing on the way in which notions of citizenship can and cannot be applied. While some stakeholders, such as consumers, primarily have individual representation to the corporation (e.g. through purchasing), others, such as suppliers, interact on a corporate basis. Similarly, in the political realm of citizenship, some representation is individual (such as that exercised by voters), whereas some is more corporate or associational (such as that exercised by lobbyists or industry bodies on political parties). Again, we will seek to identify the main modes of representation and examine their implications for stakeholders' status as citizens.

Mechanisms of *participation* are something that we examined in detail in Chapter 2, but here we are concerned with participation in the governance of the corporation, rather than its participation in societal governance. This means looking at the means by which stakeholders can protect their rights and other interests by having some kind of influence on the governing body of the corporation. These can be either mechanisms that are a formal part of the stakeholder relation – such as shareholder voting at the Annual General Meeting, or collective bargaining by employees – or more informal mechanisms such as stakeholder dialogues.

Finally, the overarching issue of *democracy* is central to most modern concepts of citizenship, and again, has been a key theme in the discussion around stakeholder involvement in controlling the corporation. Here we are interested in the extent to which the different stakeholders can and should be attributed some degree of democracy in their relations with the firm, and whether notions of stakeholder democracy or 'corporate democracy' can be legitimately applied.

In the six sections that follow, we will examine these key themes for each of the main stakeholders in turn, identifying commonalities, divergences and integrative concepts. This discussion is summarized in Table 4.1, which also identifies the main concepts that are relevant in each of the specific stakeholder literatures.

Table 4.1. *Nature of stakeholders' citizenship relations towards the corporation*

Stakeholder	Key concepts in the literature	Basis of citizenship status	Nature of citizenship entitlements	Nature of citizenship participation		
				Representation	Formal mechanisms for participation	Informal mechanisms for participation
Shareholders	Corporate governance; shareholder democracy	Ownership contract or proxy	Property rights	Individual; collective through fund managers	Board of directors; AGM; finance market	Dialogue
Employees	Organizational citizenship; industrial democracy; employee involvement; co-determination	Employment contract or proxy	Contractual rights; human rights	Individual; collective through trade unions	Collective bargaining; works councils; supervisory boards	Participatory work practices
Consumers	Market governance; consumer sovereignty	Transactional relationship, purchasing contracts, soft forms of membership	Contractual rights	Individual; collective through consumer associations	Market	Consumer activism; market research
Suppliers	Market governance; network governance; partnership sourcing; self-regulation; keiretsu	Transactional relationship, supplier contracts, (partial) ownership contract	Contractual rights	Corporate	Market; interlocking ownership	Negotiation; supplier audits
Civil society organizations	Civil regulation; stakeholder dialogue; business–NGO partnership	Public perception and societal expectations, partnership agreements	Civil rights	Collective/ associational	None	Boycotts; partnerships; dialogue

Shareholders as citizens

At first glance, it might appear an exaggeration to conceive of shareholders as citizens in relation to corporations. After all, not only is their interest almost entirely economic, as nominal 'owners' of corporations, their basic property rights and associated interests are already firmly established by this relation. Economists present the situation in terms of a principal (shareholder) and agent (manager) relation, whereby the agent acts on behalf of their principal to protect their investment. Thus, in most models of corporate governance, managers have a legal responsibility or fiduciary duty to act in the interests of shareholders.

Despite the empirical realities of this economic relation, there are, however, a number of reasons why we might start to think of shareholders in more political terms. To begin with, while the underlying ownership relation of shareholders to the corporation is an economic one, this does not mean that we can divorce it from issues of power (Engelen 2002). Just as citizens authorize governments with the power to protect their interests, so too do shareholders empower managers to protect theirs. So, in the same way as economists may well impose the notion of principals and agents on citizen–government relations (Mitchell 1990; Stigler 1971), the metaphor of citizenship has some traction in the other direction. The vertical relations of power between shareholders and the governing body of 'their' corporations signify more than just an economic exchange of resources to create value.

This political dimension is most evident in the notion of *shareholder democracy*, which is a commonly discussed topic in corporate governance (Parkinson 1993: 160–6). The basic idea behind the term is that a shareholder of a company is entitled to have a say in corporate decisions, rather than just blindly entrusting their agents to act on their behalf. The shareholder relation is not one simply of anonymous market transactions, but one where individual shareholders can exercise power to further their interests. As in systems of mass representative democracy, given the vast number of shares, and the dispersion of share ownership, the influence of a single shareholder is rather small. With little real voice, their main option to express their views on management decisions is through 'exit' (disposal of their shares). However, with institutional investors or holders of larger share packages the situation looks considerably different, since they are able to bring their collective shareholder power to bear through participation, either formally at shareholder meetings or more informally between these through dialogue with senior management.

This has been most strikingly evident in recent years in the area of executive pay, where companies such as GlaxoSmithKline (GSK) and Unilever have witnessed shareholder revolts at the excessive 'fat cat' salaries proposed for chief executives. In the case of GSK, Europe's largest drug-maker made UK corporate history in 2003 when, for the first time, a majority of shareholders voted against the board's remuneration policy. Institutional actors have also been active in the area of top management appointments where in 2004 alone, shareholders succeeded in ousting Michael Eisner as Director of Walt Disney Co., while French shareholders secured the removal of the entire Eurotunnel board. Social responsibility initiatives have also been the subject of shareholder engagement. For instance, socially responsible investment funds now increasingly engage in extended dialogue with corporate leaders over issues such as human rights, diversity, etc. In recent years, high profile successes have been scored by religious funds, such as the Interfaith Centre for Corporate Responsibility (ICCR), an association of 275 faith-based institutional investors with an estimated combined portfolio value of around $110 billion. Each year ICCR members sponsor over 100 shareholder resolutions on major social and environmental issues, and have been credited with successes including enhancement of diversity management at Motorola.

In practice, the actual ways of influencing the board of the corporation and the institutions of proxy vary across countries. Whilst the Anglo-Saxon model of corporate governance (which is typical in the US, UK, Australia and Ireland) features dispersed and frequently changing shareholding, the continental European model (typical of Italy, Germany and Spain) and the Asian model (typical of Japan and Korea) feature more concentrated and fixed ownership. The current wave of private equity takeovers of corporations combines economic promise with yet more narrow ownership and governance systems. This means that the different models of governance resemble relations of citizenship in different ways.

The Anglo-Saxon system particularly resembles the citizenship model in terms of *processes of participation* in governance and *mechanisms of accountability*. Periodic voting by shareholders and public reporting of performance by the board are not so different from the political democratic process. This is particularly so for liberal conceptions of citizenship, but insofar as shareholders also join boards, build coalitions and engage in dialogue with senior managers to further their interests, their participation in governance can extend beyond the liberal minimum. Where the Anglo-Saxon model particularly differs from the citizenship model of governance is in the *allocation of participation rights*. Democratic forms of political governance grant all designated citizens a guaranteed, and (in principle) equal opportunity to participate on the basis of their membership of the community; however, corporate governance allocates participation according to the principle of legal ownership (Kerr 2004). Not only are voting rights allocated per share (rather than per shareholder), the legitimate interests of other stakeholders (or other 'citizens') find no place in the system of governance without share ownership. Similarly, while citizens retain membership, and therefore commitment to the polity, shareholders can easily exit.

In other models of corporate governance, such as those found in Germany or Japan, where there is more commonly a network of mutually interlocking owners, including banks and other firms, and where stakeholders other than shareholders are represented in the system of governance, the parallels with citizen relations are somewhat different. Here, the central focus for shareholders is the long-term preservation of influence and power, which shares more with the thicker forms of participatory citizenship. Moreover, the wider allocation of participation rights (to employees and other constituencies sometimes including respective governments) secures a longer-term commitment to the polity, and enables a variety of forms of participation, which may be more or less legally enforceable. Therefore, unlike in the Anglo-Saxon model, the basis for the allocation of participation rights is not simply legal ownership, at least not in a way directly analogous to ownership by shareholders. Within the arena of the corporation, there are a number of parties who have made firm-specific investments and carry risk in the same way as shareholders do (Blair 1996: 13). Thus, the form of 'ownership arrangement' of other stakeholders is different to that of shareholders, but may co-exist with it (Boatright 2004). As Engelen (2002: 400) argues:

> Most legal traditions recognize not only 'formal' ownership titles as constituting legally enforceable claims, but also 'informal' rights and responsibilities that are the result of reciprocal expectations. In many legal traditions workers

> possess ownership rights, such as control and co-determination rights, as *workers* and not as *investors*. The Dutch and German Co-Determination and Works Council Acts are a case in point, as well as the co-governance rights of labour unions in Dutch and German corporatism. The same holds for (local, regional and national) governments, communities and other 'stakeholders'; they too possess ownership rights – co-determination rights and income rights – whether or not their involvement with the firm is proprietary in the legal sense. (*Original emphasis.*)

We will explore these ownership arrangements for the various stakeholders in more detail in the subsections below. The important point to note here is that the allocation of participation rights in these models of governance may still arguably be based on a form of ownership, but one substantially different to the legal title that forms the basis of shareholder rights. In fact, in this way, the allocation is probably more akin to the membership basis of citizen entitlements, i.e. recognition of stakeholder entitlements in the continental European and Asian models of governance is as much to do with their relational rights and obligations, as it is their formal legal status.

More recently, Benz and Frey (2007) have argued that for good corporate governance, shareholders might specifically benefit from the introduction of public governance mechanisms. Similar to our analysis here, they argue that 'the CEO corresponds to the head of government, the company board to the members of the cabinet, and shareholders are corporate citizens convening in a town council meeting' (Benz and Frey 2007: 95). By suggesting a return to fixed salaries for executives, a specific division of power within the firm, rules of succession similar to governments, and a range of other elements of public governance, Benz and Frey basically make the case that the processes of governing the firm in the interests of their shareholder–citizens would liken private corporations increasingly to public or governmental institutions.

In sum, the metaphor of citizenship when applied to shareholders can be used both to open up, and to close down, discussions about the nature of participation and democracy in the governance of corporations. On the one hand, it holds a certain degree of potential to envisage new ways of conceptualising the basis on which rights to participation are allocated. On the other, while it offers a clear agenda for asserting and reinforcing exclusive shareholder rights to participation, it does so within a limited conception of democracy, and a very minimalist conception of ownership.

Employees as citizens

As we have already argued earlier in this chapter, employees are the stakeholder group that has been most extensively exposed to citizenship terminology and thinking. This is most explicit in the stream of literature concerned with 'organizational citizenship', but is also evident in the wealth of discussion about workplace democracy, employee involvement and co-determination. The metaphor of citizenship has been rather powerful in the relation of firms to employees as key elements of the status of employees resemble that of the status of citizens in a polity.

The concept of organizational citizenship emerged in the late 1980s, and since this time has been the subject of an extensive outpouring of literature, mainly predicated on defining and testing models of 'organizational citizenship behaviour' (OCB). The widely cited original definition by Organ (1988: 4) suggests that organizational citizenship behaviour is 'individual behaviour that is discretionary, not directly or explicitly recognized by the formal reward system, and that in the aggregate promotes the effective functioning of the organization'. Essentially, the idea of OCB is that some employees will take it upon themselves to go beyond the expectations of their formal role and act for the benefit of the organization without any expectation of recompense. This may include a range of behaviour from helping others, to being a 'good sport', committing loyalty and spreading goodwill, scrupulously adhering to rules, going above and beyond the call of duty, being actively involved in company affairs and developing oneself for the benefit of the company (Podsakoff *et al.* 2000).

In the main, despite its explicit reference to citizenship behaviours, this literature has actually tended to steer away from any meaningful engagement with the concept of citizenship. Indeed, the metaphor of the employee as citizen in this literature is predominantly a one-sided one, perhaps best captured by its designation as the 'good soldier' syndrome (Bolino 1999; Organ 1988). Thus, employee rights and representation do not feature at all, whereas attention is primarily focused on selfless acts for the benefit of the organization. It is interesting that in the mixing of citizenship metaphors with those from sport ('being a good sport') and the military ('being a good soldier', 'beyond the call of duty'), employees are reduced to being means to others' ends, without any conception of the reciprocal relations of rights and responsibilities that bind employees and employers, not to mention citizens and governors.

argue that the company successfully managed to avoid collective agreements for eighteen years and continues to resist works councils.

The question of the legitimacy of employee participation in governance clearly remains contested, and varies across business systems, albeit in a context where there are considerable pressures for convergence towards the Anglo-American model of governance (Dore 2000; Lane 2000a; 2000b). A different though related set of arguments focuses less on the legitimacy of extending participation rights on the basis of ownership entitlements and more on the *morality* of including employees in governance. Collins (1997), for example, argues for the 'ethical superiority and inevitability' of participatory management, while Boatright (2004: 1) suggests that 'employee participation in decision-making is regarded by many as morally preferable to control of corporations by shareholders'. In the main, such arguments predominantly rest on the idea that greater democracy, egalitarianism, freedom and autonomy within the corporation are preferable because these are qualities that we value in political systems (Collins 1997). More specifically, we can say either that employees should *prima facie* have an inalienable right to participate in decisions that affect them (self-determination) or that democracy is required to justify the authority relations of power within the corporation (between the governed and the governors) (Boatright 2004).

Although it is clear that in the political realm we tend to place considerable normative value on concepts such as democracy, the success of such arguments will very much depend on the legitimacy of comparing an organizational system with a political system, and the equating of employees with citizens of the state. This, as we explored in the earlier part of the chapter, can go either way, depending on which elements of the two systems are compared. However, it is notable that even in the rather conservative pages of the *Harvard Business Review*, the idea of 'building a company of citizens' through the Athenian model of citizenship has been promoted as a new democratic model of management (Manville and Ober 2003).

The final set of arguments relates to the economic benefits of employee participation, but there is some ambiguity about the results of experiments in workplace democracy (Harrison and Freeman 2004). On the one hand, there is the expectation that more democratic organizations will benefit from more committed and responsible employees, and that enhanced levels of discretion will lead to more innovative firms with a better-skilled workforce. For instance, Engelen (2002: 402) argues that, 'co-decision making by works councils improves the quality and availability of knowledge, prevents short-sightedness and short-termism, puts managers under a beneficial pressure to legitimatize their decisions, and generates loyalty and involvement among workers'. On the downside, critics argue that democratic processes are time- and labour-intensive and could lead to suboptimal decisions with ultimate negative effects on performance and efficiency. Moreover, as Kerr (2004) argues, the very notion of democracy sits uneasily with the way most companies are set up and function. Those in power, in most cases shareholders and senior management, cannot be expected to voluntarily give up their power. At best, business firms can be 'democratic hybrids' combining bureaucratic systems asking for obedience with pockets of democratic self-determination by employees (Courpasson and Dany 2003).

Finally, commentators highlight the contextual rationalities under which democratic forms of governance are likely to work. Kerr (2004), for instance, highlights the particular role of industries and sectors in enabling or constraining workplace democracy. He argues that democratic processes are more likely to contribute to performance and efficiency in industries that depend on a highly skilled and creative workforce, or in service industries that require close attention by employees to individualized customer preferences. In a similar vein, Soskice (1997) adumbrates the role of national culture and institutions, warning against the transferral of the continental European model of co-determination to Anglo-Saxon countries given the dependence of the former on key institutions, such as long-term financing, effective vocational skill development and deeply entrenched rules and rituals of participation. On balance, the debate on workplace democracy is marked by some optimism, but is shot through with various contingencies, caveats and cautions that offer a profound challenge to the prospects, and indeed the value, of democracy among employee stakeholders.

Consumers as citizens

Once we move away from shareholders and employees, the idea of other stakeholders inhabiting citizen-like relations of power within the realm of the corporation rests on less solid foundations, but also offers some interesting considerations that are worthy of attention. The third of our stakeholder groups, consumers, are typically regarded as one of the corporation's most important constituencies, but they are also the site of some of the greatest controversy and change in relation to citizenship. As we have seen in the last chapter, the privatization and marketization of public services has reconfigured an increasing range of citizen relations into relations of consumption. So, for instance, various social service recipients from hospital patients to university students have begun to be readily conceived of as 'consumers' in much the same way as are consumers of car servicing or hairdressing.

The consumer's role in the governance of the corporation is one predicated on markets. In contrast to the hierarchical form of governance in citizen–government relations or employee–employer relations, market forms of governance rely on incentives, rewards and sanctions granted through consumer preferences. If consumers like or do not like what corporations are doing, then in principle they can vote with their wallets and encourage or discourage such behaviour (Persky 1993). In a way, consumers are like 'economic voters' wielding 'purchase votes' that influence the management of the corporation to engage in particular behaviour (Dickinson and Carsky 2005; Smith 1990). Although typically this is behaviour associated solely with the quality, price and availability of product offerings, 'ethical' or 'political' consumers in some parts of the world have also focused on broader social issues such as labour conditions, environmental impacts and fair trading arrangements with suppliers (Harrison *et al.* 2005).

The underlying assumption here is that consumers are 'sovereign' over producers – in the 'accepted sequence' (Galbraith 1974) of the market they express their needs and desires as a demand that firms then respond to by supplying them with the goods and services that they require. This defines relations of power for the consumer, which is particularly evident in early usage of the term 'consumer sovereignty', most notably that of Hutt, who is usually credited with coining the term. As Persky (1993: 184) explains in his retrospective of the term:

> Hutt defined consumer sovereignty as follows (1936, p. 257): 'The consumer is sovereign when, in his role as citizen, he has not delegated to political institutions for authoritarian use the power which he can exercise socially through his power to demand (or refrain from demanding).' Hutt's double use of the word 'power', while a bit inelegant, made clear what he was most concerned about. Consumer sovereignty gives power to consumers … Hutt

(p. 257) saw this power as an expression of democratic values in achieving 'the social control which maximises liberty and justice'.

The notion of consumer sovereignty is central to neo-classical economics, but in the main Hutt's original message about citizens' power, participation and freedom has now been replaced by an emphasis on market efficiency. In the context of perfect markets, at least, consumer sovereignty should ensure fairness in individual transactions and efficiency in the allocation of resources by the economic system (see Smith 1990). However, within the system of market governance, consumers also have certain freedoms and contract-specific rights (that are usually protected in some way through the law) such as rights to safe and efficacious products, truthful labelling and fair pricing.

At the very least, the idea of sovereign consumers voting on corporate decisions suggests some equivalence with political models of citizenship, but there are important qualifications that limit the applicability to consumers. To begin with, consumption is typically an individualistic and self-interested activity that is at odds with some of the more collective elements of citizenship. In many respects, individuals operate from different values, or moral frames of reference, as consumers than they do as citizens: 'we act as consumers to get what we want for ourselves. We act as citizens to achieve what we think is right or best for the community' (Sagoff 1986: 229). Or, as Fitchett (2005) puts it, 'consumers ... have no formal obligation to represent the interests of any other group as part of the legitimate practice of consumption, and nor do they hold in trust the resources or intentions of others ... Thus, the consumer has no ethical responsibility other than the satisfaction of his or her own needs, wants and desires.'

Some commentators in the areas of ethical and political consumption have tried to counter this by arguing that consumers can incorporate more collective responsibilities by electing to purchase fairly traded or environmentally benign products – thereby suggesting the possibility of 'citizen consumers' (Dickinson and Carsky 2005; Harrison 2005). While this may be true, there is little equality among citizen consumers since 'economic votes' are allocated on the basis of financial strength rather than any egalitarian principles (Dixon 1992; Persky 1993). The notion of voting rights being predicated on economic resources appears distinctly undemocratic as a system of governance.

Another major consideration is that consumers have only limited opportunity (or it seems, interest) to form collective representation or engage in active participation in the governance of the corporation (Fitchett 2005). In contrast to employees, the individualized nature of market transactions offers little scope for collective action among consumers, for example in pressing for better or cheaper products. Most market relations are thoroughly individualized. Having said this, there seem to be few structural constraints on consumers seeking collective representation. It is notable, for instance, that consumer associations and consumer activism of one sort or another (e.g. boycotts) have 'been high profile in most reasonably affluent societies for decades' (Gabriel and Lang 2005: 39). In a few incidences, direct action against corporations has contributed to significant changes in corporate decision-making, including the withdrawal of Premier Oil and Triumph (the lingerie firm) from Burma in 2002. Moreover, formal supporters clubs and other consumer groups have long been associated with particular sporting and recreational organizations, and even aspirational brands such as Apple and Harley Davidson have inspired the formation of 'brand communities' among devoted consumers. These associations enable a more collective engagement with the organization, albeit one that may not necessarily only utilise the market to do so. As such, then, while individual representation remains the norm in market governance, there are also opportunities for other forms and channels of influence.

This leads to the question of what mechanisms there might actually be for consumers (whether individual or collective) to actively participate in the governance of the corporation. On the one hand, the market is the principal way in which formal participation is enabled, albeit of the relatively limited form of 'exit' (much like shareholders). On an empirical level, the idea of consumers having some sovereignty over producers, and being able to effectively cast their economic vote on matters of concern, is hardly fully borne out in practice when the power differentials between corporations and consumers are so great; when the consumer's interaction with the firm is so fleeting; and when the consumer's decision involves such a range of competing demands and interests. On the other hand, informal participation of a richer kind may be possible through the associations mentioned above or, for the individual consumer, through the market research activities of the corporation. However, this is likely to be at the discretion of the corporation, and typically involves only a minority of consumers. This means that, on the whole, 'consumers are poorly placed to exercise an active governance role' (Fitchett, 2005: 20).

One exception to this generalization is, of course, through the movement of consumer cooperatives, as opposed to the other main form, workers' cooperatives. Consumer cooperatives were founded in the UK in the mid-nineteenth century. Their basic organizational form is that registered members vote on major policy decisions and elect a board which, in turn, oversees the running of the cooperative in accordance with the Rochdale Principles, which capture many themes of social responsibility. Their emphasis tends to be upon service to the consumer members but may also return a modest profit to the consumer members. The larger examples tend to be in general retailing (e.g. UK, Switzerland, Japan, Italy) but some specialize in, for example, recreational equipment (e.g. Canada, the US) or organic dairy products (e.g. Switzerland). In other cases they are very small concerns (e.g. the only shop in a community). The European Community of Consumer Cooperatives reports 60,000 different retail outlets serving 20 million consumers (http://www.eurocoop.org). While these cooperatives certainly offer the structure for consumers to direct the companies' policies regarding price, product and other social outputs preferred by the consumers, the extent of participation in practice may be limited.

Ultimately, any consideration of the role of consumers as 'citizens' within the corporation can only really be provisional. At present, the very nature of 'consumer' and 'citizen' appear to be increasingly difficult to disentangle. Consumers are increasingly being exhorted to bring their citizenship mentalities to bear on their (ethical) purchase behaviour, while citizens are increasingly being recast as consumers of public services and other entitlements. Thus, consumption may be a vehicle for expressing or channelling citizenship, just as citizenship may be reconfigured by new forms of consumption. Perhaps more than any other stakeholder, consumers are likely to bring a range of different identities to their relation with the corporation – citizen, hedonist, purist, bargain hunter, activist, to name just a few (see Gabriel and Lang 2005). So, although the market may offer only partial governance of the corporation, the act of consumption itself opens up considerable space for the exercise of a citizen identity, as we shall explore in more detail in the next chapter.

Suppliers as citizens

As we have seen in the previous two chapters, the responsibilities expected of corporations, especially in areas such as labour conditions and environmental impacts, have increasingly been extended to involve their suppliers. As such, suppliers are involved both in the discharge of corporate citizenship behaviours (Chapter 2), as well as the governance of citizenship rights by corporations (Chapter 3). The idea that a firm such as Nike should be responsible for what happens in its suppliers' factories also suggests a relation of power between the corporation and its suppliers, although it is evident that the nature of this relationship will vary according to relative resource dependence and other factors. While the social responsibility debate has tended to focus on firms' responsibilities for their suppliers' actions, the literature on supply chains suggests a great deal of variation in firm–supplier power dynamics, particularly regarding the balance of collaboration and compliance (Frenkel and Scott 2002). Given this variety of power relations, corporation–supplier relationships may not initially seem to be particularly suitable for analysis through the lens of citizenship, especially as it would be difficult even to determine which party was in the 'government' role, and which was in the 'citizen' role. This is a common problem where the ostensible citizen is represented as a corporate body rather than an individual (as we saw in Chapter 2).

However, suppliers, like consumers, are in economic relations of exchange with the corporation, and as such are likewise invested with certain contractual entitlements and responsibilities, as well as being embedded within formal and informal 'rules of engagement' which suggest other moral entitlements (Jones and Pollitt 1998). These include certain expectations about trust, commitment, fairness and risk between the two parties. More importantly, suppliers, like consumers, are also embedded in a market-based system of governance that means corporations can in principle govern their suppliers through their 'sovereign' purchase decisions. Suppliers, in the classic market model, are simply passive respondents to the market preferences of corporations, leaving them with little opportunity to adopt citizen-like roles. The market itself offers little opportunity for participation in the governance of the corporation, leaving suppliers with relatively limited involvement through informal mechanisms such as the contract negotiation process and supplier audit visits.

Increasingly, though, firms appear to be moving away from their reliance on traditional adversarial relationships with suppliers, based upon short-termist, transactional arrangements in the market. In some contexts, these have been gradually replaced with more partnership-based approaches that emphasize long-term relationships based upon mutual trust and collaboration (Durán and Sánchez 1999). Such partnership models of sourcing enable a greater degree of participation by suppliers in corporate decision-making on various issues, including innovation, product development and logistics. This suggests a more citizen-like relationship, where suppliers may enjoy more insider status, albeit a status not shared equally by all suppliers. In this sense, the informal, partial and voluntaristic nature of partnership sourcing may offer a greater degree of participation and protection of rights, but also may have a deleterious effect on supplier 'democracy'.

The insider status afforded to partnership suppliers is most evident in the Japanese model of governance, which is predicated on a *keiretsu* model of intra-organizational relations. In this context, suppliers are integrated within a networked enterprise group that enables long-term reciprocal relations with corporations, and involves interlocking ownership and a degree of institutionalised mutual participation in decision-making. Japanese suppliers are thus conferred with rights of membership and participation in the corporation, much as citizens are within a political community. Consequently, the relevance and applicability of the citizenship metaphor for suppliers is, as with shareholders and employees, largely determined by the variety of capitalism evident in a particular context.

Civil society as citizens

Civil society organizations (CSOs) have been among the most vociferous critics of the lack of democracy and accountability in corporations. As direct representatives of citizens' interests (at least in principle), CSOs are perhaps the most obvious stakeholders to be considered from a citizenship perspective. However, of all the stakeholder groups, CSOs probably have the least tangible relation with the corporation, and, in the absence of ownership or economic relations, what does it mean to say that a non-governmental organization (NGO), religious association, or community group is a citizen within the arena of the corporation?

On the one hand, the citizens that CSOs are ostensibly representing are citizens of the state, not of the corporation. This stands in marked contrast to shareholders, employees, customers, or suppliers who may all lay claim to some degree of membership of the corporation. On the other hand, CSO relations with corporations may, on the face of it, be more likely to be driven by citizen values than the other stakeholders, since the latter are all driven primarily by economic values. Thus, while their status as citizens of the corporation is less based on contractual relations and entitlements, they still assume a citizen-like relation to the corporation because they are, or represent, citizens of a polity in which corporations have a government-like position along the lines discussed in Chapter 3. Furthermore, CSOs represent citizens' interests and are a pivotal element in processes where corporations participate in societal governance in ways and forms adumbrated earlier in Chapter 2. CSOs thus base their legitimacy as citizens of the corporation on the fact that they represent hitherto externalized stakes which otherwise would have been ignored by the company. This is the obverse of the oft-claimed motivation for corporate citizenship that corporations require a social licence to trade. In as much as this is the case, it could be envisaged that civil society plays a role in defining the parameters of this arena. Thus, CSOs have a potentially important, but relatively fragile role as citizens in and around the corporation.

Civil society has long been regarded as a key arena for the enabling and exercising of citizenship, and is now receiving increased attention in this respect (Fung and Wright 2001; Fung 2003a). As the 'third sector' after the public and private sector, civil society has represented a means for self-development, active involvement in the community, as well as a form of collective representation to, or resistance to, government and other powerful actors through associations (Fung 2003a; Warren 2001). Although this has long included corporations, in recent years, CSOs such as Christian Aid, Friends of the Earth, Greenpeace, Oxfam, World Wildlife Fund (WWF) and various others have appeared to give an increasing proportion of their attention to corporations and rather less to governments. We discussed this in some detail in Chapter 3 in terms of corporations acting as a channel for the exercise of citizenship. Here, though, we are not so much interested in the broad societal role of corporations, but in the individual CSO's ability to influence an individual corporation to protect a particular set of interests.

The important point to recognize in this respect is that in contrast to other stakeholders, CSOs lack any institutionalized or formal mechanisms for participation and influence in the corporation. As a result, the main form of engagement in the past was boycotts and other direct actions aimed at corporations. More recently, CSOs have also engaged in stakeholder dialogues, partnerships and other more collaborative arrangements with corporations in order to press their interests, and effect a form of 'civil regulation' (Zadek 2007). Involvement in these partnerships remains at the discretion of the corporation, but it does at least offer the potential for the inclusion of wider citizen values in the governing body of the corporation. In some instances, the partnerships between companies and civil society organizations represent major long-term, strategic initiatives that are akin to admitting civil groups into the governance of the firm. For example, companies such as Unilever have cooperated on this level with the WWF in the Marine Stewardship Council. Similarly, Greenpeace has been a key partner for the German company Foron in the development of eco-friendly refrigerants, as well as for the energy company nPower in the development of renewable electricity marketed under the Juice brand.

A more formal institutionalization of civil society interests into corporate governance is represented by the emergence of 'social enterprises'. While different to the corporate form that we are primarily interested in in this book, social enterprises represent something of a hybrid of civil and commercial organizations and offer an alternative perspective on how civil interests might be incorporated into the corporation (Seelos and Mair 2005). Similarly, the current UK debate on the legal recognition of the 'community interest company' – featuring citizen groups represented on the board – offers another such fresh perspective (Low and Cowton 2004).

Ultimately, given that CSOs essentially act on behalf of third party interests, the question of the accountability of CSOs themselves is also a crucial one. This issue has been raised with increasing regularity in recent years (Hilhorst 2002). This is perhaps not surprising when one considers that CSOs have often been the parties most vociferously questioning the accountability of corporations. Debates about CSO accountability have largely mirrored the same questions that have been raised in relation to corporations. For example, who exactly is an organization such as Greenpeace supposed to be serving? Are the interests of its managers aligned with those of its principal constituents? To what extent and to whom is Greenpeace responsible for the consequences of its actions? This suggests that we can conceptualise CSO managers as 'agents' for a broader collective of civil society 'principals' in the same way that we do for corporate managers and shareholders (see Doh and Teegen 2002). Likewise, we can model CSOs as representative of different stakeholder interests just as we can with corporations (e.g. Hilhorst 2002).

Given such a range of stakeholders, issues of accountability, participation and democracy are clearly quite complex. Still, it is, in fact, the accountability of CSOs to their supposed beneficiaries that tends to raise the most debate. A number of problems are evident here (see Ali 2000; Bendell 2000; Hilhorst 2002), including accusations that: Western CSOs purporting to represent the interests of those in less developed countries have imposed their own agendas on local people without adequately understanding their situations and needs; the participation of beneficiaries in agenda setting, defining priorities and making strategic decisions is often limited; the need for financial support and other resources can focus CSO's interests on donors' priorities rather than those of their intended beneficiaries; beneficiaries typically lack effective mechanisms to voice approval or disapproval of CSO performance; and direct involvement with corporations may work to co-opt CSO priorities away from their beneficiaries.

In some ways, then, it would appear that many CSOs have tended to be equally as inattentive to issues of participation and democracy among their citizens as many corporations have. Given their largely positive impact on society, their moral orientation and comparatively high levels of popular trust, it could be argued that perhaps these issues are less crucial. However, given the growing importance of their role in society in general, as well as their involvement in business specifically, these questions are only really likely to gain in significance otherwise CSOs too will be accused of power without responsibility. What we see, then, with civil society is that it has the potential to provide a platform for citizens to engage with corporations, but that the mode of engagement, both between citizen–CSO and CSO–corporation, does not *necessarily* offer a very solid basis for the exercise of citizenship.

Conclusion

As we have seen, the idea of stakeholders as citizens can be quite a powerful one in the broad discussion about corporate governance, and in particular regarding our understanding of participation and democracy in corporate decision-making. The political metaphor of citizenship helps us to explore and refine our thinking about the allocation of rights to stakeholders, and about appropriate forms and norms of participation in corporate governance.

A citizenship perspective, we would argue, serves as a powerful tool to frame and understand the complexity and diversity of a firm's relations to its multiple stakeholders. It first of all provides a lens for disclosing the very basis of the relationship and the fundamentals on which the status of being a stakeholder is grounded. A citizen-like status for a stakeholder, as we have shown, is predicated on specific rights and to have a clear understanding of these differences in status of stakeholder–citizens is vital for managing these relations. This is particularly significant in situations where lines between stakeholder groups and claims become blurred: when Nike refused to comply with one of its customers' wishes to have the word 'sweatshop' embroidered on his customized pair of trainers, he was addressing a contentious human rights issue in the company's relation to its employees–suppliers (Crane and Matten 2007: 339). What turned the case into a public relations disaster for Nike, though, was the fact that the company basically infringed one of the contractual rights of their customer – namely to use and to pay for the option of customizing his product according to his own preferences.

Furthermore, this case also highlights the value of citizenship thinking as our approach conceptualizes not only the status and the entitlements of stakeholders more precisely but also opens up stringent ways of thinking about the concomitant processes of stakeholder participation. A citizenship perspective, in fact, opens up the opportunity of tapping into a rather rich heritage of both theoretical and practical approaches to design effective modes and mechanisms of citizenship participation in the process of societal governance. This perspective is helpful already in the narrow context of this chapter where we conceived the arena of a firm and its stakeholders as a polity. Here, citizenship thinking offers substantial and promising avenues of developing specific approaches to governing the firm as well as its relations to internal and external groups. As we have argued throughout this chapter, lessons from the way governments interact with their citizens can be applied to the firm–stakeholder context in a similar fashion.

The latter becomes even more valid if stakeholder collaboration takes place in the contexts outlined in Chapters 2 (corporations as citizens) and 3 (corporations as governments). If companies become more involved in societal governance as citizens, those 'fellow citizens' with whom they will interact are in most cases likely also to be stakeholders of the company. In a similar vein, those citizens for whom corporations take over from government aspects of governing their citizenship entitlements almost by definition have a stake in the company. In as much as these contexts become more of an empirical reality for companies the discussed trajectories of approaching stakeholders as citizens presents the logical consequence.

At the same time, as a sense-making concept, the notion of stakeholders as citizens has certain drawbacks. In particular, the metaphor of citizenship takes on a rather different complexion in each stakeholder group, and it is only partially successful in integrating multiple stakeholder relations. Stakeholder relations as a whole do not resemble any particular single model of citizenship. Models of citizenship do not help to illuminate any specific aspect of stakeholder relations across all stakeholder groups. And, different models of corporate governance resemble different types of citizenship relationships.

One of the main problems with extending notions of citizenship to the full range of stakeholders is that only employees really maintain a relatively consistent and unitary membership of the corporation, and even they may be embedded in multiple citizen relations with corporations. Although there are exceptions, most stakeholders enter a relatively transitory and promiscuous relation of citizenship with the firm. Consumers bring their citizen identities to multiple corporations in many and various ways, and easily switch allegiances. Their power, therefore, is, paradoxically, in their capacity to exit from a particular relationship. While this is analogous to citizens' role in the electoral process, it is not reflective of the engagement of other forms of democratic citizenship. Shareholders usually operate a portfolio of stocks. Governments interact with all corporations to some extent. Even employees, who may be 'citizens' of a single firm, may also be shareholders in other firms, customers of yet more, and engage with still others through membership of civil society organizations. Thus, insofar as citizenship is a useful analogy for stakeholders, only a conception of citizenship that allows for multiple interconnected citizen relations is appropriate. This, of course, takes us away from traditional views of citizenship that are based on stable relations of power between citizens and governments of nation states. Instead, we might look towards reconfigurations of citizenship that have emphasized the importance of identity, ecology and global community, rather than the nation state as the main arena of citizenship. It is to these that we now turn in the second part of the book.

Notes

1. In fairness to Freeman, while the corporation is predominantly presented as the focal point in his book, he also indicates that 'the managers in a corporation' are actually a more precise focus (Freeman 1984: 209).
2. This alludes to the fact that the heartland of this approach lies particularly in those countries bordering the river Rhine: France, Germany, The Netherlands, Switzerland and Austria. In a broader sense, though, key features of this capitalist approach can also be traced in the Scandinavian countries as well as in Italy, Spain and Portugal.

PART B

Corporations and citizenship reconfigurations

5 *Citizenship identities and the corporation*

Shake your conscience. Drink with commitment.

Mecca Cola advertising slogan , www.mecca-cola.com/en/index.php, July 18, 2007

Introduction

So far in this book we have tried to map out main avenues of applying the notion of citizenship to corporations. There are some relatively consistent, well-established and robust understandings of citizenship in political science and political philosophy, which can be taken – as it were – from the shelf and examined with regard to their applicability to corporations. However, we have also noted the contingency and dynamics of citizenship. This is perhaps nowhere more true than when we turn to the identities that underpin or challenge citizenship.

> The modern conception of citizenship as merely status held under the authority of the state has been contested and broadened to include various political and social struggles of recognition and redistribution as instances of claim-making, and hence, by extension of citizenship. As a result, various struggles based upon identity and difference (whether sexual, racial, ethnic, diasporic, ecological, technological and cosmopolitan) have found ways of articulating their claims to citizenship understood not simply as a legal status, but as political and social recognition and economic redistribution (Isin and Turner 2003: 2).

This relatively recent emphasis on citizenship reference frames other than that of the nation state has led to a broad debate on a variety of transformations in the nature of political communities. While some of these new frameworks are linked to concrete developments, such as the deterioration of the natural environment or the advent of globalization (Chapters 6 and 7) many of them are constituted by distinct cultural characteristics of certain groups. This debate has led to a plethora of work around the phenomenon of 'cultural citizenship' (Kalberg 1993; Stephenson 2003; 2001) which in essence explores, analyzes and conceptualizes new ways in which cultural identities have become the key element of constructing political communities. Central to the debate on cultural citizenship are new cultural identities which form the basis of membership in the political community, and thus confer citizenship status on their holders.

These citizenship identities are premised on social identities that their advocates seek to politicize. Citizenship identity captures the way groups understand and project themselves as internally integrated and distinct from others in the polity. These characteristics are then used as a basis for making claims either to share the wider citizenship status from which they have been excluded or to win special citizenship advantages or exemptions in terms of entitlements and/or process. This is because although 'formal citizenship in Western democratic societies is presumed to confer a universal set of rights and duties ... citizenship on the books and citizenship in action are not coterminous' (Calavita 2005: 407). One can possess formal status as a citizen yet be excluded (in law or in fact) from certain civil, political or social rights, or from forms of participation in the political process that are available to others.

Citizen identity characteristics are usually: based on some long-term, often inherited, attributes; combined with activities and practices which reinforce the inherent characteristics; and not only require internal affirmation but also external recognition of the distinctive identity. The specific bases for social, and in turn, citizenship identity vary – and indeed there has been a proliferation of such identities emerging in political realms across the globe. In the emergence of liberal democratic politics, religion and gender were prominent citizenship identities. In the nineteenth and twentieth century struggles against empire and colonialism, nationalism was a key basis for identity. Subsequently, bases for identity-based citizenship claims have included ethnicity, sexual orientation, disability and age. Identity has become yet more kaleidoscopic as people assume multiple identities. This may reflect the increase in people with multiple nationalities and ethnicities resulting from migration but also from the recognition of people's multiple and shifting identities when they remain in one social place. The key point is not *what* the basis for identification is, but rather *that* individuals in groups are constituted in some distinctive context, and that this can be a basis for inclusion in a polity as a citizen, or a basis for claiming that their distinctiveness requires special recognition or remedy in order to enable them to enact full citizenship roles.

This contrasts with the more universal conceptions of individuals which are sometimes implicit in economics and politics. The significance of identity for economics is that it challenges the assumption that business owners, managers, consumers, employees or investors, for example, make market calculations on the basis of commonly-held motivational frameworks. Instead, identities bring different value- or interest-based vantage points into economic transactions.

Likewise the significance of identity in politics is that it forms a basis for defining or challenging the scope and limits of citizenship premised on assumptions of universal political features alone. As Iris Marion Young observed: 'the attempt to realize the universal citizenship ... will tend to exclude or put at a disadvantage some groups, even when they have equal citizenship status ... insisting that as citizens persons should leave behind their particular affiliations and experiences to adopt a general point of view serves only to reinforce that privilege; for the perspectives and interests of the privileged will tend to dominate this unified public marginalizing or silencing of other groups' (Young 1994: 391).

In this chapter we will see how companies either place themselves or find themselves in positions which are critical to the ability of people of different identities to fulfil aspects of their citizenship, be it in forms of self-expression or in the ability to be employed. This is notwithstanding the assumption that some managers might hold the view either that market decisions are based on universal and abstract criteria or that it is the responsibility of governments to define and provide for citizenship possibilities of different social identities.

Social identities as a basis for citizenship identity

In this section we explore the sorts of social and citizenship identities that have emerged that corporations may need to address. We consider, first, identity as consisting of attributes, second identity as a resource, and third we examine responses to proliferating social and citizenship identities.

Identity is usually understood as some basis for associating with one group of other humans on the basis of some attribute which also differentiates this group from others, be they the majority or minority.

Thus, from Aristotle until the late nineteenth century it was frequently taken as axiomatic that citizenship should be accorded to male members of society. Over the last two centuries, in particular, women's suffrage movements have challenged this view and have offered an idea of citizenship which embraces women.

However, feminist claims have developed such that equal citizenship is not simply regarded as a question of an equal vote or right to stand for election. It has addressed a whole range of issues concerning both the conditions of continuing inequality, which can and should be addressed, as well as the condition of gender difference which needs to be taken account of in advancing citizenship. These include the projection of women in media, employment conditions and remuneration, and the role of women in reproduction and care. Hence corporations, for better or worse, have become involved in debates about the citizenship of women, as they are major advertisers, employers and providers of goods and services. For instance, multinational fast food companies in Saudi Arabia operate separate entrances and seating areas for men and women, leading to accusations by some that they operate a form of 'gender apartheid' that serves to reinforce inequality in women's status as citizens (King 2001).

Other biological forms of identity include race, ethnicity, some forms of disability and sexual orientation. In many countries, citizenship has been defined either by law or practice in racial or ethnic terms. Civil rights groups in numerous countries initially campaigned for equal political rights assuming that this was the key to citizenship. But, having won these rights, on finding that aspects of their lives were still slow to change, such groups broadened their conceptions of citizenship to focus on, for example, employment and remuneration conditions, which again brought corporations into the reckoning. In the case of disability and sexual orientation, while citizenship has not usually been proscribed on this basis, those identifying as disabled, or gay, lesbian, bisexual or transgendered (GLBT), have focused on such issues of recognition, and legal equality concerning their practices, and the resources and conditions for them to function fully as citizens. Again, corporations in their roles as employers and as providers of retail and employment environments have been asked to accommodate such agendas. In the UK, for instance, all service providers are required by law to ensure that there are no physical barriers stopping or making it unreasonably difficult for disabled people to access or use their services.

Some bases for identity may not be biological but social. Thus, religion, nationalism and ethnicity reflect membership of social groupings which, heavily or even exclusively, reflect inherited affiliations, but which individuals can choose to adopt or discard. These social bases for citizenship identity can either characterize dominant groups in society who wish to maintain their religion, nationalism or ethnicity as the basis for citizenship, or groups at the margins (be it numerically or in terms of access to power) who wish to challenge the dominant basis for citizenship identity. This could either be to substitute one basis for identity for another or to amend or supplement the dominant basis in order to better establish and legitimize their own identity. Again, this can extend beyond the formal concomitants of citizenship to include employment rights, rules about investment and trade, consumption and representation in marketing. These issues have confronted business in such societies as Northern Ireland, Belgium and Canada as well as more dramatically in the Middle East and pre-democratic South Africa, for example.

Other forms of social identity may more strongly reflect choice over such matters as consumption. There has been much written about the social connections formed through brand communities (Muñiz and O'Guinn 2001), neo-tribes (Cova 1997), and other cultures of consumption (Kozinets 2001). As Cova (1997) suggests, brands provide 'linking value' for individuals who self-identify within communities based around their consumption. Thus, more postmodern bases of identity have been rooted in consumer preferences for such products as Harley Davidson motorbikes (Bagozzi and Dholakia 2006a), convenience foods (Cova and Pace 2006), car clubs (Algesheimer *et al.* 2005) and open source technology brands (Bagozzi and Dholakia 2006b).

In all these cases, corporations are critical to the ability of individuals to define their social identity by consumption, although there are clearly limits to the political nature of such engagements. For consumer communities to represent genuine citizenship identities, they need to be the basis for claims to status, entitlements or processes of participation within the polis. This perhaps becomes more evident when consumer communities coalesce around avowedly societal issues, such as fair trade (e.g. in collectives such as 'fairtrade towns' and 'fairtrade universities'), or anti-corporate protest (e.g. through boycotts and ethical consumption) (see for example Handelman 2006), but at the same time, there may also be a political function to brand communities based on consumption of cars, motorbikes, open source software, or many other product categories. We need only observe the political nature of groups such as the US National Rifle Association to see how the consumption of a specific product can be the basis for citizenship claims and entitlements. Again, in all these developments, business is centre-stage in debates about social and citizenship identity.

We have seen that identity is not only an attribute but also a resource. As a result, identity is something which is mobilized for political purposes, be it by groups seeking to win greater autonomy and power (e.g. European nineteenth-century nationalist movements) or by groups seeking to defend their status or other resources from other claimants (e.g. the Afrikaans National Party in the Republic of South Africa). Identity is therefore not only a basis for mutual recognition and association of the group in question, but also a basis for differentiation from and mobilization against either another group or simply those not sharing the attributes.

This is relevant for business. First, they can become caught up in identity politics. Thus McDonalds has been portrayed as antithetical to French national identity in terms of its impact on consumption and retailing traditions as well as more generally representative of American values which subvert French ways. This went beyond rhetorical criticism when one of the company's outlets was destroyed by José Bové and members of his militant farmers union in 1999. Shell in Nigeria has become identified by sections of the Ogoni people as not only economically exploitative but also as associated with the federal government's oppression. It is therefore regarded as a key player in the separatist aspirations of these people. Second, companies themselves can use identity as a resource, a concept which we will explore in more detail below.

Identity politics is not unambiguously either a good or a bad thing. On the one hand it can be associated with greater social autonomy and flourishing. This is captured in the word 'liberation', widely used by women's, gay and nationalist movements. It has been associated with the achievement of status and respect with established systems for women, GLBT and adherents to minority religions, for example. Conversely, it can be associated from the outside, at least, with the absence of toleration and mutual distrust as in the sectarian politics of Northern Ireland, Lebanon and the former Yugoslavia, for example. It can also be associated with excessive pressure for conformity as the group strives to maintain its differentiation – the resource for those who wish to mobilize identity politics.[1] Thus John Stuart Mill (1946), one of liberalism's greatest advocates, feared that nationalism may insulate its members from the social, political and economic benefits of modernity.

Modern societies have responded to the claims of identity politics in a variety of ways. Some, like France, have tended to impose a form of national and secular identity in order to deter national break-up (e.g. in the suppression of the Breton and Languedoc languages and culture) and to preserve a strong sense of the modern French identity (e.g. in the laws concerning foreign language films, legislation on the wearing of religious symbols at school). Other conceptions of citizenship have effectively, rather than formally, excluded groups from citizenship as experienced by native and black North Americans who suffered fundamental restrictions on their citizenship even in the twentieth century, notwithstanding constitutional assumptions about their political equality. More recently, the US has shifted from its 'melting pot' approach to immigration, in which distinctive citizenship resources were discouraged, to the elevation of Spanish to the status of an official language following the wave of Latin American immigration.

Notwithstanding the fact that some forms of identity are more readily inherited than others, it is certainly true that there is an element of choice about which identity or identities people assume. The attachment to identities is therefore complicated by the fact that many people, especially in post-industrial societies, have multiple identities and that these are in flux. We now turn to focus on the relationships of business to such developments.

Corporations and citizenship identity

As we have shown, corporations have played a significant role in the development and articulation of many different citizenship identities. However, it is clear that the nature of this role will vary in different contexts. Three types of role are evident: corporations *reflecting* citizen identity; corporations *enabling* citizen identity; and corporations *inhibiting* citizen identity.

Corporations reflecting citizen identity

Corporations that identify with a particular citizenship identity (or are identified with it by others) can be said to reflect citizenship identity. In the first part of the book (Chapter 2), we saw this playing out in the ascription of the citizen metaphor to the corporation, i.e. we explored whether corporations were like citizens because they possessed similar characteristics to 'real' citizens. However, this line of thinking can be extended beyond traditional national citizen identities to encompass alternative or micro identities based on race, religion, gender, sexual orientation or other forms of social identity. Hence, just as a company may be seen as an American or Japanese company because it is like American or Japanese citizens in significant respects, so may a company be regarded as a Jewish company, an African-American company, a Mormon company, a gay company, and so on because it shares something with these types of citizen identities. Moreover, individuals who patronise such firms (or who boycott them) may interpret their engagement with the company as an act of identification with and solidarity towards their fellow citizens.

As we have said, probably the most obvious way in which corporations reflect citizenship identities is in their association with a particular country, region or nationality. This is particularly true of publicly owned companies which operate under national or regional company names. But this often extends to formerly or partly publicly owned companies such as 'flag carrier' airlines (e.g. American Airlines, Air France, British Airways, Singapore Airlines, Malaysian Airlines). It is also true of other companies that extol their national identity through branding and promotion. For instance, IKEA actively promotes itself as a Swedish company while Marlboro has long been associated with images of the American west. As a corporation with a national identity, the claim for citizenship like other American, French, Singaporean or Swedish citizens might be seen as more credible or persuasive.

Over time, however, national identity may be seen as less attractive to companies who may want to vary these associations in order to appeal to other constituencies in other ways. For instance, British Airways, with its distinctive Union Jack tailfins and advertisements that extolled customers to 'fly the flag', moved to introduce 'world art' tailfin designs in 1997 in order to represent itself as a global airline rather than just a British one. The initiative, however, met with considerable controversy, even incurring the wrath of ex-prime minister Margaret Thatcher (who famously declared, 'we fly the British flag, not these awful things'), and was eventually dropped in favour of a restyled Union Jack logo. Ultimately, British customers preferred the airline to reflect their traditional citizenship identity rather than engaging with a more cosmopolitan transnational identity. However, this appears to run counter to a wider shift to more globally oriented brands, illustrated by the usages of ANZ bank rather than Australia and New Zealand, HSBC rather than the Hong Kong and Shanghai Banking Corporation, BP rather than British Petroleum, and various other similar transformations of corporate identity.

Sometimes, rather than reflecting a national citizen identity, businesses can reflect a minority citizenship identity and/or one in adversity. Thus Ellis Marsalis Senior, the grandfather of the famous Marsalis jazz brothers, came to prominence in New Orleans because he founded and ran a hotel business which catered for black commercial travellers who otherwise experienced impediments to their citizenship rights of free movement and equal treatment. Since this time, there has been a significant growth in 'minority-owned businesses' that reflect the racial citizenship of their owners, especially in countries like the US, where the population of such enterprises grew dramatically during the 1980s and 1990s, more than doubling their share of US firms from less than seven per cent in 1982 to almost fifteen per cent by 1997 (US Small Business Administration Office of Advocacy 2001). Indeed, minority owned businesses are evident in many countries and in many industries, often supplying products and services specific to their citizenship (such as Kosher or Halal food), but perhaps more frequently simply reflecting the broader racial mix of the countries in which they are formed.

A remarkable phenomenon, for example in the US cities of San Francisco, New York and Boston, and the UK cities of Brighton and Manchester, is the emergence of what is known as 'the pink economy,' in which GLBT people establish businesses which enable them to reflect their identity of sexual preference around which grow supply chains and customer networks which multiply this basis of identity. A recent article cited an estimate that the pink economy is worth US$250 billion per year.[2] Moreover, there is plenty of evidence that mainstream corporations see this as an important business niche and are also reinforcing GLBT citizenship through business. Indeed, for many years, Boston has had an official GLBT chamber of commerce, the Greater Boston Business Council, which organizes networking events, group health insurance benefits, an annual business expo, and a directory of members and their businesses.

As some of these examples suggest, there may be immediate commercial benefits for firms that seek to reflect particular citizen identities with their brands. Consumers who perceive a brand as being part of their citizen community (or in the case of brand communities, being the fulcrum of their community) may be likely to exhibit significant loyalty and commitment to the brand. This is particularly the case when a brand goes further and appears to profess a political agenda associated with the community. For example, the vodka brand Absolut and the automotive brand Subaru have experienced tremendous loyalty from the gay community in the US because of their persistent willingness to advertise in gay media and appeal to gay consumers, even when other brands sought to downplay or resist their connection to gay identity due to concerns about maintaining their mainstream appeal (Sender 2005). Such brands may also be actively promoted by 'their' community, enjoying the status of a privileged citizen, for example, when governments work on behalf of companies to secure export deals 'in the national interest', or when minority business associations promote their members' interests. Examples of the latter include the Asian Women in Business Association, the National Black Chamber of Commerce, the Latin Business Association and the National Minority Supplier Development Council, as well as the above-mentioned Greater Boston Business Council for GLBT business professionals – all based in the US.

Clearly, though, corporate reflections of citizenship identity are unstable ones. They not only vary with the shifting branding strategies of marketing departments, but are also vulnerable to the market for corporate control. In the former instance, marketers may feel that an association with 'minority' interests of gay, environmental, or Latin consumers no longer serves corporate interests, and so may seek to lose their affinity with such a citizen identity. Alternatively, where the niche is attractive, faux citizen identities may be adopted by firms to capitalize on a growing market. For instance, as more mainstream businesses buy into the pink economy, an issue arises for those who want to make consumer choices strictly to support those who bear a genuine GLBT identity. It is harder for these consumers to distinguish those that 'really do' share the identity from those that identify with it for market purposes.

In the case of the market for corporate control, firms may be bought by other companies that do not share the same citizenship. In the automotive industry, for example, mergers and takeovers have led to the 'Swedish' automotive brand Volvo and the 'British' brand Jaguar falling under the ownership of the American company Ford, and the iconic 'British' Mini brand falling under the control of the German firm, BMW. Acquisitions of 'environmentalist' companies such as Body Shop, Ben & Jerry's, Seeds of Change, and Green and Blacks (by the mainstream corporations L'Oreal, Unilever, Mars and Cadbury's respectively) can also threaten their connections with alternative environmentalist citizen identities. The fact is that just as individuals may develop a range of citizenship identities, so too is it increasingly difficult to assign to corporations a unique citizenship status (and all the entitlements and duties that go with it), especially in the case of large multinational actors that produce a multitude of product lines to various target markets in hundreds of countries across the globe. This is clearly a challenge for corporations seeking to appeal on the basis of their citizenship identity, as well as for consumers seeking to connect with, or reward, companies that share their identity. The allocation of citizenship status based on identity to corporations is highly precarious, especially if it offers support to marginalized or at-risk identities. However, corporations can take a more active role in enabling the citizenship of different social identities, as we shall now discuss.

Corporations enabling citizenship identity

Corporations can go further than simply reflecting citizen identities in their corporate identities. There is also plenty of evidence that companies can actually enable marginalized social identities to acquire or develop their citizenship. They can do this in several ways: (i) by *enabling de facto citizenship status*; (ii) by *providing citizenship entitlements through employment and business opportunities*; (iii) by *providing products and services* used to enhance citizenship status, entitlement, and/or process.

The *enabling of de facto citizenship status* can occur when a company provides employment to non-citizen immigrant or migrant workers, and in doing so provides them with a status that enables them to gain certain entitlements of citizenship. The offer of a job, whether to legal or illegal non-citizens, is often the first step to securing citizenship status for those whose identity would not normally provide them with such rights.

Perhaps the most dramatic illustration of this is in the 'Brinco' (Spanish for 'jump') boutique sneakers, in part designed to assist migrants get across the Mexican border to the US. They are in the colours of the Mexican flag and contain a compass, a flashlight, a pouch for money or pain-killers and a rough map of the border region.[3] More widely, and relatedly, the employment of illegal immigrants and migrant workers, for example, in the southern states of the US and in southern Europe, can be a first step to citizenship. Here, a job, albeit one that is usually poorly paid, insecure and lacking social benefits, can provide some degree of de facto citizenship status while in the country. Although the illegal Mexican worker in Texas may be exploited, some benefits of American citizenship may be available to him or her, such as schooling for their children, participation in markets and the ability to enjoy a degree of security and public order. In well-developed immigrant communities, there may even be the potential for legal representation and protections as well as political participation.

The role of corporations here in facilitating this granting of de facto citizenship status is, on the face of it, limited, but at the same time it is clear that if businesses refused to break the law (or take advantage of poor enforcement) by employing illegal workers, there would be fewer incentives for illegal immigrants to enter the country to find work. Moreover, in doing so, corporations themselves, either explicitly or implicitly, are ascribing some level of de facto citizenship status (albeit usually of a second-class and economic variety) to legal non-citizens.

At times, though, the corporate role is even more pronounced. For example, the sheer number of Mexican workers in the US has led to periodic amnesties for illegal immigrants who have acquired employment. Thus, companies are providing what in retrospect can be regarded as a passport to legal citizenship status. Hence, as Tancredo (2004: 13) suggests, 'our political and legal institutions are subtly encouraged to follow the economic institutions in treating the illegal resident the same as the legal resident. The United States is thus moving toward de facto citizenship as a replacement for traditional citizenship. This movement is slow and subtle, but its signs are unmistakable.'

Most corporate involvement in enabling citizenship identity through de facto status is arguably more subtle, but no less profound, than the granting of status to non-residents and illegals. The granting of employment opportunities to those identifying as women, racial minorities, GLBT and disabled people is widely seen as an important step on the path to more equal citizen status and entitlements for such groups. At one level, simply the ability to participate freely in labour markets is an essential constituent of contemporary citizenship. Beyond this, employment provides opportunities for subsequent participation in other (consumer) markets, and helps develop the type of cultural capital necessary for progressing into certain other arenas of citizenship such as running for political office. Quite simply, jobs – and in particular good quality jobs – help prevent disadvantaged groups from becoming 'second class citizens'. This, of course, relies to a large extent on the corporation being able to provide, through employment, appropriate citizen entitlements to those with non-dominant identities, as we shall now discuss.

Providing citizenship entitlements through employment and business opportunities is a significant issue on the diversity and equal opportunity agenda. As we saw in Chapter 3, where we considered 'corporations as governments', firms have long been involved in the provision of citizenship entitlements in the workplace. For citizenship based specifically on identity, corporations can clearly have a significant role to play in providing a richer experience of entitlements such as equality, freedom from discrimination, freedom of expression (as well as various others) by ensuring that their racial minority, GLBT, disabled, female, or religiously identified employees enjoy such freedoms in the workplace.

While legislation may typically provide the baseline for such entitlements, firms can both go beyond legislation in this arena, as well as actively supporting legislation and living up to the spirit rather than the letter of regulation. Turning, for example, to the case of women at work, there is evidence that many Western companies are seeking to recognize the gendered character of work experience and opportunity and are introducing policies to better enable women to fulfil their employment potential. They thereby contribute to a richer experience of women's employment rights beyond those required by government legislation. Such a situation can be seen for various other citizenship identities, notwithstanding the numerous counter examples of corporations inhibiting the expression of citizenship identity in other instances, as we will see below. The point here, however, is not so much that corporations will act like governments in the role of providing entitlements (which was our basic premise of Chapter 3), but that the emergence of citizenship identity movements may often take place outside of the traditional state–citizen duality anyway. The battle for equality, for instance, is just as likely to take place at the workplace, in the realm of the corporation, as it is in the realm of state politics.

There are also examples of corporations that seek to provide citizenship entitlements through work, not directly within the corporation but either through self-employment or through dedicated companies. An example of the first is that of Hindustan Lever (the Indian subsidiary of Unilever), which works with government agencies and non-governmental organizations (NGOs) that provide micro-credit to women as a means of alleviating poverty. As a result tens of thousands of women are selling Unilever products, often alongside their own, in thousands of villages throughout South Asia. Although they are not Unilever employees, the company assists the women with training and marketing and provides a relatively reliable source of income. Care India endorses this as they see the women as benefiting from learning about retailing, distribution and marketing.[4] Moreover, they have acquired significant market status in societies where this was often discouraged.

Beyond the direct provision of entitlements in the workplace and markets, it is also striking how the reinforcement of citizenship identity through business has also enabled constituencies to engage more fully in citizenship outside their business in broader identity politics. For example, it should also be noted that the elevation of women in business can also feed into their more effective formal political participation, as evidenced by the career paths of numerous female politicians that have crossed over from the corporate sector. In the area of business associations based on identity grounds (e.g. gay or Hispanic business associations), the battle for entitlements in the workplace has also at times led to deeper political engagement through the association. As a spokesperson for the Boston GLBT chamber of commerce commented, this started in the 1990s with a group of Boston gay and lesbian professionals meeting to form a network and to discuss GLBT issues in the workplace. However, the network has grown to include not only 700 individual business people but also corporate members that sponsor Gay Pride events and annual awards ceremonies. This citizenship identity has therefore now developed as the GLBT business community sees that leveraging its economic power 'can do more to change corporate America than holding rallies … You have to work at changing the power structure … We've evolved from simply viewing big business as the enemy to thinking that we need to work with big business. We're being seen as important constituents'.[5] Now such political figures as the

Mayor of Boston and gubernatorial candidates speak at network meetings. This represents a threshold change, first, from when gay and lesbian people felt excluded from business because of their citizenship identity; second, from when business became a means by which they could reflect their citizenship identity; and third, to when business could be leveraged to engage in political activity.

The enhancement of citizenship status through the provision of *products and services* can happen quite innocuously, for example, by simply providing certain opportunities as part of the firm's normal business. Some of the seventeenth- and eighteenth- century English coffee houses were identified by Habermas (1989) as critical in the emergence of 'the public sphere' by allowing a space for free speech (see also Sennett 1996). That these businesses were often threatened with closure by governments illustrates some of their significance for the most basic form of citizenship participation, free exchange of ideas. More recently, AOL Time Warner's decision to provide free software, e-mail and other services to broadband customers as part of its marketing strategy thereby enables its customers to access vast amounts of information and participate in a range of activities relevant to their citizenship.[6] In terms of alternative or minority citizenship identities, media and technology companies have provided the products and services necessary for a wide range of communities to meet, organize and articulate their political values and aspirations in ways that would have been impossible a few decades ago.

These enabling environments for the expression of citizenship identities often will be developed in a self-conscious way by the corporations that we identified above as those that reflected the identities of 'their' community. Hence, gay entrepreneurs may start up gay websites and magazines, Jewish butchers may provide kosher meat to Jewish consumers, and so on. A particularly striking example is provided by the case of Islamic banking, which has operated for some time in Pakistan, Malaysia and Dubai, but is now spreading and attracting Western banks. This obviously allows a citizenship identity to be reflected, since the banking products must be approved by scholars who issue fatwas (religious rulings) that a product is Sharia compliant. This requires that money does not lead to debt and that interest is not simply earned on money alone (or 'riba', which is why gambling is against Sharia law). Instead the money must be backed by assets (i.e. equity banking) and allow earnings on a cost plus fixed profit basis. However, the availability of these products is described precisely in terms of enabling a form of citizenship by identity as illustrated by a lawyer working in the industry: 'These days even a Muslim who is not very devout will choose a Sharia-compliant product because it enhances his status in the community ... Most Muslims don't want to live in an Islamic state. But if you offer them ways to assert their identity today that are not too hazardous, like with Islamic banking, there is a lot of demand'.[7]

Beyond simply providing products and services, though, corporations also play a broader role in articulating the existence of communities based on identity. Marketers and journalists actively construct the existence, for example, of a 'gay market' or a 'Hispanic market' through press releases, magazine articles, or even directories of products, services or publications. As Sender (2005: 5) suggests in relation to the gay market:

> The gay community ... is not a pre-existing entity that marketers simply need to appeal to, but is a construction, an imagined community formed not only through political activism but through an increasingly sophisticated, commercially supported, national media. Marketing has thus been instrumental in the very formation of groups, including politically inflected groups.

Marketing activities aimed at identity-based groups provide visibility and, under some conditions, legitimacy to them. So when publications such as the *Hispanic/Latino Market Advertising Guide* proclaim that the Hispanic market is 'the fastest growing segment of the US Market', they help to suggest that there is an identifiable, relatively homogenous community of Hispanics that represents a viable marketing niche. Such communities can then potentially gain political and other types of status and power through their perceived economic significance: 'in a capitalist society, market incorporation is of the utmost importance because it summons a social legitimation approaching that of citizen' (Peñaloza 1996: 33). Of course, the causality here is difficult to disentangle – clearly recognition as a defined market will often follow the creation of a politically constituted community as has been suggested for both the gay and African-American markets in the US (Peñaloza 1996; Sender 2005). However, further civil and political gains can be made by communities through enhanced market visibility and attention from corporations, suggesting that the two are intrinsically intertwined. As Sender (2005: 242) powerfully argues in relation to the GLBT market, 'the distinction between business and politics is bogus: marketing images of and to GLBT people must necessarily involve both'. This intimate connection between business and identity politics also, of course, brings with it a downside to those seeking to articulate and validate certain identities. Just as corporations can enable citizenship identity so, too, can they inhibit it.

In some cases even the distinctions between the commercial and identity-based manifestations of citizenship become quite obscured, as in the case of the long-standing Cooperative movement in the UK. This organization is both a member of the Labour Party as well as a prominent retailer, banker, insurer and funeral provider, which returns profits to members and seeks to differentiate itself with its egalitarian social standards (e.g. in social reporting, supply chain transparency). Another, more recent, example comes from the far right UK party, the British National Party, which has announced that it will sell life insurance through 'Albion Life Insurance' to boost its own finances.[8] Interestingly, the name of the financial intermediary thus far remains veiled, presumably as it would fear punishment from other citizenship identities. Both cases illustrate that products and services enabling citizenship identities can represent a mix of characteristics which mean different things to different groups and, moreover, are dynamic in their representation of particular characteristics which are of appeal to specific societal subgroups.

Corporations inhibiting citizenship identity

Corporations have often been associated with inhibiting citizenship, in that people's self-identifications with a citizenship based on religious, racial, gender, or sexuality types have been hampered by the actions of corporations. This can happen in four ways: (i) by *excluding* those with certain identities from employment in the corporation or from accessing its products and services; (ii) by ensuring that such identifications do not *prosper* within the organization; (iii) by failing to acknowledge and *represent* citizen identities in corporate communications or *misrepresenting* them; (iv) or even producing products and services that are actively used to *suppress* certain citizenship identities. Let us look at each of these in turn.

The process of *excluding* those with certain social identities from employment in corporations is illustrated by the rather familiar cases of companies in the southern states of the US, Northern Ireland and apartheid South Africa conforming to the expectations of dominant social identities, be they white or protestant, and disadvantaging those with other identities. However, there is evidence of such exclusion, or its more subtle manifestations, in many other contexts. In numerous countries and industries GLBT employees have suppressed their sexuality at work out of fear of reprisal. In some organizations, the outward expression of certain religious affiliations has been outlawed, e.g. by prohibiting the wearing of turbans, the Hijab, or kippah head coverings. British Airways, for example, found itself in the middle of a major media storm in 2006 when it asked a Christian member of staff to conceal her crucifix on a necklace because it contravened the company's uniform policy requiring that all jewellery and religious symbols on chains should be worn under employees' uniforms.[9] Similar exclusions can affect customers with non dominant identities, such as GLBT people who have found it necessary to obfuscate their domestic arrangements in order to obtain mortgages, women or people of colour who have been refused entry to golf clubs and restaurants, or Muslims who have been denied permission to board aeroplanes. Sometimes companies find themselves having to make choices among identities, as the UK Co-operative Bank found when it told Christian Voice to close its account because 'its discriminatory pronouncements' concerning gay rights were deemed incompatible with the bank's ethos.[10]

At one level, these experiences could just be viewed in terms of discrimination, but in a wider political view, corporations here are potentially involved in a more fundamental inhibition of citizenship identities. When those who self identity as black, lesbian or Christian experience inequality, unfair treatment or obstructions to accessing employment or services, their entitlement to some of the basic rights of citizenship are threatened. While corporations may well argue that this is a problem for governments to deal with through equal opportunities legislation, it cannot be denied that business sometimes has played a role in preventing certain citizenship identities from achieving free expression and participating in the workforce and in markets.

A more subtle sort of complaint that is made against companies is that while they may formally and behaviourally be prepared to employ people with a diversity of social identities, they do not create working conditions that enable them to *prosper* and, more specifically, to enjoy their full citizenship rights to equal consumption, employment, autonomy and recognition. A good example of this is the case of gender which has been a prominent instance of identity politics, particularly since the advent of liberal feminism of Mary Wollstonecraft, and of John Stuart Mill and Harriet Taylor in the late seventeenth and mid-eighteenth centuries respectively. It has informed powerful social movements throughout the world premised on the common identification with women's distinctive roles in reproduction and the social roles which have tended to go with this, particularly in industrial society, in the form of child-caring and home-making. While these roles have been regarded as sites both of alienation and of fulfilment by feminists (Somerville 2000), their key role is that they provide a powerful basis for identification and association with other women and difference from men.

A recurring complaint among feminists is that even despite their achievement of the status of citizenship in democratic countries, women have not fared well at the workplace. This is often presented in terms of the corporations being male-dominated and therefore unsympathetic to women's claims, and of governments being unwilling to legislate to require companies to improve women's lot at work. Feminists demonstrate that corporations are hostile to women's issues by comparing women's inferior experiences of the workplace with those of men and by comparing women's inferior experiences of the private sector with those of their counterparts in the public sector. First, there has been the complaint that women have tended to receive lower wages for performing the same jobs as men. In welfare democracies this issue has tended to be addressed through equal pay legislation, though because women are less likely to be in continuous employment even in these cases a sexual pay gap remains. Secondly, and relatedly, there is the complaint that women do not enjoy similar levels of career development as men and do not reach the most powerful positions in companies. This is manifest in the very small proportion of chief executives and board members who are women, and the relatively small number of female senior executives (Singh and Vinnicombe 2005). Hence the glass ceiling is both evidence of companies not addressing gender issues at the workplace and also an explanation for these issues not being addressed. The top jobs are held by those who are either advantaged by women's poorer conditions or who are simply blind or hostile to these. Recent opinion poll data in the UK revealed that large numbers of women would be prepared to enter the labour market if employers provided more flexible employment conditions so that they could combine paid work with their caring responsibilities.[11]

Although corporations are therefore often regarded as unresponsive to female identity, most liberal feminists would regard this as simply reflective of the mores and practices of the wider family. Central to women's workplace experiences are their roles in reproduction and childcare which have not been sufficiently recognized, rewarded and compensated for. Hence the perception that '[t]he equality of women and the institution of the family have long been at odds with each other' (Somerville 2000: 2). Corporations simply reflect these wider mores not simply by exploiting women but also by failing to build their wider roles into the rewards and conditions of the workplace. Marxist feminists, however, would regard the corporation as not reflective of a social phenomenon but as its creator and maintainer. Both perspectives, however, share the view that companies' practices have tended not to reflect the social realities of gender identity and thereby compound (for liberals) or structure (for Marxists) deficiencies in women's citizenship experience.

A third way in which corporations may inhibit citizenship identities is by failing to *represent* citizen identities, or *misrepresenting* them, in corporate communications of one sort or another. As we discussed above, the exposure of certain identities in advertising and other forms of corporate communications is often presented as a way in which those identifying as such become normalized and accepted in society – and thus more able to enjoy the kinds of citizenship entitlements experienced by more dominant groups. Thus, for example, the portrayal of African-American people in US television adverts, or gay men in British television adverts, has been identified by some as a major milestone in their achieving equal political status in society. However, just as corporations can choose to include such identities, so too can they exclude or distort them in their communications. The latter can happen when corporations are seen to rely on 'negative' identity stereotypes, such as persistently portraying women as housewives, or racial minorities as low status workers. Even ostensibly 'positive' stereotypes used in adverts, such as the affluent white gay man, the athletic black sportsman, or the multi-tasking executive mother, can be argued to render others who identify as gay, black or female invisible or under-represented. Marketing can 'minoritize' among identity-based communities and privilege an 'ideal' version of the identity over others (Sender 2005).

As with the processes identified in the previous sub-section, a major theme here is the question of whether advertisers create social identities and social attitudes towards them or merely reflect pre-existing identities and attitudes. This is a theme that has been taken up in a range of literatures, summarized by Richard Pollay (1986: 33) as one manifestation of the 'distorted mirror' idea of advertising – namely that 'some of our cultural values are reinforced far more frequently than others. Hence, while it may be true that advertising reflects cultural values, it does so on a very selective basis, echoing and reinforcing certain attitudes, behaviors and values far more frequently than others.' For many proponents of various forms of identity politics, then, the involvement of corporations in creating and reflecting citizen identities through markets and through marketing is a double-edged sword. While it can offer some degree of mainstream recognition and acceptance, it can also lead to problems of misrepresentation, and the potential replacement of the political goals of identity movements with simple consumerism. There is understandably a degree of caution about the problems of assimilation and the relative benefits and drawbacks of becoming a target market, whereby political values and aspirations are reduced to consumer preferences.

Finally, another way in which citizenship identity can be compromised by companies is when they support or supply products and services to repressive regimes that *suppress* particular citizenship identities. This has been widely discussed in relation to companies involved in supplying products to the Nazis, for example in Edwin Black's (2001) controversial study of IBM's involvement in the Holocaust:

> IBM, primarily through its German subsidiary, made Hitler's program of Jewish destruction a technologic mission the company pursued with chilling success. IBM Germany, using its own staff and equipment, designed, executed, and supplied the indispensable technologic assistance Hitler's Third Reich needed to accomplish what had never been done before – the automation of human destruction ... IBM's subsidiary, with the knowledge of its New York headquarters, enthusiastically custom-designed the complex devices and specialized applications as an official corporate undertaking.

This phenomenon has also been illustrated recently in the cases of Yahoo, Microsoft and Google accepting Chinese censorship rules for their operations in China. More broadly, Amnesty International has identified internet repression in such countries as Iran, Tunisia, Israel and Vietnam.[12] The most conspicuous case was the Chinese Journalist Shi Tao, who got sentenced to ten years in a labour camp, at a trial based on evidence made available to the Chinese courts by Yahoo. Reporters Without Borders in 2006 listed no less than 54 'cyber dissidents' in China. Interestingly, the contestation about this corporate role has led to intense controversy in the larger business community itself. Domini Social Investment, together with Boston Common Asset Management, recently filed a shareholder resolution with Cisco, whose surveillance routers and 'Policenet' devices enabled the Chinese government to monitor electronic communications on the internet. The resolution asked the company to report on how the firm ensures its products and services are not being used to commit human rights violations, and received nearly twenty five per cent support from shareholders concerned with investing in a company whose management avoids uncomfortable confrontation with government regimes (Crane and Matten 2007: 484–5).

Of course, there are always questions about the veracity of such accusations, as well as, more fundamentally, about whether corporations as economic entities should take a stand on such political questions. Should firms be responsible for what their governmental customers do with their products, and to what extent are they obliged to obey the law in the countries in which they operate if this goes against the laws and expectations of their home country? These are the types of underlying questions that prevail in assessing the role of corporations in suppressing citizenship identities through their products and services. Our point here is not to answer such questions, but simply to highlight the thoroughly politicized agenda that firms can run into through such behaviours.

Conclusion

In this chapter we have explored the way that citizenship has been transformed by the politics of identity, and how citizenship identities have been reflected, enabled and inhibited by the corporation in various ways (see Table 5.1). What we have observed, then, is a range of different roles and processes inhabited by the corporation in identity politics, many of which are implicit and which have gone unrecognized and un-noted by those in the business community, but have also been identified and questioned by those seeking to understand or advance the

Table 5.1. *Corporate roles and citizen identity*

Corporate role with regard to citizenship identity	Examples
Reflecting citizen identity	• Use of national/regional/cosmopolitan symbols; • Minority orientation (by ethnicity, consumption preferences).
Enabling citizen identity	• Impacts on de facto citizenship status; • Provision of citizenship entitlements (through employment, business opportunities); • Provision of products and services to enhance citizenship.
Inhibiting citizen identity	• Excluding those with certain identities from employment, products, services; • Ensuring that such identifications do not prosper, failing to represent, or misrepresenting, citizen identities in communications; • Producing products and services that are used to suppress citizenship identities.

position of different identity communities. What is clear is that in a capitalist society, corporations are inevitably involved in the reconfiguration of citizenship along the various constellations of identity, even if their actual role and responsibility here remains a matter of debate. The politics of identity cannot be entirely severed from the manifestations of identity in product and labour markets, however much corporations may claim their involvement is in business, not politics, and however much activists for identity groups claim their interests are in politics not business (Sender 2005).

Ultimately, though, the corporate role is one that cannot be designated as either normatively good or normatively bad – such assessments have to be made on a case by case basis. Sometimes it appears that corporations can play an incredibly important role in the process of conferring political status to certain communities formed on identity lines, in others their role can be far more malign. In many instances, it is not even so much the role or impacts of the individual corporation that we need to examine, but the aggregate effects of markets, industries or industrial regions on particular groups.

Notes

1. It should be noted that it can also be associated with fear within the group, as illustrated by intra-group 'policing' as evidenced in Northern Ireland.
2. *Boston Business Forward*, 26 August 2006: http://www.bizforward.com/bos/issues/2001-12/pinkeconomy/.
3. 'Migrants put their best shoes forward', *San Francisco Chronicle*, November 18, 2005: A2.
4. C. Prystay, 'With loans, poor South Asian women turn entrepreneurial', *The Wall Street Journal*, May 25, 2005, accessed from http://www.hllshakti.com/sbcms/temp5.asp?pid=46802618&nid=48412296&stid=24682101.
5. *Boston Business Forward*, 26 August 2006: http://www.bizforward.com/bos/issues/2001-12/pinkeconomy/.
6. *The Economist*, August 5, 2006: 11.
7. 'Make money not war', *FT Magazine*, September 23/24, 2006: 21.
8. See www.bnp.org.uk.
9. See 'Cross row stokes Christian anger', BBC News, October 15, 2006: http://news.bbc.co.uk/1/hi/uk/6051486.stm. Following pressure from political and church leaders, British Airways reversed the ban.
10. See 'Faith news', *The Times*, June 25, 2005, 75.
11. Equal Opportunities Commission, *Can we afford not to care?*, May 2006, London.
12. 'Today, our chance to fight a new hi-tech tyranny', *The Observer*, May 28, 2006, 8.

6 Citizenship ecologies and the corporation

Free trade as freedom for corporations is based on the forced alienation of rights to land, water and biodiversity that common citizens hold as a birthright.

Vandana Shiva, 'How free is free India?', *Resurgence Magazine*, June 1997

Introduction

In the last chapter, we saw how the corporation had been involved in the reconfiguration of citizenship around identity. In this chapter, we continue this exploration of the role of corporations in alternative forms of citizenship by focusing specifically on ecological ideas of citizenship. Such notions have been percolating in and around the environmental studies literature and in debates about citizenship for some time now, but are far less developed than identity based concepts or, as we shall see in the following chapter, cosmopolitan ideas of global citizenship. That said, ecological perspectives on citizenship draw from and contribute to both of these other sets of ideas, without being subsumed by either. Therefore, there is clearly something of a distinctive literature, or more accurately a set of related literatures on citizenship that are specific to the ecological domain, and it is these literatures that we shall explore here in order to outline some further thoughts on the corporation and citizenship.

Although the literature dealing with ecological perspectives on citizenship is less developed than for our other two reconfigurations (identity and globalization), we have chosen to dedicate a chapter to the ecological perspective here mainly because environmental issues constitute such a major part of the debate on corporate power and responsibility. Business, sustainability and the natural environment are no longer the strange bedfellows they once were. At a practical level, most large corporations now publish some kind of environmental or sustainability report extolling their performance against a wide range of environmental impacts, while huge swathes of industry across the globe have adopted environmental management systems of one sort or another, such as the Eco-management and Audit Scheme (EMAS) and International Standards Organization (ISO) 14000 Standards. Governments and non-governmental organizations (NGOs) continue to press for more sustainable business, and universities have begun to incorporate sustainable business courses into their curricula. Scholarly attention in the area mushroomed in the 1990s and continues unabated, giving rise to numerous books, articles, conferences and dedicated journals and research centres.

At present, most of this interest focuses on the technical dimensions of managing corporate environmental impacts, whether through pollution abatement, product redesign or process reengineering. However, corporate involvement in environment issues has also impacted at the political level, for instance in business self-regulation (Orts 1995), and the development of governance regimes for environmental problems such as climate change (Levy 1997; Levy and Egan 2000). Clearly, then, we can see that certain aspects of corporate involvement in citizenship are likely to have ecological dimensions.

In corporate discourse, the notion of 'corporate citizenship' that we explored in Chapter 2 has emerged as a central concept in how firms frame their relation to sustainability issues. This is most evident in corporate reports and communications dealing with sustainability, which have increasingly incorporated citizenship terminology, and suggested that efforts towards sustainability are a result of, or synonymous with, 'good' corporate citizenship. For instance Novo Nordisk, the Danish pharmaceuticals company, claimed in its 2002 report that 'Managing a sustainable business implies taking broader responsibility than delivering healthy returns on investments. A profitable business is the basis for sustainable development, but as a responsible corporate citizen the commitment goes beyond narrow business concerns.'

However, in this chapter, we start from a different place. Rather than seeking to reveal the ecological dimensions of the mainstream citizenship intersections with corporations that were introduced in Part A, we explore the potential of what might be regarded as 'green' or 'ecological' citizenship for examining corporate power and responsibilities.

These are relatively new ways of thinking about and conceptualising relations of citizenship, but have become an increasingly popular way of framing debates in environmental politics (Dobson 2003). At a basic level, ecological citizenship is concerned with the status, entitlements and processes of participation that citizens enjoy in relation to the natural environment. However, as we shall see, the various terminologies of environmental citizenship embrace a wide spectrum of opinion on the shape and relative importance of these features. In this chapter, we therefore explore these different perspectives and examine the specific role that corporations have, or could have, in shaping, enabling or constraining the exercise of such citizenship. In so doing, the chapter develops some of the ideas introduced in the last chapter about corporations contributing to the transformation of our notions of citizenship, but here we will focus specifically on the reconfiguration of citizenship attached to ecological spaces. It also tackles the rather different problem of how corporations might think about relevant communities of citizens from an ecological perspective, and how the entitlements of those citizens might be considered.

The chapter begins with an outline of the nature of citizenship and the environment, and examines the relevance of citizenship as a connection to place(s), and possibilities for citizenship to be applied to ecological communities, rather than citizenship being simply an attribute of people within nation states. We will suggest that ecological citizenship can be both about a reterritorializing of citizenship, as well as a profound deterritorialization of citizenship, depending on the perspective adopted. Applying these perspectives to corporations, we then explore the impacts of corporations on indigenous peoples' notions of place, identity, knowledge and property. This will provide the opportunity for exploring the notion of corporations as vehicles for exporting, transplanting and reconfiguring conceptions of citizenship. The chapter then goes on to identify the implications of ecological citizenship for expanding the stakeholder set to include non-humans and future generations. Finally, we explore the reconfiguration of the corporate community that agendas of re-localization and ecological deterritorialization might suggest.

Citizenship and the environment

The recognition and development of a form of citizenship appropriate for environmental issues and politics has spawned a growing stream of academic literature across the politics, philosophy, ecology, law and sociology disciplines. Although some authors seek to make conceptual distinctions between alternative labels here – for instance, Dobson (2003) distinguishes between 'environmental citizenship' and 'ecological citizenship' – for the sake of simplicity we will use 'ecological citizenship' as a catch-all term in this chapter.

This stream of literature has been characterized by a considerable degree of heterogeneity, and often a fair degree of imprecision, about what exactly ecological citizenship might constitute. In general, though, it is possible to discern three main strands, each of which characterizes ecological citizenship rather differently (see Table 6.1). First, there is the notion grounded in pre-modern ideas of identity and status being intimately tied to a certain physical territory or ecological environment rather than to a nation state and/or government (Curtin 1999). Second, there is the notion of citizenship being grounded in the modern apparatus of liberal or republican citizenship and focusing predominantly on environmental rights (Shelton 1991) or the common good (Sagoff 1988) respectively. Third, there is the notion predicated on non-territoriality that seeks to establish an entirely new basis for citizenship (Dobson 2003). Let us briefly examine each in turn.

Ecological citizenship as intimate connection

The idea that citizenship is tied to a physical place largely rests on a view that valorizes spatial and community connectedness, and that is profoundly sceptical of the enlightenment project of political rights and liberalism. Espousing a kind of 'land ethic', writers in this vein have viewed modern notions of citizenship to be an imposition on the traditional embeddedness of indigenous communities within ecological environments. For instance, for the Maori of New Zealand, citizen power 'derives from a connectedness to *whenua* (land), to *marae* (sacred gathering places), to the *papakainga* (consecrated land) and to their *urupa* (traditional burial grounds)' (Lunt *et al.* 2002: 356), not from political status based on relations to a sovereign authority. Hence, as Deane Curtin contends, traditional community ties have been threatened by 'the increasingly global reach of Western liberal individualism' (1999: xi) and the 'extension of a calculus of individual preference satisfactions' (1999: xiii). Put simply, the importing of Western ideas of entitlements predicated on relations with the state, coupled with the whole machinery of government, capitalism and scientific progress (see for example Merchant 1989), is claimed to have usurped traditional ecological connections.[1]

Table 6.1. *Three versions of ecological citizenship*

	Intimate connection	Extension of rights and obligations	Non-territorial obligation
Normative basis of citizenship	Eco-communitarian self-determination	Can be based on either liberal or republican model of citizenship	Obligations of citizens are relative to their ecological footprints
Character of membership	Ecological embeddedness – membership status is predicated on connections with the local physical environment	All those affected by environmental decisions, including non-humans and future generations	Community of obligation is continually constituted according to material impacts on the environment
Location of citizenship	Local physical environment	Variable and issue-specific – can range from local to transnational	Transnational ecological footprint
Main focus in examining citizenship relations	Spiritual relations with place rather than political relations among actors	Vertical relations between citizens and authorities	Horizontal relations between citizens

As a result, it is suggested that there have been 'devastating consequences for pre-modern tribal society', especially in the colonies, and most acutely in those dominated by white-settler communities (Turner 2001: 205). This has subsequently prompted numerous policy interventions in the twentieth century 'designed to acculturate, to assimilate or to accommodate aboriginal peoples' – none of which has proved entirely satisfactory (Turner 2001: 205). What we see then is a picture of pre-modern community ties being supplanted by modern political relations of citizenship, that in turn have been unable to successfully embrace those communities still based on ecological connectivity.

To some extent, then, it is probably a misnomer to label such pre-modern ties as 'citizenship', since the term itself is intimately connected with the modern project. Curtin (1999: xii), in fact, warns of the dangers that have been posed by the dominance of a moral language of liberal individualism for making sense of alternative understandings of culture in relationship to nature. Indeed, most authors are fairly careful to avoid using the language of citizenship to actually describe ties of this kind from the past. However, the language of citizenship *is* typically invoked to label 'new' forms of emerging ecological citizenship that either seek to accommodate aboriginal communities, or take inspiration from them.

For instance, let's take the example of Curtin's (1999) notable work that urges us to rethink 'the question of ecological citizenship'. Curtin traces and critiques Western impositions on eco-communities across the globe, identifying what he calls the 'institutional and systemic violence' intrinsic within a range of societal shifts including commercial exploitation, the 'green revolution' of industrialized agriculture and even well-intentioned Western progressive movements for social justice and deep ecology. Each of these, he contends, has contributed to a radical de-localization of social, cultural and political identity and action.

As an antidote, he offers the possibility of a new form of ecological citizenship that he calls 'critical ecocommunitarianism'. In so doing, he argues for a rekindling of a sense of place through cultivating an informed and humble citizenry that is genuinely committed to preservation (Howland and Robertson 1999), and which begins with the authority of local communities to 'define their own values and participate in their transformation over time' (Curtin 1999). In this perspective, then, ecological citizenship represents a profound re-territorialization of citizenship that starts not with the political territory of the state, but with a re-imagining of an intimate relation between communities and an ecological territory. As such, while it emphasizes aspects of participation, this form of ecological citizenship roots the will to participate in an emotional and spiritual connection with a natural environment.

Ecological citizenship as an extension of rights and obligations

The second form of ecological citizenship that we are concerned with is one that primarily focuses on extending the modern apparatus of traditional liberal or republican citizenship to incorporate environmental concerns. In the former case, the issue is one of appending the Marshallian framework of individual citizen rights with a further set of 'environmental rights' (Shelton 1991). Such entitlements essentially provide for the protection of the individual citizen against the effects of pollution and environmental degradation (Dean 2001). 'Ecological citizenship is expressed as a right to a safe, "natural" environment' (Turner 2001: 205). It is arguable whether an extra category of rights is really necessitated by the environmental entitlements of humans, since 'in so far as social rights cater for such basic human needs as clean water, it is possible to reclassify certain social rights as environmental rights' (Dean 2001: 492). However, it would be hard to deny that certain entitlements of citizenship are specifically about environmental issues, while others have even gone so far as to include a right *of* the environment itself within the debate (Shelton 1991).

The latter republican approach focuses more on evaluating the types of obligations towards the common good, and political processes of participation, that are necessary to enable democratic involvement in environmental decisions (Lidskog 2005; Light 2003; Sagoff 1988). These are based on a reconceived idea of the relations of citizenship, as Light (2003: 51) here attests:

> Citizenship, conceived along classical republican lines, identifies a role for residents of a place by articulating a range of minimal obligations they have to each other for the sake of the larger community in which they live ... Adding an environmental component to a classical republican model of citizenship becomes then the conceptual basis for a claim that the 'larger community', to which the ... citizen has obligations, is inclusive of ... space, place, and environment, as well as people.

As such, the pursuit of an ecologically sustainable society in this view is to some extent about 'sacrificing personal inclinations or preferences to the common good' (Dobson 2003: 96), and in having a voice in matters that concern one's environment (Lidskog 2005). Thus, whether the focus is on rights or obligations, the classic traditions of citizenship appear to offer a plausible way forward for addressing environmental issues, albeit with several key problematics, as we shall now see.

Typically, variants of either approach have to attempt to tackle the thorny issues of where to draw the boundaries of membership of an ecological political community, and who to confer with citizenship status in the context of environmental issues (Hilson 2001). In the former case, the boundaries of membership are difficult to establish given that environmental problems can be at times very local (e.g. noise) and at others, thoroughly deterritorialized (e.g. global warming). So, for instance, Lidskog (2005: 197–8) argues that, 'today's environmental problems demand that citizenship must be – at least partly – extracted from its location within the nation-state ... the meaning of citizenship cannot be restricted to a national context'. Alternatively, Light (2003) takes a more local approach and applies civic republicanism to develop an ecological citizenship for urban communities. In essence, it would appear that in contradistinction to traditional citizenship where the boundaries of membership are firmly fixed and permanent, the boundaries of ecological citizenship are shifting and issue specific.

Similarly, it is critical to address the question of whether to include future generations and non-human species into the ecological community (Smith 1998). The concept of intergenerational justice is central to notions of sustainability. Therefore, it is necessary to carefully consider how to extend the obligations of citizens towards their fellow (unborn) citizens in an ecological context. This, as Mark Smith (1998: 30) shows, is a question subjected to 'intense disputes' but which, he concludes, must at least lead to new guidelines on acting with restraint to avoid future harms. Equally, obligations to animals, plants and the ecosphere more broadly are typically promoted by ecological thinkers, but again this potentially prompts us to go beyond the traditional communities of citizenship. It is worth noting that the debates here are mainly around the conferring of *rights to*, or *obligations towards*, future generations and non-humans; it is, after all, rather difficult to argue for meaningful *obligations of* animals, trees, unborn babies and other non-sentient beings. As such, it highlights some of the limitations and difficulties of applying existing concepts of citizenship to the environmental realm.

Unsurprisingly this has given rise to the development of alternative directions for the conceptualization and application of ecological citizenship.

Ecological citizenship as a new non-territorial obligation

Finally, then, the third strand of literature on ecological citizenship seeks to go beyond pre-modern and modern forms of citizenship to map out fundamentally new conceptual terrain in citizenship. It primarily does so by focusing on the problem of non-territoriality, and the issues this raises for identifying an appropriate political space. Probably the most well worked out example of this approach is offered by Andrew Dobson (2003) in his book *Citizenship and the Environment*.

Dobson centres his ideas about ecological citizenship on Wackernagel and Rees' (1996) concept of the ecological footprint – 'a quantitative assessment of the biologically productive area (the amount of nature) required to produce the resources (food, energy, and materials) and to absorb the wastes of an individual, city, region, or country' (Venetoulis *et al.* 2004: 7). The ecological footprint is by now a fairly well-known tool for estimating the amount of productive land area that is required to sustain a specific human population in terms of its resource consumption and waste assimilation (Wackernagel and Rees 1996). So, for instance, it has been estimated that the ecological footprint of the United States is 9.57 global hectares per capita, while that of Brazil is 2.39, and that of Bangladesh 0.5 (Venetoulis *et al.* 2004). Similarly, footprint analyses have also been conducted for cities such as Almada in Portugal, and regions such as the San Francisco Bay area in the US (Venetoulis *et al.* 2004) and even development projects and sporting events (Collins and Flynn 2005).

Calculations of ecological footprints are important if we accept that the amount of nature available to support populations is limited, and that some populations may 'over-occupy' ecological space unsustainably. Thus, from a citizenship point of view, Dobson suggests that the concept of an ecological footprint gives us a relevant community of obligation. Because we rely on the productive area of the footprint to maintain our own existence, it is this area that circumscribes our relations of citizenship with those upon whom we impact. Hence (Dobson 2003: 106) concludes that:

> The 'space' of ecological citizenship is therefore not something given by the boundaries of nation-states or of supranational organizations such as the European Union ... It is, rather, produced by the metabolistic and material relationship of individual people with their environment. This relationship gives rise to an ecological footprint which gives rise, in turn, to relationships with those on whom it impacts ... They may live near by or be far away, and they may be of this generation or of generations yet to be born ... By definition then, ecological citizenship is a citizenship of strangers.

Crucially, then, Dobson also makes clear that the relations of citizenship according to his conception differ quite markedly from those articulated in the traditional models of citizenship. First, the principal concern is with horizontal relations between citizens, rather than the vertical relations between the individual citizen and the political authority. Second, status and membership issues are downplayed since the community of citizenship is produced rather than given, i.e. citizens are not allocated a fixed membership of a given community, but continually constitute their community of obligation through their material impacts. Third, the differential size of footprints suggests that impacts on other citizens are asymmetrical, and that therefore one's relevant obligations are also asymmetrical. This, again, is in marked contrast to more traditional forms of citizenship that valorize symmetrical relations of reciprocity. Different citizens will have different burdens of obligation depending on the size of their footprints, while those who occupy less than their quota of ecological space may have no such duty at all.

Dobson's theory of ecological citizenship therefore extends and reworks our thinking about the meaning of citizenship in quite challenging ways. This is also true of all of the three perspectives on ecological citizenship outlined here. Each brings a new perspective to the mapping out of relations of power and responsibility within political communities. The focus on intimate connections seeks to break the connection between responsibility and vertical relations of power. It does this by attaching responsibility (e.g. to the environment) back to emotional, cultural and spiritual connections rather than simply to political institutions. The approach that focuses on stretching traditional models of citizenship challenges our conventional ideas about community membership and status. It does this by potentially extending the relevant community to encapsulate non-human species and future generations. The final approach that starts with an idea of a deterritorialized obligation is perhaps the only one that seeks to make a radical break with the past; and here, fundamentally new ways of drawing the political community, and of considering horizontal relations of power and responsibility are surfaced.

Such developments may well be significant for our understanding of citizenship, but the question that remains for us to answer is what do they have to do with corporations? This is the question to which we will now turn.

Ecological citizenship and the corporation

How do these new views of citizenship help us to rethink or evaluate corporate power and responsibility? Do they offer any substantial fresh thinking on such debates? Do they help us to consider what it might mean for a corporation to be sustainable, or to be a good citizen on the planet? In our view, the answer is a qualified yes. The ecological perspectives on citizenship certainly do open up some important new avenues for thinking about corporations, but at the same time, it must be cautioned that these avenues are unlikely to be the ones that corporations anticipate going down when they commit to sustainability initiatives. In all, three new considerations are brought to the fore regarding corporate responsibility and power by ecological citizenship. These are: responsibilities for exporting liberal citizenship; rethinking the stakeholder set; and reconfiguring the community of the corporate citizen.

Responsibilities for exporting liberal citizenship

In our discussion of ecological citizenship as intimate connection, we saw that certain aboriginal cultures were based on a world view that tied social, moral, spiritual and political relations to a physical place. The disintegration of these relations could be seen to be associated with the introduction of Western models of liberal citizenship, scientific and economic 'progress', and transformation to capitalist modes of production and exchange. While this has largely been a political project, corporations have long been implicit (and at times complicit) in such developments, particularly as engines of the industrial revolution and, more recently, of economic globalization. To illustrate why this might be the case, let us look at a few examples.

Liberal citizenship is a largely Western invention, and is 'intricately interwoven with the nation-state and welfare institutions' (Elliott

2001: 47). If we trace the exporting of the citizenship model to, say, India, we can see that much of the initial apparatus of liberal citizenship was introduced by the British East India Company, which enjoyed virtually governmental status and responsibilities in the territory. The company operated its own armed forces, maintained civil law and ultimately introduced Westernized judicial and penal systems to India. Moreover, although it remained a dead letter well into the twentieth century, the Charter Act of 1833 provided that no Indian subject of the Company would be debarred from holding any office under the Company by reason of their religion, place of birth, descent or colour – thereby establishing liberal notions of rights into the country.

A second type of example comes from the role of corporations in influencing the way that liberal entitlements such as property rights become applied to aboriginal cultures. This story has been played out across the former colonies, most notably in conflicts about mining and extraction, and in assigning intellectual property rights to traditional knowledge (Shiva 2001).

For instance, before the British state colonized Australia over 200 years ago, the Aborigines who inhabited the lands did not specifically characterize their relation to the lands in terms of what we would call 'property rights'. Rather than assign certain territories to individuals, or even certain tribes or families, the main relation of aboriginal communities to 'their' land is via sacred sites, so-called 'dreamtimes' or 'story places', which are important elements of aboriginal beliefs and rituals. However, the establishment of corporate mining operations on these lands during the twentieth century, by companies such as Rio Tinto and BHP Billiton, led to the destruction of their spiritual integrity as well as the extraction of billions of dollars worth of resources from Aboriginal lands with little or no form of compensation. This is because, until 1992, Australian law upheld the principle of *terra nullius* (a Latin term meaning 'empty land'), which basically assumed that the Aboriginal people did not own the land before the white settlers arrived, despite having lived in the country for more than 40,000 years. Although this principle was overturned in 1993 by the Native Title Act, there is still considerable contestation over various mining projects because of different perspectives on the nature of entitlements, title and property among aboriginal people, as well as between them and other property 'owners' and lease-holders, Australian governments and corporations. Moreover, Aboriginal people have little option but to engage in a debate with mining corporations based on the liberal notion of property rights since this is the relevant cornerstone of citizen entitlement in Australia. Although this has led to the development of a range of more positive engagements with Aboriginal communities by mining corporations, such as compensation packages, aboriginal employment programmes and the introduction of traditional knowledge and place names into local site management, the reliance on Western concepts of citizenship also potentially has major drawbacks for Aboriginal interests, as Banerjee (2000: 21) contends:

> The question of cultural sites is a complex one involving multilayered interconnections between country, people, language, kinship, community, and spiritual and political systems. It is impossible to reduce this rich and complex cultural landscape to lines on a map based on Western notions of geography and property. Aboriginal notions of land and country are epistemologically and ethically incongruent with Western notions. The process of 'accommodating' Aboriginal interests into a capitalist, colonial framework is simply an imposition of an alien knowledge system and a subjugation of local knowledges.

In the case of traditional knowledge, therefore, a similar situation has begun to emerge where multinational corporations in the agricultural, pharmaceutical and biotechnology industries have, through international trade organizations and agreements such as Trade Related Aspects of International Property Rights (TRIPS), helped to impose the agenda of intellectual property rights onto indigenous knowledge. By traditional knowledge, we mean the knowledge accumulated over time by indigenous communities that is manifested in a range of medicines, know-how, tribal art work and songs (Ghosh 2003). This may relate to the extraction and preparation of genetic resources such as plants and medicinal herbs for human usage, for example in medicines and cosmetics (Cottier and Panizzon 2004).

Once multinational corporations seek to exploit particular uses of plants that have been known by traditional communities for centuries and patent them as their *own* inventions, such knowledge may pass from the public domain to that of private corporations. This 'biopiracy' (Shiva 1997) can mean that indigenous communities lose their sovereignty over resources as well as entitlements to use specific knowledge. So, in order to defend against such incursions, many campaigners have sought intellectual property rights protection for traditional knowledge, arguing that the patent system needs to be revised or overhauled to account for traditional knowledge (Anon 2005). One of the more critical problems here is how to extend a notion of individual property to a collective endeavour and community knowledge accumulated over generations.

Therefore, this again may pose a problem for indigenous communities, which do not traditionally share liberal notions of individual property on knowledge (Banerjee 2003). As Ghosh (2003: 591) contends:

> The application of intellectual property rights to … medicinal know-how is arguably misguided. Scholars have also criticized the increased propertization of intellectual property to the detriment of the public domain and non-market values. For these scholars, protecting traditional knowledge through patent, copyright and trademark is another example of that pernicious trend. The argument is that the treatment of traditional knowledge artefacts as intellectual property, within the same class as pop music, the great American novel, Cipro, Mickey Mouse, and The Terminator subverts the notions of what constitutes traditional and modern.

What we see, then, is a complex debate emerging about the best way to ensure that indigenous communities are treated fairly and do not suffer injustice at the hands of multinational corporations – but also a parallel debate about how to prevent these very protections from fundamentally reshaping traditional notions of citizenship and the public good. Corporations may not deliberately seek to export the architecture of individualized liberal citizenship, but in so far as they are the drivers of an expanded and reconfigured property rights regime through their actions, they are necessarily implicated in the process of exportation. Clearly, such considerations could potentially suggest new social and political responsibilities for corporations (to some extent similar to those we considered in the previous chapter), but one would also have to seriously consider what prospects there might be for meaningful progress. After all, the very bases of citizen entitlement – individual versus collective – are extremely divergent, and the corporation is, by its nature, thoroughly enveloped in a liberal consensus on the virtue of property as an individual right of ownership and exploitation.

Rethinking the stakeholder set

The second consideration surfaced by concepts of ecological citizenship is that of rethinking the stakeholder set. For some time now, there has been an active debate on how to identify legitimate stakeholders for the corporation (Mitchell *et al.* 1997). As part of this debate, the question of whether the environment itself is a stakeholder has been raised a number of times (Driscoll and Starik 2004; Phillips and Reichart 2000). From an ecological citizenship perspective, however, the issue is not so much whether the environment is a stakeholder in a general sense, but whether actors such as non-humans and future generations should be admitted into the moral community of the organization.

Clearly, corporate decisions about farming or animal testing on the one hand, or fossil fuel extraction, carbon emissions and nuclear energy on the other, all raise the potential for considering these additional actors as relevant stakeholders. In a practical sense, the stakes of such groups will obviously have to be articulated by others (such as civil society organizations). But, this does not necessarily detract from their potential status as members of the corporate moral community. We need only consider the case of infants, or adults with severe mental health problems, to realise that an inability to articulate one's stake does not mean that the firm should not consider one's interests.

So, if the status of these additional stakeholders in the corporate moral community were acknowledged, what kind of additional responsibilities would be posed for firms? This is a tricky question, but some proposals can be developed by looking to the ecological citizenship literature and adapting it to fit with corporate responsibilities. For instance, responsibilities to future generations could draw on Daniel Callahan's guidelines, cited in Smith (1998: 31), to give the following principles:

1. Corporations should not act in ways that jeopardize the existence of future generations.
2. Corporations should not act in ways that jeopardize the ability of future generations to live in dignity.
3. Corporations, in defence of their own interests, may have to act in ways that jeopardize future generations, but should do so in ways that minimize this risk.
4. In determining whether corporate activities do jeopardize the existence or dignity of future generations, corporations should act in responsible and sensitive ways as if each action with uncertain consequences could harm one's own employees.

In so far, then, as concepts of citizenship enable us to think more clearly about status and entitlements with respect to corporations, the extension of citizenship to include non-humans and future generations offers a further challenge that can to some degree be accommodated. However, there are some broader challenges here that also have to be dealt with regarding the definition of the corporate community. If we take some of the ecological citizenship concepts seriously, then we might go beyond simply incorporating one or two new communities into our stakeholder set, but rather we might radically reconfigure the moral community of the corporation. This might entail either a re-localizing, or a deterritorialization, of the corporate moral community.

Reconfiguring the community of the corporate citizen

As we have seen in Chapter 2, ideas of location and community membership are quite important for establishing the citizen-like qualities of corporations. Most notably, for the purposes of identifying their 'nationality', it is usually necessary to locate a corporation in the country of its headquarters. Similarly, individual factories, offices, warehouses and shops are clearly located in a readily identifiable physical environment, and a community of fellow citizens. In general, though, corporations are rather difficult to locate within a meaningful community, especially when they encompass a range of people, buildings and processes across multiple sites and countries. Ecological citizenship typically seeks to reconfigure the community of citizenship – and so offers some interesting avenues for rethinking the status of corporations in this respect.

If we take a view of ecological citizenship as intimate connection, then it is clear that the location of the corporation in a relevant community would necessitate a greater attention to the immediate local environment. According to this perspective, citizenship is only realized in the intimate connections between people, communities and their natural environments. One way of applying this thinking to corporations is therefore to consider the importance of embedding corporate members in ecological environments in order to foster a true sense of responsibility, respect and reciprocity for nature. For example, Whiteman and Cooper (2000) have explored the implications of 'ecological embeddeness' among indigenous communities for developing a framework for contemporary sustainability management in corporations. They argue that personal identification with one's physical place, adherence to ecological beliefs, gathering of ecological information firsthand and physical location outside in the ecosystem will promote more commitment to sustainable management among corporate managers than the modernist dislocation of individual, community and ecology.

This re-localizing of the perspective on corporations would clearly lead to some rethinking of the relevant political community for citizenship, whether we thought of corporations as like citizens or governments, or whether the corporation itself was conceived as the arena of stakeholder relations. Issues of power and responsibility would, for example, mainly be surfaced within the local ecological environment of factories and offices, rather than played out in the global economy of multinational corporations and international trade. However, it has to be said that the ontological shift necessary to re-localize corporate responsibility in this way appears somewhat optimistic in an increasingly globalized context. While more meaningful engagement with local ecologies may well help sustain a more profound ecological ethic of responsibility within corporations, the power, influence and impacts of corporations are by now so thoroughly non-local, that the re-localizing agenda could only ever play a limited role in the delineation of corporate responsibility.

A rather different reconfiguration is evident if we take up the third view of ecological citizenship as non-territorial obligation. Insofar as horizontal relations of citizens can be articulated with the concept of an ecological footprint, the boundaries of corporate responsibility could similarly be conceptualized in such a way. Just as countries, cities and regions have such a footprint, so too do corporations. Hence, an environmentally intensive corporation would have a larger footprint than a relatively benign one – and would have a more substantial set of obligations as a result.

This deterritorialization of obligation suggests a rather different model of power and responsibility than the one proposed, for example, by stakeholder theory. The relevant moral community of the corporation would be those required to sustain its current level of activity at any one time. Although in a similar vein to stakeholder theory corporations would be responsible to those affected by their actions, the 'stakeholders' or 'citizens' pertinent to corporate responsibility would not be a fixed set of people or groups but would be continually (re)produced according to the material needs and impacts of the company. As a 'citizenship of strangers' (Dobson 2003: 106), where the community of obligation is scattered all over the world, and even into future generations, the identification of those to whom corporations owe responsibilities is rather tricky, even if the principle by which responsibility is established is relatively straightforward.

The idea of responsibility being inscribed by an ecological footprint offers a quite powerful way of rethinking the social, political and moral situating of the corporation. At present, footprint analysis has begun to feature in management texts dealing with sustainable management in corporations (e.g. Hart 1997), although its uptake by corporations and those that study them has been primarily at the technical level – namely, measuring and perhaps attempting to reduce a corporation's footprint. For example, the British energy company BP produced a high profile print advertising campaign in Europe in 2005 that headlined 'Knowing your carbon footprint is a step in the right direction'. The copy of the advertisement went on to say, 'Here at BP, we're trying to reduce our footprint. Since 2001, our energy efficiency projects have reduced emissions by over 4 million tonnes'. Measuring elements of an ecological footprint in terms of carbon dioxide emissions in this way is an important technical exercise in sound environmental management. However, it is a rather different task to that of identifying dimensions of corporate power and responsibility through footprint analysis. Nonetheless, as a heuristic device for conceptualizing new forms, boundaries and counterparts of obligation among corporate and other citizens, the concept of an ecological footprint still offers considerable promise, even if much work remains to be done to see how it could be practically applied to corporations beyond specialist environmental management techniques.

Conclusion

In this chapter we have seen how ecological citizenship offers a range of different ways to explore the relationship between corporations and citizenship. This includes fresh perspectives on the role of corporations in exporting liberal citizenship and the impacts this has on indigenous communities and their knowledge and culture. It also includes new ways of thinking about stakeholders and alternative communities of obligation around the firm.

These are not, it should be noted, necessarily mutually co-existing perspectives on the corporation – and indeed arise from some quite widely differing accounts of ecological citizenship. Moreover, they are also views that have yet to make much impact on the analysis of corporate responsibility and power. To date, the corporation has not tended to feature very prominently in political analyses of citizenship and the environment, while similarly, political analyses of citizenship have yet to enter the debate about corporations and sustainability. This chapter, then, should be seen as a first tentative step in this direction – an attempt to bring together some disparate strands of literature to make new meaning about the social role and responsibilities of corporations from an ecological perspective. The ideas we have presented offer some promise for conceptual development in this respect, but there are also a number of shortcomings that would have to be resolved. First, in relation to responsibilities for exporting liberal citizenship, there is considerable promise in using ecological citizenship to refine our conceptualizations of the role that corporations play in the configuration of the social, political, economic and ecological landscape of communities. However, at this stage, there are problems in applying these understandings to develop a practical agenda for corporations. Second, in terms of rethinking the stakeholder set, our analysis provides further impetus and insight to the debate around stakeholder identification, but is less clear about the obligations this poses. Third, looking at the community of the corporate citizen, we can use ecological citizenship to identify relevant local and/or global communities, but at this stage it is difficult to foresee exactly how such projects could be realized.

All told, then, ecological citizenship is probably rather stronger in describing the types, boundaries and subjects of corporate responsibilities than it is in prescribing the normative dimensions of those responsibilities, or their operational implications. As such, the main contribution of this chapter is in identifying new ways of working out who corporations might have responsibilities to, and why, rather than exactly what those responsibilities in themselves might be. That is not to say that with further work more progress on this cannot be made, but there is much still to be done before a fully realized theory of corporate ecological responsibility is made possible.

Nonetheless, ecological citizenship theories not only open up important conceptual space for revitalizing our thinking about corporate power and responsibility, but also offer potentially important new ways in to a number of major current debates. For example, they can help us to make sense of and contribute to discussions around the role of the corporation in traditional knowledge and intellectual property rights; they also offer new ways to explore some of the world's most pressing global problems such as climate change, water provision and energy security from the point of view of corporate responsibilities and footprints. If we look, for instance, at the role of business in tackling climate change, we can see that while this phenomenon has been met with some attention in the business and society literature from a strategy perspective (e.g. Begg *et al.* 2005; Hoffman 2005; Kolk and Levy 2001), relatively little concern has been dedicated to the deeply political nature of the problem (Bulkeley 2001; Levy and Egan 2003). The first aspect of ecological citizenship, in particular notions of eco-communitarianism, offers considerable potential for investigating new modes of participation for corporations in governing global policy issues such as climate change. The second aspect of rethinking the stakeholder set can provide a framework for corporations to address the thorny issue of why and to whom they actually have certain obligations in affecting global climate change. Especially in a context where state-based attempts to define these issues, most notably the Kyoto Protocol, have failed to define an all-encompassing community of actors involved, we have witnessed some attempts by corporations to voluntarily address the issue. Finally, and closely related to the preceding point, ecological citizenship arguments can provide an approach to assess the dimensions by which their impact on global climate can be assessed and managed, as we already discussed briefly in the case of BP. In a similar vein, we would argue, notions of ecological citizenship could help frame and conceptualize future research on corporate responsibility for a host of global environmental issues, most notably global deforestation, decline in biodiversity, depletion of marine resources, or proliferation of nuclear risks.

Note

1. It is worth noting that while such ecological connections have mainly been discussed in relation to indigenous populations of colonized countries, some views of European citizenship have also centred on connections to place. For example, the eighteenth century German philosopher and literary critic, Johann Gottfried Herder, sought to replace the traditional concept of a juridico-political state with that of the 'folk-nation'. In defiance of the Enlightenment, he emphasized the importance of nature, climate and heredity in defining an innate and distinctive nationhood.

7 Citizenship, globalization and the corporation

The forces of envy, despair and terror in today's world are stronger than many of us realised. But they are not invincible. Against them, we must bring a message of solidarity, of mutual respect and, above all, of hope. Business cannot afford to be seen as the problem. It must, working with government, and with all the other actors in society, be part of the solution.

UN Secretary Kofi Annan, Address to the World Economic Forum, 5 February 2002

Introduction

Throughout this book we have frequently come across the phenomenon of globalization. Initially we discussed the rise of corporate participation in a citizen-like way in the governance of various global issues, such as global warming and the fight against pandemics (Chapter 2). We also saw a shifting corporate role towards a government-like involvement in, for instance, governing global markets for goods and services or governing civic entitlements in global supply chains in countries with weak governance institutions (Chapter 3). In Chapter 4 we analyzed the political aspects of the community formed by the firm and its stakeholders and frequently referred to the potential global reach of this new arena. In this chapter, we first analyze and theorize the impact of globalization on the corporate involvement in the citizenship arena more systematically and, second, examine the effects of globalization on the reconfiguration of the very notion of citizenship itself and the role of corporations in shaping, and being impacted by, this process. The chapter begins with a review of the rapidly expanding literature on globalization and citizenship, and presents globalization as a force for the deterritorialization of citizenship.

We apply the concept of citizenship in the context of globalization to corporations in four main ways. First, we present an overview of the role of corporations in driving globalization, through the global proliferation of products, brands and supply chains. Based on our analysis of the literature on global citizenship, we explore the current and the potential role for corporations in contributing to global governance systems and processes, both independent of, and in conjunction with, governmental and non-governmental organizations (NGOs). We then examine the role that global resistance to corporations, such as global boycotts, protests and other civil action, has played in the emergence of more global notions of citizenship and civil society. We finally turn to the expectations being placed on companies to be engaged in 'global corporate citizenship', and the efforts and claims they have made in this respect.

Globalization and cosmopolitan citizenship

Based on a growing consensus in the international relations literature (Delanty 2000; Scholte 2003) we can understand globalization as the progressive eroding of the relevance of territorial bases for social, economic and political activities, processes and relations. As such, globalization has crucial implications for the notion of citizenship. In Chapters 2 and 3 we have delineated a view on corporations in a citizenship perspective based on the two dominating schools of thought in citizenship thinking, both of which are inextricably linked to the notion of the nation state. In Chapter 2 we highlighted the process aspect of citizenship where the notion of participation in a political community and the identity of a member in a civic arena feature as the central reference point. In Chapter 3 we focused on the status and entitlements of citizens which derive from the nation state being the general guarantor of citizens' rights and the key reference point for civic duties. Both of those perspectives are fundamentally conceived and conceptualized against the backdrop of a nation state offering strong institutions to govern rights and duties. The nation state, however, in its nature, has always been a territorial state defined by sovereignty over a well-defined territory marked by discernible and more or less controllable borders.

With globalization in essence being the deterritorialization of political activities, however, the pivotal reference point of citizenship, the nation state, gets marginalized and weakened. Consequently, the very notion of citizenship has been transformed from fairly generic bi-polar notions (e.g. liberal vs. republican) to a more complex and dynamic construct (Falk 2000; Hettne 2000). The literature on citizenship in the global age is rich and manifold (e.g. Archibugi 2003; Castles and Davidson 2000; Hanagan and Tilly 1999; Hudson and Slaughter 2007; Linklater 2002; Stephenson 2003).

In the following, chiefly based on Gerard Delanty's (2000) work, we discuss four major perspectives on what is referred to as cosmopolitan citizenship in the context of globalization, all of which conceptualize different aspects of the globalization process. 'Cosmopolitanism', the common denominator of these approaches, is an understanding of the relevant political community for citizenship being the world or cosmos beyond the narrow confines of just one nation state (Delanty 2007; Linklater 2002). All these perspectives, in our view, rather than offering mutually exclusive ways of understanding the phenomenon of citizenship in the global age, provide different angles on the transformation of citizenship through globalization which, in turn, helps to locate and understand the place of the corporation in this dynamic context. In many ways, then, globalization weakens the concept of citizenship through the gradual demise of the pivotal actor, the nation state. On the other hand, though, globalization also opens up much thicker notions of citizenship allowing for a richer and multifaceted understanding of the dynamics of global political processes. Table 7.1 provides an overview of the different perspectives on citizenship in the global age. We will briefly discuss each in turn. In a final section we will then draw together the discussion with an assessment of the growing importance of the notion of human rights for cosmopolitan citizenship.

It is worth noting that the notion of cosmopolitan citizenship offers considerable overlap with those notions of citizenship which we have discussed so far in this part of the book. So, for instance, in Chapter 5 we have seen that corporations have significant impact on enacting or suppressing national identities, and with many companies operating globally now, the national identity can either be strengthened, reinforced or even suppressed through corporations. One of the key reasons for the rise and enforcement of cultural notions of citizenship is, in fact, that traditional reference frames for citizenship have been eroded by globalization. In a similar vein, we discussed the implications of ecological citizenship as a non-territorial obligation and its implications for corporations in Chapter 6. Globalization, in particular the global nature of many of the most pressing ecological issues, has been a strong

Table 7.1. *Four different views on cosmopolitan citizenship (based on Delanty 2000: 49–67)*

	Internationalism: Legal Cosmopolitanism(LC)	Global Civil Society: Political Cosmopolitanism (PC)	Transnational Communities (TC)	Post-Nationalism (PN)
Normative basis of citizenship	Universally true and applicable moral values as basis of an international order	Plurality of political (democratic) principles, cognitively constructed in similar ways within communities	Multiple cultural identities of highly mobile (mostly ethnic) communities	A constitution, enacted by the rule of law based on processes of democratic deliberation and values
Character of membership	Individuals as members of humanity ('citizens of the world')	Multiple membership in local, regional, global and virtual communities and networks; constituted by shared cultural identities, experiences and interests	Membership of ethnic, multi-ethnic and hybrid groups, flexibly defined by descent and/or residence	Membership based on residence in a territory governed by a constitutional framework ('constitutional patriotism')
Modes of governance	Government, governing in accordance to the rule of 'international law' and based on the free will and public approval of civil society	State and non-state actors on local, regional and global levels; global democracy based on multi-level governance networks	Variety of political, economic, cultural and religious mechanisms of governance, defined by the respective group	Discursive democratic processes in a territorial community defined by a common constitution
Key proponent(s)	Immanuel Kant	Richard Falk, Anthony Giddens, David Held, Manuel Castells	David Hollinger	Jürgen Habermas

driver of these new and contemporary ways of constructing political communities. Given the relevance of globalization to the transformation of citizenship we dedicate this chapter to this phenomenon and to its implications and ramifications for our specific interest in citizenship from a corporate perspective.

Such an explicit appreciation of the changing nature of citizenship on a global level, however, has met only limited attention by those who refer to this terminology in business practice and research. While we will assess the corporate usage of the citizenship metaphor later it is appropriate to point out the relative dearth of literature on cosmopolitan citizenship in the debate on corporate citizenship in the management literature. Logsdon and Wood have, however, recently suggested the notion of 'global business citizenship', which attempts to conceptualize the notion of citizenship for business corporations at the global level (Logsdon and Wood 2002; Wood *et al.* 2006). While Logsdon and Wood deserve credit for being among the first to bring a more rigorous appreciation of the political nature of citizenship into the applied literature on corporate citizenship (e.g. Wood and Logsdon 2001) their understanding of global citizenship in a business context is confined to a rather limited version of 'universal ethical principles'. While this notion is vaguely linked to what we will discuss as 'legal cosmopolitanism', it is at the same time far too limited to appreciate the multifaceted debate and numerous empirical mutations we witness when analyzing citizenship on the global level. This in turn has led to a rather constrained and vague debate on the implication of citizenship on the global level and its implications for corporate actors in this arena.

Legal cosmopolitanism

The notion of legal cosmopolitanism arguably goes back to eighteenth century enlightenment thinking, most notably Immanuel Kant's (1970) notion of international relations (Delanty 2000: 53–8). This view is predicated on the idea that each individual is part of humanity in the sense of a global community of citizens who refer their status not in the first place to the state or government but to a set of universally true and applicable moral values, which should form the basis of an international legal order. Legal cosmopolitanism is not so much concerned with national governments of territorial states; they are taken as a given. Rather, the focus is on the legitimacy that these governments derive solely from the fact that they comply with 'international law' based on the respect for those universal moral values. These governments depend (or should depend) on the consent of civil society, in which each individual exerts their free will. This view focuses on a legal framework as the key tool of governance which is applicable globally. It is not so much concerned with individual nation states and does not relate the notion of citizenship to those institutions of territorial governance. The latter are important, but only legitimate insofar as they comply with 'international law'.

Legal cosmopolitanism describes and conceptualizes some important aspects of globalization, in particular the search for globally shared and commonly accepted moral values regardless of race, culture, religion, language, ethnicity or other discriminating factors. Be it the aspiration to a 'world ethos' (Küng 2002) or, more concretely, the UN declaration of human rights, many attempts of governing the global sphere in fact are predicated on the notion that human beings world wide share a certain, potentially minimal, set of values and norms as the lowest common denominator, which should constitute the legal principles of transnational governance.

Political cosmopolitanism

In contrast to legal cosmopolitanism, political cosmopolitanism tries to understand the way globalization actually shapes, transforms and redefines political communities and institutions (Archibugi 2004; Delanty 2000: 58–63). In doing so it shifts the focus from a principle based, or moral, understanding of global humanity to an analysis of the political shifts induced by globalization. As such, political cosmopolitanism is chiefly interested in the nature of citizenship beyond the 'container of the nation state' (Beck 1999; 1998). It is argued that, rather than being a citizen of one state, individuals are, in most cases simultaneously, part of multiple communities. Some of them are global, some are regional and others are local. After all, globalization in many places has reinvigorated a sense of belonging and identity at a local level. Equally, in an age of electronic media and communications, virtual communities increasingly reflect the deterritorializing nature of globalization.

Rather than assuming universality, political cosmopolitanism acknowledges that all these different communities of which individuals can simultaneously be members are organized according to a plurality of *political*, rather than moral, principles. Citizenship here is then the simultaneous membership by individuals of different communities, each of which is governed according to a diverse range of political principles, with the contestable underlying assumption of some form of democracy as the dominating and desired platform for citizenship. The result is a global civil society (Baker and Chandler 2005), in which state and non-state actors, in particular international non-governmental organizations (INGOs), interact in a global democracy on various political levels and in different political networks.

Political cosmopolitanism is therefore concerned about understanding and explaining the most complex result of globalization. Next to the involvement of nation states, crucial decisions such as the protection of the global climate can only be brought about by a complex interaction of a plethora of actors, including supranational governmental institutions, NGOs, business, the media, academics and other civil society communities or actors. We have already discussed an example of this perspective in Chapter 6 when looking at ecological citizenship as a new non-territorial obligation conceptualizing a global community of citizens forged together by affecting and being affected by their respective 'ecological footprints'. This perspective of political cosmopolitanism, then, unlike the more generic views of citizenship discussed in Chapters 2 and 3, or the notion of legal cosmopolitanism discussed above, attempts to conceptualize the complex reality of citizenship in the context of globalization. It is rather short on normative criteria except, however, for the notion that the political governance of global civil society should follow democratic principles.

Transnational communities

A crucial feature of cosmopolitan citizens is that they are often members of highly mobile migrant communities (Delanty 2000: 63–4). One of the consequences of globalization is that it has allowed individuals and groups to easily relocate across the globe. What started with the mass settlement of European emigrants in America in the seventeenth and eighteenth centuries[1] is now a widely observable phenomenon across the globe, more recently dominated by South to North and East to West migration. There are large communities of Asians in Britain, Hispanics in the US and Chinese all over South East Asia. These communities are unified by common ethnic values which are in most cases not only cultural but also political, economic and religious. Cosmopolitan citizenship, understood as membership in these communities, thus follows dominantly ethnic and multi-ethnic lines (e.g. 'British-Asian') and is often of a strongly economic and cultural nature. Membership of these groups, however, is not only defined by descent (ethnicity) but is often a hybrid resulting from longer residency in different locations (e.g. Hispanic Californians, British Pakistanis, Chinese Malayans), which are neither fully part of the original ethnicity nor fully integrated into the current cultural environment of their residency. Transnational communities, then, are a specific example of what we discussed in Chapter 5, however in this chapter we focus on the global nature of these specific ways of providing identity as a prerequisite of membership in a community.

The crucial element exposed by this perspective on cosmopolitan citizenship lies in the fact that it is neither morally nor legally based, nor is it necessarily defined along political lines. Citizenship here becomes reconfigured along the lines of ethnicity resulting from membership in a globally migrant community of individuals. In the context of our argument, transnational communities are particularly interesting as some commentators, for example Richard Falk (1994), explicitly include highly mobile business elites in this perspective. Multinational corporations (MNCs), or the global business 'community', bring relatively homogenous values, education, lifestyle and language, and function rather like the migrant ethnic communities. Most significantly, their membership of a deterritorialized community is highly mobile across the globe. We will come back to this aspect later in this chapter.

Post-nationalism

Post-nationalism opens up a perspective on cosmopolitan citizenship which appreciates particularly the demise of nationhood as a basis for citizenship (Delanty 2000: 64–6; Sassen 2002). Globalization leads to multifaceted communities defined by local, regional, global or virtual characteristics, bound together by common cultural, ethnic, social or economic characteristics rather than shared national identities. While citizenship as nationality is based on birth, the key proponent of post-national citizenship, Jürgen Habermas (e.g. 1994; 1995; 1998), identifies a model of citizenship based on residence as a key pattern of cosmopolitan citizenship. Again, this perspective can be seen as another specific manifestation of citizenship based on the identity of a resident in a specific territorial community. He argues that post-national citizenship is the only way to maintain the idea of citizenship in a cosmopolitan context. Pivotal to this notion of citizenship are, first, a constitution, which replaces nation-based reference points for assigning status, entitlement and processes of citizens, and, second, the existence of a public sphere within which cosmopolitan citizens can participate in civic deliberation and democratic governance.

In this, Habermas' notion of citizenship is close to legal cosmopolitanism, which also acknowledges a pivotal role for a territorial government and its dependency on public approval. However, post-nationalism also conceives of civic actors beyond nation states, visible, for instance, in the notion of citizenship within the European Union or institutions of the United Nations, the latter governing cosmopolitan citizenship on a transnational basis. Post-national citizenship is akin to political cosmopolitanism in that it recognizes multiple levels of communities and actors in the governance of citizenship. However, post-nationalism is rather pessimistic about the ability of 'global civil society' to (self-) govern citizenship but reiterates the necessity to ground cosmopolitan citizens' rights and duties in a constitution based on territoriality and to create a public sphere for the discursive democratic governance of such a polity. Post-national citizenship is particularly challenging to notions of transnational citizenship. While the existence of transnational communities is one of its empirical starting points, it argues that the only way of a peaceful coexistence in a political community is that all individuals, regardless of affiliation to other (for instance transnational) communities, subscribe to a minimal consensus on status, entitlements and processes of participation for citizens in the public sphere. Recent debates in many Western societies about the appropriate integration of and demands on ethnic and religious minorities show that both these views of citizenship can create quite significant contestation.

Cosmopolitan citizenship and human rights

So far in this section we have discussed four of the main approaches to cosmopolitan citizenship. All of them try to provide an answer to the question of how citizenship is reconfigured in a world where the pivotal reference point of extant citizenship thinking becomes increasingly brittle. With the partial exception of legal cosmopolitanism, however, the different approaches have focused more on the political and institutional implications of cosmopolitanism, and have taken for granted an underlying consensus on common normative values, constructed by different forms of democratic and discursive processes. In other words, while cosmopolitan citizenship provides different perspectives on the processes of citizenship, the actual status and entitlements of cosmopolitan citizens have been rather neglected in our discussion.

Early notions of liberal citizenship have attempted to define the relation of the individual within a community by assigning certain citizenship rights based on a political understanding of the individual as embedded within a (democratic) nation state. With the dissolution of the traditional reference point for citizenship and its replacement by a rather complex array of membership(s) in different communities on various levels, the very notion of citizenship rights has increasingly been replaced by the broader and more general notion of human rights (see here and in the following; Delanty 2000: 68–80). Citizenship rights are based on a political understanding of the individual while human rights are based on a more general ethical conception of the individual. With the traditional political reference points for citizenship being eclipsed by globalization it is hardly surprising that human rights have risen to centre stage in cosmopolitan citizenship.

Human rights are increasingly relevant as a topic for global corporations and it is therefore appropriate to emphasize that the notion of human rights in cosmopolitan citizenship is by no means unproblematic. We will highlight three areas of difficulty. First, there is the problem that we do not have a consensus on what human rights are, and how they are defined in breadth and depth. Unlike legal cosmopolitanism, we cannot assume a common global understanding of human rights. Though there are suggestions on how to solve this problem, which we will discuss further in this chapter, it is important to note that despite the centrality of human rights as a substitute for clearly defined citizenship rights, the ethical debate on the definition of this construct is ongoing and as yet unresolved.

Second, there is some debate about the very notion of human rights as a Western or even Eurocentric concept. Though there are certain commonly shared values between cultures globally, there are still significant differences remaining, based on different notions of human dignity and different balances of individual and collective rights. Much of this critique stems from a post-colonial perspective which treats human rights as little more that just another way of imposing Western values and concepts on other parts of the world. We will revisit this point later on in the context of corporations and human rights.

A third impact of the wider debate on human rights is the emergence of what some have called legal pluralism. For instance, the implementation of the European Charter for Human Rights has led to quite significant impacts on the way nation states within the European Union govern citizenship rights. Furthermore, human rights are the core concern of a plethora of INGOs, global civil society actors and supranational organizations that impact quite significantly on national governments – a development that has led some to identify the end of citizenship (Soysal 1994). Though some of these developments might, of themselves, be beneficial in the context of our analysis of citizenship, they have obfuscated the sense of what citizenship rights are and which actors are responsible and accountable for their implementation.

Corporations as drivers of globalization

In the preceding section of this chapter we have reviewed the literature on the effect of globalization on citizenship and discovered that the emerging construct of cosmopolitan citizenship is in many aspects quite different from the ideas of citizenship within nation states. Our conclusion so far is that citizenship, taken to the global stage, becomes a more multi-faceted, ill-defined and complex phenomenon. A number of basic features, such as the status of individuals and their rights as citizens, are difficult to translate to the global level. In short, globalization transforms – and arguably weakens, obfuscates or blurs – crucial features of the concept of citizenship.

In this section we show that globalization is not a given; it is a phenomenon that is constructed, shaped and boosted by corporations. As a result, we argue that corporations, in having such a notable influence on globalization, can also be seen as indirectly driving the transformation of citizenship in the global age. This argument will form the basis of our further analysis of the role of the corporation in citizenship on the global level, in which we contend that many of the factors that have informed the transformation of citizenship result in part, at least, from corporate action.

As outlined earlier, we understand globalization to be the increasing deterritorialization of social, economic and political relations, activities and interactions. In the following, we will outline some of the key factors which have led to this deterritorialization trend and analyze the role corporations have had in shaping these factors (Scherer and Palazzo 2008; Scholte 2003). Table 7.2 provides an overview of the discussion.

The discussion on globalization as a new phenomenon only really unfolded in the early 1990s. Two crucial conditions at the *political* level were: first, the end of the Cold War and the associated division of the world into two hegemonic blocks; and second, the tide of more neoliberal economic policies in many of the big industrial nations in the West (see Chapter 3). Together, these allowed for the creation of a more homogenous global political and economic space characterized by (forms of) democracy, capitalism and free markets, and an increased influence of private actors, less regulation for business and lower bureaucratic and tariff barriers to cross-border activities. The liberalization of international trade is particularly manifest in the rise of transnational political and economic regimes, the most striking example being the enlarged European Union (EU-25), although it entailed some increased bureaucratic and tariff barriers in extra-EU relations. All of these political developments have paved the way for what some refer to as a 'borderless world' (Ohmae 1990), where goods and services, people and ideas can move relatively freely from one territory to another.

The role of corporations in bringing about these political changes, however, is contested and arguably more indirect. While corporate lobbying has certainly informed many of the Western democracies' policies in the 1980s, a key driver of liberalization and the harmonization of regulatory and fiscal regimes has been the attraction of foreign direct investment (FDI) and its promise of wealth creation, employment and tax revenue to their governments. Corporate influence, though, is more direct in shaping global trade regimes with representatives of corporations and the growing number of global business associations and coalitions being involved in the World Trade Organization's (WTO) trade negotiation rounds (Geppert *et al.* 2006).

Likewise, corporations have had an indirect effect on events leading to the fall of the Iron Curtain. Much of the consumer dissatisfaction with living conditions in many Eastern Bloc countries in the 1980s had been fuelled by increased awareness of the living standards in the West, manifest in consumption patterns that had been met by corporations, and which had been showcased to people in the East by the daily

Table 7.2. *Corporations as drivers of globalization, i.e. deterritorialization*

	Manifestations of deterritorialization (examples)	Corporations as drivers of deterritorialization
Political factors	• Libertarian politics in the 1980s (see Chapter 3) • Fall of the Iron Curtain • Rise of transnational political and economic regimes (e.g. EU, NATO, ASEAN, NAFTA)	Corporations have indirect roles as they are not the key decision-maker on these issues but often make powerful impacts through: • Lobbying • Direct corporate power over FDI (employment, tax income etc.) • Participation in liberalizing bodies (e.g. WTO, GATT, Doha Round) • Growing number of global business associations
Technological factors	• Communications technology (e.g. internet, mobile telecommunications, TV) • Transport technologies • Markets for cheap energy • Impacts on the emergence of global side effects (e.g. climate change, risks resource depletion)	Corporations operate, develop and control those key technologies, e.g. • Energy industries • Airlines, shipping and haulage companies • Media industry • Most production processes controlled by corporations
Social/cultural factors	• Converging global culture and belief systems • Homogeneity of cultural products (e.g. film, media, literature, music, sports) • Converging education models (e.g. MBA, Bologna process) • Erosion of language barriers	Corporations contribute to and act as a channel for spreading a global culture through, e.g. • Global cultural industries • Global advertising campaigns • Globally standardized products • Encouragement of a more homogenous business culture
Economic factors	• Abolition of trade barriers (e.g. GATT, EU) • Rise and spread of multinational corporations (MNCs) • Homogeneity of fashion trends and consumption patterns • Rise of world wide markets for capital, commodities, products and services, labour.	Corporations are the main sources and key actors within the context of the economic aspects of globalization • Global supply chains • Key sources of FDI • Extensive use of global markets • Global recruitment strategies

programmes and commercials of Western television and media. Anecdotally, among the very first impressions of the West for many East Germans, when overrunning the checkpoints on the night of 9 November 1989, were free bananas, coffee packs and chocolate bars handed out to them by Western food multinationals.

Another crucial driver of globalization has been the availability of *technologies*, which have enabled the rapid communication of information and movement of capital, labour and products over large distances. The obvious examples are the internet and mobile telecommunications, which enable communication and the development of business and social relations regardless of territorial basis (Giddens 1990; 1999). Equally, there has been an enormous increase in air traffic and other forms of transport. All this has been facilitated by technological progress, particularly in the area of energy extraction, production and distribution. On the flipside, technology has also led to significant side effects (Beck 1992), many of which are also global, such as global warming and the risk of nuclear pollution, epitomised by the Chernobyl accident. For many authors (Beck 1997a; Goldblatt 1997; Linneroth-Bayer *et al.* 2001; Matten 2004) these deterritorialized side effects of modern technology have been a key driver of globalization.

Needless to say, most of these technologies that enable communication, transport and travel, or lead to undesired global side effects, are developed and utilized in the sphere of corporations. This is certainly the case in transport and energy industries but also increasingly in the telecommunications, internet and media industry, where private corporations dominate the field and the number of state-controlled media is increasingly in decline. Overall, corporations certainly provide the majority of the technological infrastructure for social, cultural and economic drivers of globalization, to which we now turn.

For many authors, the key drivers of globalization are *social* and *cultural* in nature. Quite a number of scholars use accounts of the transformation of remote villages in Asia or Africa by Western products, logos and cultural products as indicative of a more homogeneous global culture (see various papers in Boli and Lechner 2000). Similarly, an increasingly standardized popular culture and set of belief systems seems to be reflected by films, music and sports events, which are simultaneously appreciated and consumed all over the world. Likewise, we witness an increasing convergence in education patterns, partly facilitated by political efforts to harmonize education systems (such as the Bologna Process in the EU) or by highly mobile elites obtaining degrees from universities in Western Europe and North America. These developments are underpinned by an increasing literacy in the English language, in part enabled by and in part enabling the global spread of culture, in particular in film, media, literature and popular music.

Corporations have a crucial influence on this global spread of a homogenized culture. Most of those cultural products are sold by corporations on a world wide scale, accompanied by global advertising campaigns spreading corporate logos and slogans to the remotest places of the planet (Klein 2000; Ritzer 2003). Furthermore, amid the drive for the global standardization of products an increasing number of homes, schools, workplaces and public spaces are shaped in the same fashion and style making high streets, campuses and holiday destinations look more similar all over the world (Bakan 2004). In many ways, as some have argued (Falk 1994; Stephenson 2003: 126–49), the business world itself is an epitomization of this development. Multinational companies employ MBAs and other graduates coming from similar academic institutions and converging educational systems working with the same software products, speaking the same language and implementing the same business ideas. Arguably then, corporations are key drivers and facilitators of an increasingly deterritorialized world in which culture and social environments become increasingly detached from their original territorial bases.

Though sometimes difficult to distinguish from political forces, the *economic* drivers of deterritorialization have often been seen as the most contested side-effect of globalization. Typically, proponents of this take on globalization refer to the lowering of trade barriers between countries and the growing number of developing countries which, in order to attract FDI, have tried to turn themselves into more attractive investment locations by lowering tariffs, taxes and requirements for social protection of workers or the preservation of the environment (Korten 2001; Mokhiber and Weissman 1999; 2001; Scherer and Smid 2000). Multinational corporations (MNCs) and their subsidiaries are obviously key actors in a world where economic decisions are predominantly shaped by economic criteria as they seek to produce goods and services at the most cost effective locations. In a similar vein, markets for capital, financial services and commodities are global in nature: to participate in these markets it is no longer necessary to be physically present in a specific location.

By establishing and managing global supply chains and being the key sources of FDI, corporations' role in facilitating and managing a global economy is crucial. So, for instance, Wal-Mart in 2004 was the eighth biggest economy as a trading partner with China, ahead of Australia, Canada and Russia (Jingjing 2004). Furthermore, private corporations are not only the key actors within global markets but in many cases they also own the infrastructure that facilitates the exchange of supply and demand, such as airlines, shipping or telecommunication companies.

The role of corporations in global governance

In the first part of the book we analyzed the role of the corporation in the governance of the citizenship. We delineated three perspectives through which we investigated citizenship as a framework to understand the roles and responsibilities of corporations: as if they were citizens (Chapter 2); their role in the governance of citizenship (Chapter 3); and the opportunities they provide for stakeholders to behave in a citizenly fashion (Chapter 4). In the following, we will apply these three views to the global level and examine the potential of corporations as citizens in the context of cosmopolitan citizenship through the four main schools of thought in cosmopolitan citizenship outlined earlier in this chapter.

Corporations from the perspective of legal cosmopolitanism

Legal cosmopolitanism, as argued above, is predicated on 'international law', a universally accepted set of norms and values which should govern citizens globally as well as those actors which govern citizenship, most notably nation states. The most common manifestation of such global sets of norms could be seen in the notion of 'human rights' as manifest in the UN convention on human rights. The relationship between corporations and human rights has been discussed recently with a number of publications (Frynas and Pegg 2003; Sullivan 2003), conferences and watchdogs dedicated to the topic. It characterized the former UN High Commissioner for Human Rights, Mary Robinson's, 'Realizing Rights – Ethical Globalization Initiative' and various business and human rights groups, e.g. Amnesty International.

Many MNCs are very active in implementing this perspective by drawing up human rights policies. Shell, for example, sees this as an integral part of its corporate social responsibility (CSR) related activities.[2] More broadly, this approach is adopted by the 2,500 plus companies that have signed up to the ten principles of the UN Global Compact (Wagner 2004) and those that have signed up to other third party codes of conduct (COC) or codes of ethics, such as the Organization for Economic Cooperation and Development (OECD) Guidelines for MNCs or the International Labour Organization (ILO) conventions (for an overview see Bondy *et al.* 2006). In doing so, these companies have committed themselves to what is commonly regarded as a basic set of global values and principles (Frankental 2002).

While our discussion so far just adds corporations to the actors of legal cosmopolitanism, this perspective also reveals a more direct and active influence of corporations in transforming notions of citizenship. Many MNCs have drawn up industry codes of conduct for their industries or have, together with civil society actors, developed third party codes of conduct to enable yet other corporations to implement global standards (Mullerat 2005). A particularly delicate role of MNCs emerges where they operate in states where human rights are disregarded. The classic example is the role of MNCs in apartheid South Africa. By adhering to the Sullivan Principles they finally withdrew from the country and added to the international pressure that finally led to regime change in 1994. These tensions between companies and oppressive governments have recently been discussed in the context of companies such as BP in Azerbaijan, Shell in Nigeria and Chevron and Triumph in Myanmar, which have been expected by their Western critics as well as some stakeholders to enact human rights standards beyond those of the respective national governments. A growing number of companies adopt a government-like role by attempting to impose global rules and principles with regard to human rights and labour standards on their suppliers in countries whose governments neglect human rights.

The general tension in fitting corporations into a framework of legal cosmopolitanism, however, seems to be that, as Delanty argues, 'from the discourse of internationalism . . . cosmopolitan citizenship has been subordinated to a state-centred world' (2000: 58). Thus, allowing corporations into this framework in a role other than that of a citizen abiding by 'international law' exposes a crucial deficit. Corporations are private actors and their sphere of influence is not constituted by other citizens. Moreover, these other citizens have not given their public approval to corporations to govern. This ultimately exposes questions about the legitimacy of corporations acting as another 'leviathan' alongside governments, many of which are to subject to some degree of public approval.

Corporations from the perspective of political cosmopolitanism

Political cosmopolitanism acknowledges that globalization has significantly undermined the capacity of nation-state governments to govern on a global level. Rather it assumes a plethora of civil society actors and transnational organizations participate in global governance alongside those traditional, territorially based actors (Levy and Kaplan 2008; Ruggie 2004; Scherer *et al.* 2006). In this picture, it is not very difficult to locate corporations and in fact a significant number of contributions in the literature on cosmopolitan citizenship have discussed the potential and limitations of business as an active player in global governance (Bock and Fuccillo 1975; Henderson 2000; Koenig-Archibugi 2002; Moon 2002; Ronit 2001).

We can conceive of corporations as active participants in global governance alongside other civil society actors. There is a growing number of business–NGO partnerships designed to solve complex issues in the governance of societies (Bendell 2000; Warner and Sullivan 2004), in particular in the global South (Ashman 2001; 2000). This approach is also part of the UN Global Compact which, besides committing corporations to ten principles, also provides extensive opportunities for business deliberation with other civil society actors referred to as 'learning forums', and inter-organizational networks (see McIntosh *et al.* 2004). In a somewhat different vein, corporations also act as a global civil society group of their own by forming interest groups which engage in global civil society on behalf of business. A powerful example here is the Global Climate Coalition, an interest group formed by major MNCs in the oil business to represent business interests with regard to global climate change and in particular the Kyoto Protocol (Begg *et al.* 2005; Kolk and Levy 2001; Levy and Kolk 2002). The Fair Trade movement can be seen as such a multi-level policy network, combining a plethora of business, civil society and governmental actors to ensure fair labour and market conditions for producers of commodities in the global South (Davies and Crane 2003; Moore 2004; Nicholls and Opal 2005).

Business not only participates in governance issues pertaining to their immediate commercial interests; private companies are also increasingly sharing the governance of wider societal concerns and needs. Classic examples are the role of business in fighting global diseases, particularly in the global South, such as malaria or HIV/Aids. Though the partnership approach is still dominant in these business initiatives (Lamont 2002; Lamont and Williams 2001; LSE & Wellcome Trust 2005), the power differentials in resources, research and development and technology often assign corporations a leading role in these projects. A good example would be the Global Business Coalition on HIV/Aids where many of the world's biggest MNCs have come together to tackle this global pandemic (Leisinger 2005; Rosen 2003).

Another recent area of interest, where corporations are explicitly seen as actors participating in, if not replacing, longstanding governmental activities is the 'bottom of the pyramid' (BOP) concept of C. K. Prahalad and others (Hart 2005; Prahalad 2005; Prahalad and Hammond 2002). At the core of this approach is the insight that most Western MNCs, particularly those producing mass consumer products such as food, detergents, cars and mobile phones, only serve the upper five to ten per cent of consumers in emerging or developing markets such as China, India, Brazil or Nigeria. A huge market of up to four billion consumers, however, has remained untapped just because, these authors argue, Western corporations only transfer their longstanding business models to countries where consumer behaviour follows familiar patterns. The list of successful examples of industries targeting the bottom of the pyramid includes banking, communication technology, consumer electronics and transport.

From a governance perspective, the proponents of the BOP approach argue that a business model which is attuned to the needs and contingencies of emerging markets does not only provide these formerly disenfranchised people access to much coveted products taken for granted in the developed West, but also allows these people more stakes in the process of actual wealth creation. The latter is because much of the BOP thinking is predicated on the assumption that successful business models would also require significantly larger parts of the value chain to be located within these markets geographically. In particular, BOP thinking is increasingly seen as a more successful replacement of the traditional development model which is largely based on (Western) governments transferring aid to governments in the developing world, which has failed to substantially reduce global poverty levels. This approach is by no means uncontested (Blowfield and Frynas 2005; Michael 2003), however it can be regarded as a good example of corporations assuming a key role in fighting global poverty and, as it were, collaborating and competing with governmental actors in search of more efficient approaches to address global poverty (Hoffman *et al.* 2005). A particular boost to this approach has come from various initiatives to involve business in the implementation of the Millenium Development Goals (e.g. Nestlé 2006; Timberlake 2005).

Some corporations have taken up this challenge of becoming active participants in different roles in global governance. The lens of political cosmopolitanism, however, exposes some of the problematic implications of corporate participation in global governance. In particular, nation states, especially in the developing world, depend on corporations for wealth creation, economic development and FDI, which arguably translates into political power for the corporations (Korten 2001; Scherer and Smid 2000). This threatens to turn this new world of political cosmopolitanism into an uneven playing field. Moreover, there are only limited possibilities for democratic participation of stakeholders in corporations' pursuit of their private interests.

Corporations from the perspective of transnational communities

The perspective of transnational communities exposes the fact that globalization has created the opportunity (and sometimes the threat) for groups of people to relocate to other parts of the world or to pursue a highly mobile lifestyle. They thus transcend the boundaries of nation states as the traditional arena of governance of citizenship and may develop intra-group citizen-like patterns of interaction. The application of this perspective to business would lead us to conceptualize the 'business community' – a term often used by corporate leaders to refer to their organizational field (Bakan 2004) – as representing such a transnational community. This would allow us to understand businesses world wide as a community, bound together by common interests, interactions and institutions pretty much in the sense that new institutionalism characterizes the 'organizational field' of business, consisting of competitors, suppliers, educational institutions and (self-)regulatory bodies (DiMaggio and Powell 1983; Geppert *et al.* 2006; Meyer and Rowan 1977; Morgan 2001).

In this perspective individual corporations could be understood as members of a larger, transnational community in whose governance they participate. There are clear indicators of such a community emerging, including attempts to define status and entitlements of members as well as defining processes of members participating in the governance of the community. For instance, the burgeoning field of industry codes of conduct and other forms of business self-regulation clearly points to the civic nature of the business community. The ongoing efforts to standardize and homogenize business practices, most obviously in the International Standards Organization (ISO), illustrates another approach to governing the 'business community' (Guler *et al.* 2002). Standards relating to the wider responsibilities of business to society (e.g. the environmentally focused ISO 14000 series, the emerging ISO 26000 standard on CSR) represent an effort of global business to govern its members' behaviour and to define their responsibilities not only *within* the business community but also *with regard to other* communities. In addition, business has impacts on business education, as many of the larger and influential business schools rely heavily on corporate funding, which in turn contributes further to the 'business community's' governance of itself. The annual meeting of business leaders at the World Economic Forum in Davos can be regarded as one of the strongest manifestations of such a community as well as of the ongoing effort to govern the behaviour of business as citizens of a global community. We will come back to this point later in this chapter.

More narrowly, a single multinational corporation can even be conceptualised as a transnational community, much in the sense we conceputalised the firm and its stakeholders as a political community in Chapters 2 and 4. A growing literature conceptualizes MNCs as 'transnational social spaces' (Geppert *et al.* 2006; Morgan 2001; Pries 2001), premised on these businesses being global communities in themselves. In this way they resemble transnational ethnic groups by virtue of their global values and cultures which are often implemented by formal value statements or more detailed codes of ethics and conduct. Furthermore, many MNCs have fairly elaborate systems of education, training, communication and multi-level meetings, all of which serve the end of ensuring the globally homogenous governance of highly mobile and diverse transnational communities (Bâelanger 1999).

More narrowly still, corporations are also social spaces where a variety of – in the literal sense – transnational communities meet, collaborate and interact. In this perspective, then, corporations face the challenge of governing their relations to their stakeholders as members of transnational communities in a civic pattern. In Chapter 5 we discussed in some more detail the various ways in which corporations become involved in constructing or suppressing civic identities. Key expressions of corporations living up to this challenge would include implementing diversity programmes catering to different ethnic or religious preferences among their employees or customers. Other expressions of corporations' governance through everyday activities would be through catering to the needs of ethnic communities by offering teaching in specific languages, and catering for specific diets and food preparation needs of these transnational communities.

The lens of transnational communities identifies the civic nature of business as transnational social spaces and exposes challenges for business to govern these spaces in a citizenly manner. There are, however, limits to this perspective. First, business as a whole and single MNCs tend only to be communities in the virtual sense and, furthermore, tend to be bound together mainly by economic, rather than social criteria. Second, and relatedly, contestation about the political role of companies is not so much concerned with the internal governance of the corporations but with how business as a community is embedded in and interacts with other national and transnational communities.

Corporations from the perspective of post-nationalism

The central point of post-nationalism in the context of cosmopolitan citizenship is that citizenship is configured no longer on the basis of nationality or descent, but is governed by the constitution of a polity whose members belong to it on the grounds of residency. Applying this perspective to corporations provides a rather limited range of possibilities and, if anything, exposes some of the greatest dilemmas of governing transnational actors which are characterized by transcending one of the defining criteria of post-nationalism, namely residency.

If we think of corporations as citizens this would certainly imply that they comply with the 'constitution' of the country where they are based. In the case of MNCs, however, this claim also exposes companies to rather contradictory claims, if the legal frameworks in home and host countries differ. Following the arguments of the preceding sections, one might suggest that MNCs, as citizens of their home countries in Europe,

East Asia or the US, should implement the values of the home countries throughout their global operations. This would be consistent with the logic of the US Foreign Corrupt Practices Act, which makes bribery an offence for MNCs even if it happens abroad (Donaldson 1989: 31). However, despite many endeavours of MNCs, these attempts to impose their values on subsidiaries governed by different 'constitutions' can prove to be quite problematic. Many efforts of MNCs to implement responsible practices are sometimes discounted as a new form of colonial imposition of Western values on other civilisations (Blowfield and Frynas 2005). This perspective would be particularly salient if we assumed that corporations should treat their stakeholders in a citizen-like fashion. This would lead corporations to respect the fact that some of their global stakeholders would be subject to different sets of values, manifest in the customization of products (consumer stakeholders) or work practices (supplier or employee stakeholders). In summary, the notion of a residency-based 'constitution' for governing corporations exposes problems for globally active corporations rather than suggesting fruitful avenues for addressing the deterritorialized character of governance within these organizations. In this sense, then, globalization exposes the often complicated and controversial debates in corporations as to which principles should govern their global operations and their engagement with stakeholders globally (see also Chapter 4).

Within the framework of post-nationalism, however, there are aspects which are akin to the cosmopolitan aspect of citizenship and, thereby, have quite significant impacts on the corporate governance of and participation in citizenship. Habermas' idea of citizenship in a post-national setting also rests on the assumption that the very values of a 'constitution' can only be determined and implemented on the basis of discursive deliberation and democratic processes within a society. This idea, which we discussed in the context of Chapter 2, has met increasing attention in the CSR literature recently. As Scherer and Palazzo (2008) argue, such a political framing of corporate social responsibility is a crucial element for the legitimacy of corporate activities within (global) society: 'in a world of different cultures and values, a philosophical foundation of first principles of social life is an unnecessary and futile attempt'. They suggest that corporations (as citizens, we would add) should be part of deliberative processes in society and participate in civic deliberation (see also Scherer and Palazzo 2007). Examples could be stakeholder consultations, employed by apparel manufacturers in order to establish norms and values for the governance of their suppliers in the developing world (Wokutch and French 2005). In governing citizenship, whether as members of society or regarding the organization of their stakeholders, corporations in a post-national setting would implement mechanisms for civic deliberation and organizational democracy (Fung 2003b) with regard to which values should govern, for instance, their codes of conduct or production strategies. This aspect of participation and deliberation renders the implications of cosmopolitan citizenship similar to the role of corporations as understood by political cosmopolitanism.

Summarizing the diversity of lenses on corporations in a cosmopolitan setting

While globalization, on the one hand, has weakened many notions of citizenship we see a new emerging arena of citizenship at the global level which in many respects enriches the concept of citizenship. From the four key perspectives on cosmopolitan citizenship, corporations are both affected by these new features of citizenship as well as actively involved in shaping and enacting the very notion of citizenship at a global level.

The perspective of legal cosmopolitanism highlights the necessity of founding and implementing the status and fundamental entitlements of individuals in a global context and we have seen that corporations not only face certain expectations along these lines but also contribute actively – sometimes even pivotally – to the enactment or suppression of key facets of citizenship at the global level. Political cosmopolitanism sketches out new mechanisms of civic participation and again we see corporations as key players next to governments and civil society. As a transnational community, business in general, but in particular MNCs, constitutes a key arena in which new global forms of citizenship are enacted. From a postnational perspective, there are mechanisms in which corporations, as surrogate citizens, can legitimately participate in the governance of society. At the same time, however, each perspective also uncovers the limits to corporate roles in the global citizenship arena. Arguably though, together these perspectives also provide a conceptual backdrop for developing alternative approaches to some of the current contestations about the corporate role in global governance. We will investigate this point more closely in the following section.

Countervailing powers? Global movements critical of corporations and global capitalism

Locating the corporation in the context of cosmopolitan citizenship has yielded a multifaceted picture. Of the four different perspectives it is the rather messy and complex political cosmopolitanism which focuses on the embeddedness of the corporation in a network of global civil society. This is arguably the perspective which most explicitly integrates and conceptualizes corporations as key actors in cosmopolitan citizenship. Among the key actors on the cosmopolitan stage we can identify nation state governments, intergovernmental organizations (IGOs) including transnational governmental institutions, INGOs and MNCs (Boli and Thomas 1997).

All of these actors within the arena of citizenship on a global level face a number of problems. We confine ourselves here to two main issues. The first problem of global civil society actors is that of *representation*. This may seem less pressing for citizens who, in principle, are represented by national governments which are accountable and transparent. Even in these cases, however, on the global stage governments can defy what would be norms of representation on the domestic stage, illustrated by the debate on recent decisions to go to war in Iraq and Afghanistan in many democratic societies. With INGOs such as the WTO or transnational governmental institutions such as the EU this problem exists in a similar fashion. Even NGOs are increasingly exposed to contestation about their mandate and how far they are actually representing those constituencies they claim to represent (Bendell 2005). This problem is most blatant in the case of the centrepiece of global governance, the UN, in which undemocratic countries are in the majority.

Second, global civil society actors face the problem that most of their governance of citizenship is *voluntary*. This represents quite a deep-seated tension with the very notion of citizenship, where status and entitlements were once considered 'inalienable rights' (in the words of the 1776 US Declaration of Independence) and therefore something which – in its original inception – nation state governments are obliged to respect. On the global level, mechanisms to make the governance of citizenship mandatory by any of those global civil society actors have so far been very limited and are currently mostly derivative of the fact that one group of key players, namely democratic nation state governments, have the mandatory commitment to govern citizenship and to be accountable to their national citizens.

In the following, we address both problems with specific regard to the corporation as an actor in cosmopolitan citizenship and to the role of a key surrogate in addressing citizenship issues, namely global civil society organizations.

We have discussed the role of civil society actors, in particular NGOs, at various places in this book. In this chapter we confine ourselves to one particular group of actors which is commonly alluded to as the 'anti-globalization movement' (AGM, for an overview see Eschle and Maiguashca 2005). The AGM consists of a variety of groups, organizations and activists including NGOs, academics, trade unionists, journalists and politicians (the latter mostly in the global South). The birth of the movement is generally regarded to be the protests during the 1999 WTO meetings in Seattle ('the Battle of Seattle'), which also exposed violent action as one of its features. The movement is rather heterogeneous, reaching from global campaigning organizations such as ATTAC (Birchfield and Freyberg-Inan 2005), to local resistance groups such as the Zapatistas in Mexico (Higgins 2005).[3] Despite their label – allegedly attributed to the movement after Seattle by the American media – it is a global network of organizations which are primarily concerned with the side effects of globalization and which seek to shape globalization in a different fashion. As Eschle (2005: 27) argues, the movement has 'focused more centrally on phenomena associated with *economic* globalization: the increasing power of corporations, the growing role of international financial institutions, and the policies of trade liberalisation and privatisation propounded by the latter and benefiting many of the former'. The movement regards these as producing economic inequality, social and environmental destruction and cultural homogenisation. Globalization is also regarded as a process which leaches power and self-determination away from people and governments, in other words, as being anti-democratic. Corporations, then, are not the only target but a central one for AGM members because they see corporations as contributing to a globalization 'from above' rather than 'from below'. The movement thus is not against globalization per se: after all, it is itself quite deterritorialized. However, it is interested in shaping globalization so as to allow meaningful involvement of cosmopolitan citizens in global civil society.

As some of the world's most powerful economic actors, corporations have always been a central target in the AGM's striving for attention and change. The corporations' 'representation deficit' is particularly telling here: if they act as citizens or, more poignantly, as government, they only appear to represent the company's shareholders and, at best, its stakeholders. MNCs, particularly, find it hard to demonstrate that they represent a significant proportion of the people who are actually affected by their governance of their citizenship, be it through investment, employment practices or lobbying of local governments.

Turning to the AGM, its own methods of representation are varied. On the one hand there are conferences and meetings, such as the World Social Forum[4] designed as an alternative annual summit to the World Economic Forum (WEF) in Davos. On the other hand, actors within the AGM increasingly try to voice their interests through protests at global gatherings of governments (such as the EU or G8 summits), of financial institutions (such as the WTO meetings) and of corporate leaders (such as the WEF). The rationale for this second group of strategies is that their presence at these meetings provides the media coverage on which it depends to move corporations (and other actors) towards responding to their demands. There is clearly some ambiguity within the movement about the often violent nature of some protests, which are legitimated by – in the words of this chapter – the need to make the representation gap visible.

The second problem the groups associated with the AGM address is the voluntary nature of corporate involvement in governing citizenship in the interest of individual citizens. By publicly exposing and campaigning against corporations the AGM aims to put public pressure on companies to engage in a more desirable way for governing citizenship. The key 'hostage' of protesters here is the brand value particularly of large MNCs, which can suffer quite significantly from these activities, as the recent example of the protest against Google's collusion in censorship in China illustrated. Other avenues of exerting pressure on companies have been selected efforts by global protest movements to buy shares of companies and then try to use the annual general meeting as a platform for exposing the corporations.

The direct involvement of corporations with the AGM so far has been limited. The increasing efforts to adopt the notion of 'global corporate citizenship' as discussed in the next section can be interpreted as a response of companies by depicting their efforts at more responsible behaviour given their place in the arena of global civil society. On a more project-based level, however, we have seen a number of direct partnerships between business and NGOs in areas of primary concern to the AGM, such as the rights of indigenous people in the context of extracting industries (Warner and Sullivan 2004).

Global corporate citizenship?

As discussed in Chapters 1 and 2 the language of citizenship has been embraced enthusiastically by the business world. There is now a 'cosy consensus' (Norman and Néron 2008) around citizenship as the label of choice for corporations framing their activities in CSR, sustainability, governance or ethics. In part, our interest in citizenship has been triggered by the spread of the terminology. In this section, then, we take a brief look at how the 'business community' uses the terminology of citizenship on the global level, normally referred to as 'global corporate citizenship'.

The seminal document on global corporate citizenship is 'Global Corporate Citizenship – The Leadership Challenge for CEOs and Boards' initiated by the World Economic Forum in 2002 and signed by forty six CEOs or Chairpersons of the world's biggest MNCs, such as Coca Cola, Deutsche Bank, DHL, McDonalds, Renault and UBS (World Economic Forum 2002). It laid the foundation for the 'Global Corporate Citizenship Initiative' (GCCI) of the WEF which since then has produced a number of projects in implementing the ideas. It is interesting to see that the GCCI deliberately refrains from defining global corporate citizenship and just uses it as a label:

> Although the statement uses the language of corporate citizenship, we recognize that definitions and approaches vary, with terms such as corporate responsibility, sustainable development and triple-bottom-line also in common usage and different conceptions of what each of these terms means in practice. Our aim is not to focus on specific definitions . . . (World Economic Forum 2002: 1)

This approach is mirrored by most companies adopting the language of global corporate citizenship, as the example of Microsoft in its 2005 'Citizenship Report' indicates:

> The terms 'Global Citizenship' and 'Corporate Citizenship', which are used throughout this report, are interchangeable with similar terms such as 'Corporate Social Responsibility' and 'Corporate Sustainability'. (Microsoft 2005: 1)

Thus, many corporations only allude to global citizenship as a label while deliberately avoiding in-depth engagement on the implications of citizenship. This rather vague use of global citizenship is also reflected in the literature on global corporate citizenship, where it is couched variously in terms of: sustaining the licence to operate (Warhurst 2004); a partnership approach to stakeholders (Nelson 2000); and an orientation of CSR towards values, the public interest (Post 2002) or hypernorms (Logsdon 2004). Similarly, some authors refer to 'business citizenship' when discussing global corporate citizenship (Logsdon and Wood 2002; Wood and Logsdon 2002; 2001) but apply limited notions of citizenship. As we have argued in Chapter 2, the language on (global) corporate citizenship in business and most parts of the academic debate is either re-labelling corporate philanthropy ('limited view') or a re-packaging of extant notions of CSR ('equivalent view').

In the context of this chapter, however, the popularity of the citizenship terminology is most remarkable as it exposes the desire in business to stress elements of membership, partnership and participation in global civil society. Corporations thereby appear to have embraced the approach of political cosmopolitanism (outlined above) as they position themselves as one of a number of members of this global political community – in other words, as a 'global corporate citizen'. This language is most dominant in the UN publications on the Global Compact as well as in the way businesses talk about their involvement in the Compact, as exemplified in a recent statement by one of the Compact's key representatives (Power 2006).

Although corporations appear to be actively embracing the idea of global corporate citizenship, they are keen to avoid any impression that they aspire to roles commensurate with those of governments (Matten and Crane 2005a). This is well-illustrated in Microsoft's 'Citizenship Report' (Microsoft 2005). Microsoft's licence to operate has been challenged by the US government and the EU Commission concerning its position as a monopolistic technology provider – a role which is an increasingly vital element in the governance of society. Consequently, it is not surprising that the company's twenty-three page document features no less than forty six references to governments. The wording carefully avoids any implication that Microsoft assumes an equal or superior position to government. For example, it states that the company is in 'proactive collaboration with other industry leaders, governments, community-based organizations, and nongovernmental organizations (NGOs)' (4); and that 'Microsoft and the Namibian government have been implementing a joint project' (5) depicting the organization as a modest partner and helper. The company presents its services as strengthening governments: 'Microsoft will transform the way governments interact with their citizens and citizens with their governments' (11). Even when referring to the recent law suits and court rulings in the US and Europe (16–17) the company presents itself as complying as a member of these respective political communities.

Another example of the careful avoidance of any confusion of the corporate role with that of governments is a statement by the managing director of the logistics company DHL:

> Some observers on globalization have remarked that governments are finding it more challenging to deliver social development. This is especially the case in developing countries, where there is a growing demand for companies to expand the boundaries of their responsibility. Corporate social responsibility is not a substitute for the rightful role of democratic governments to set up regulatory frameworks and social welfare programmes for the benefit of society. (World Economic Forum 2005: 11)

Thus, the corporate discourse on global CC avoids any implication that business might equal or replace governments in their governance of citizenship.

A similar tendency is evident in companies' adoption of a citizenly approach to their stakeholders. While stakeholder interests are expressly appreciated, corporations prefer to take a 'responsible' attitude to these as an expression of citizenship rather than reviewing the status and entitlement of stakeholders.

There are also limits to the way corporations use the language of citizenship to describe partnership projects – arguably one way of strengthening the participation of stakeholders in the governance of the corporation (World Economic Forum 2005). It is also striking that the Global Compact, a flagship of global CC, was set up without any trade union involvement and it has only subsequently and reluctantly integrated these stakeholder voices (Baker 2004). Trade unions could be regarded as key to the establishment of citizenship in stakeholder relations as their existence is a formal acknowledgement of the status of employees within the corporation and is closely related to the definition and protection of their entitlements. Thus global corporate citizenship can still be rather paternalistic and pre-occupied with voluntarism.

In summary we argue that despite its embrace of citizenship terminology the global business community has yet to fully engage with the practices that we might have expected to accompany the rhetoric. The use of the citizenship metaphor to stress embeddedness, participation and co-operation in global civil society sometimes appears rather shallow. Moreover, there is little evidence that corporations have fully embraced the implications of their political roles, both with regard to the government-like functions that they perform and to the status and entitlements of their own stakeholders.

Conclusion

Analyzing the impact of globalization on citizenship has revealed a complex yet urgent context for the new political roles of corporations. First, we see that citizenship as a concept and a political practice has undergone quite dramatic changes through globalization. Relatively generic concepts such as human rights dominate debates about status and entitlements. But the new arena of participation in global civil society presents a multifaceted and even messy array of actors with very different power resources, bases of legitimacy and interests. The debate on cosmopolitan citizenship also emphasizes new ways of enacting citizenship, new modes of participation and broader and multiple reference points for what constitutes the relevant political community.

If anything, one could argue that cosmopolitan citizenship not only provides a new conceptual space for locating corporations in this global arena but also, empirically, it yields an active role of corporations in transforming numerous global aspects of citizenship. Arguably, then, cosmopolitan citizenship provides a launch pad for considerably thicker notions of citizenship, particularly regarding corporate roles therein.

Second, we have not only revealed how corporations are affected by and react to new forms of global political organization, but also how they have undertaken active roles in the very shaping of cosmopolitan citizenship. We not only refer to the ways in which business drives the underlying process of globalization, but also to the key roles of private companies in governing a plethora of policy issues, including fighting diseases, addressing environmental risks, and shaping global (self-) regulation.

Our discussion, however, has also exposed the opportunities for and limitations to corporations actively undertaking new political roles. The modest aspirations of corporations in their language of global citizenship could be interpreted either as appropriate or diffident from a citizenship perspective. But when new political roles are assigned to or assumed by corporate actors, there remain deficits of transparency, accountability, self-restraint and openness to civic deliberation and control which a citizenship model might be expected to entail.

Notes

1. We acknowledge that global migration of larger communities has been an age-old phenomenon. However, earlier migrations took place in political contexts where political communities were not organized following the post-enlightenment notions of status, entitlements and processes of participation which are central to our analysis.
2. See the relevant sections of www.shell.com.
3. ATTAC (Association for the Taxation of Financial Transactions for the Aid of Citizens) is one of the leading anti-globalization campaign organizations, see www.attac.org.
4. http://www.wsf2008.net.

8 Conclusion

The good citizen should know and have the capacity both to rule and to be ruled, and this very thing is the virtue of a citizen

Aristotle, *The Politics*, Book III

Introduction

This book has been an exploration of ways in which corporations and citizenship might come together. The purpose behind this endeavour was to cast some light on how we might conceive of the firm as a political actor in society, and how we might regard its roles and responsibilities in such a context.

At first glance, however, the results of this exercise might seem somewhat inconclusive. Our analysis suggests that there is some mileage in thinking about corporations as citizens, and also as governments, as well as arenas of citizenship – although we have also shown that there are significant limits to conceiving of corporations in such terms. Moreover, we have yet to determine whether any of these three applications is more suitable than the others, or even whether they are mutually exclusive perspectives. Similarly, while we have clearly shown that it can be helpful to explore how corporations have become involved in the reconfiguration of citizenship along identity, ecological and globalized lines, it is unclear if there is anything to be found in common across these different reconfigurations. Thus, we have an interesting and multi-faceted account of corporations and citizenship, but what in the final analysis does it all mean?

In this final chapter, we seek to dig beneath the surface of these findings and reveal some deeper-level conclusions raised by our analysis. The main thrust of these conclusions is to make sense of the fragmented picture provided by the earlier chapters and to carve out new conceptual ground in the study of corporations and citizenship. Specifically, we will do two things. First, we identify the implications of applying a citizenship perspective to the analysis of the political dimensions of the *corporation*. In so doing, we will establish that the corporation is essentially uncategorizable within the existing domain of citizenship. Rather than acting as a lens, citizenship offers a kaleidoscopic view of the corporation that helps to reveal different characteristics at different times and for different purposes. Corporations are not citizens, they are not governments and they are not arenas of citizenships – but in some respects, and under certain conditions, there is a close enough resemblance to each for us to be able to consider corporate roles and responsibilities in new and at times quite powerful ways. We suggest that ultimately this prefigures the need for a redefinition of the corporation to take account of its ambiguous political role. Later in this chapter we will provide a few initial thoughts on the kinds of directions this project might take.

Second, we go on to examine what the previous chapters tell us that is new, unique or distinctive about *citizenship* when considered in the context of the corporation. One conclusion here is simply that the domain of citizenship has yet to adequately account for the tremendous rise in prominence of the corporate actor in contemporary society. The existing concepts and theories provide a partial but incomplete and ultimately somewhat unsatisfying account of the political role of the corporation. Perhaps more importantly, though, our analysis suggests that the corporation itself is not simply a passive object within the domain of citizenship, but acts to shape and construct relations of citizenship – sometimes actively or deliberately, at times accidentally or passively. Ultimately, corporations are transformative in and of political arenas. This helps to explain why it is so difficult to place the corporation in the realm of citizenship. In attempting to do so, we also have to recognize that the introduction of corporations changes those very relations of citizenship that we are interested in.

This chapter will proceed to elaborate on these themes in more detail. The next section looks at the implications for understanding the corporation, the following one explores the implications for citizenship, and then we close with a discussion of the significance of these findings for redirections in theory, policy and practice.

Understanding the corporation

What is a corporation? The question we attempted to answer in the first part of the book was whether, from the perspective of citizenship, the corporation is a citizen, a governor, an arena of citizenship, or perhaps none at all. The answer, it seems, is all of these – but none of them entirely. Concepts of citizenship have not been developed with corporations in mind, and so there is, it appears, no easy way to locate a role for them among the traditional actor spaces of citizenship and governance. However, when we apply any of these three metaphors they do help us to perceive certain characteristics of the corporation with more clarity, and they approximate a close enough fit to enable us to develop some fairly substantial proposals for assigning particular rights and responsibilities to corporations – as we have attempted in Chapters 2 and 3 in particular – providing we do so within the context of specific relationships with other actors.

The potential of the three citizenship relations

The idea that corporations can approximate to all three of the metaphors used to examine citizenship relations in Part A is perhaps not so surprising when one considers that the landscape of citizenship itself is characterized by an interpenetration of roles among actors. The very idea of citizenship is predicated on a notion of citizens and governors both being involved in governing and being governed, as expressed by Aristotle in the opening quote of this chapter. There is no strict demarcation of roles: governments are governed by the electorate to act on their behalf, while citizens participate in governing through various forms of political participation, such as constituting political organizations, expressing preferences, engaging in debate and running for office. Corporations, we suggest, can similarly inhabit the actor spaces of both governors and citizens – and in fact by focusing on corporate actors, we can see even more clearly how these actor spaces may interpenetrate. Indeed, it would appear that the rise in political significance of the corporation may even be a contributing factor in the advanced interpenetration of these roles. Once we admit corporations to the realm of citizenship, they serve to further blur the boundaries between what it means to be a citizen or a governor.

If we look also to our third metaphor – corporations as arenas of citizenship – it is again not so surprising that this identity can fit simultaneously with our other two if we examine the nature of conventional citizenship actors a little more closely. Many such actors when constituted into organizational forms such as local governments, political parties, pressure groups and the like, not only represent mediating institutions for citizens and governors, but also replicate certain aspects of the organizational form of a political arena. Civil society groups, for instance, play a part in enabling citizens to participate in governing, and also can be subjected to a similar kind of analysis that we applied to the corporation in Chapter 4. Their various constituencies – clients, employees, funders, etc. – can be conceived of as citizens, with the organization's board of governors representing a form of 'government'. Once more, this should be expected. Political institutions such as these are to some extent modeled on the ideal of the citizen state in order to engender appropriate status, entitlements, participation and ultimately democracy for their constituents.

Reconfigurations of citizenship and the corporation

In terms of the reconfigurations of citizenship that we explored in the second part of the book, our discussion in Chapters 5 to 7 has added further perspectives on the corporation. Clearly, the kaleidoscopic picture of corporations that we have developed from a citizenship perspective is in large part a result of the kaleidoscopic nature of the concept of citizenship itself in contemporary debates. It is particularly significant that the reconfigurations of citizenship we discuss are less oriented along legal and political lines, present a less sharply defined and hierarchical arrangement of actors, and the rules of application are much more open than in classic liberal or republican notions of citizenship. It is therefore little surprise that corporations arguably fit more smoothly into these new ways of conceptualizing the political nature of communities than in the traditional models emphasized in Part A. In fact, we have seen that corporations can play key roles in citizenship reconfigurations. Pivotal aspects of gender, sexuality, ethnicity or class-based citizenship are either enacted or can at times be suppressed by corporations. Corporations, rather than governments, are seen as the central object of civic concern in many communities affected by ecological challenges, such as climate change or genetic engineering. Or, in the cosmopolitan context, corporations have not only been among the most important accelerators of globalization but have subsequently become regular participants in the multi-actor and multi-level setup of global governance.

The purpose, then, of this discussion in the second part of the book is not to distill a specific metaphorical meaning, for instance, of what a 'corporate citizen' could possibly be from a certain perspective. Rather these perspectives allowed us to identify links and connections between otherwise distinct social and political phenomena. This is mirrored by the fact that identity, ecology or globalization as constituting principles of a new political architecture are not mutually exclusive perspectives; in fact in a number of respects they are even intertwined and actually borrow from each other. In many ways, then, these contemporary reconfigurations of citizenship suggest a potentially wider set of political roles for corporations than those discussed in the first part of the book, albeit with less clear cut responsibilities.

Towards new responsibilities?

Given the preceding discussion, it is clearly important to acknowledge that our ambivalent findings regarding the corporation are not so surprising given what we already know about citizenship. However, this does not detract from the fact that corporations do not fit easily within a single pre-defined political role – and more importantly, that this makes it extremely challenging to assign definitive rights and responsibilities to them. Since the corporation is knowable yet uncategorizable as a political actor or institution, corporate responsibilities are inherently contestable. If we look at the corporation one way, we might suggest one set of responsibilities, whereas if we look at it another way, we may suggest another set entirely. Each of these sets is legitimate within a specific debate about specific relationships with other actors, but they are not transferable to all.

As a result of the lack of congruence between these different perspectives, a lot of decisions may simply fall back on corporate discretion. For example, in the context of a decline in government capacity or the appearance of a government vacuum, there are few accountability or directional mechanisms to assist a company in knowing whether to fill the gap or remain aloof. There are few ways in which corporations' stakeholders can signal in a representative or authoritative fashion whether they consider that the corporations have an obligation to fill the governance gap and within what accountability parameters this should be enacted. Corporate roles in identity politics can be de-problematized with recourse to the argument that such practices are simply labour or product market choices, while social and ecological responsibilities to the community, whether localized or delocalized, are underpinned by few formal mechanisms of citizen representation.

This is not to say that greater consensus about corporate responsibilities in the political context cannot be generated in time, or even legally codified. But, this would require firmer agreement than we have at present about the political role and status of the corporation among those seeking to define its responsibilities. In this book, we have set out some of the considerations and parameters within with such a debate (or debates) might take place. For example, for those seeking to assign duties and entitlements to 'corporate citizens' we have set out the main issues at stake, such as how to ensure that corporations exercise restraint when participating in political processes. For those seeking to assign responsibilities to powerful quasi-governmental corporations, we have shown that while corporations have significant roles to play in the delivery of entitlements, their ability to guarantee, enforce and enable democratic participation of citizens is currently rather limited. In the purview of corporations as arenas of citizenship, we have shown the importance of addressing the differences in status, entitlements and participation that are evident across and within different stakeholder constituencies. In identity politics, we have shown the types of roles that corporations play in such spaces. For those seeking ecological protection, we have articulated specific ways that corporations might be implicated within different modes of reform. For those focusing on the global level of analysis, we have set out some key mechanisms and conditions under which corporations can participate legitimately in global governance.

So what at this stage can we say a responsible corporation should be, or do, from a citizenship perspective? This is ambiguous but at a minimum requires the acknowledging and managing of its political role – or at least of the relevance of politically derived concepts such as rights, governance and democracy to corporate responsibilities. Ultimately, we would suggest, the corporation is, at least in some respects, a *governing organization* – that is, it participates in some forms of governance as a 'citizen'; it actively governs in some respects as a 'government'; and it organizes governance for stakeholders as an 'arena of citizenship'. Similarly, the corporation participates in the governance processes by which citizenship identities are enabled or inhibited; it is involved in governing the degree to which spatially or temporally defined communities of people around the globe can enjoy a healthy ecological environment; and directly participates in the governance of global political issues and basic human rights.

What we conclude, then, is that corporations and citizenship are inextricably intertwined. As we have tried to demonstrate throughout this book, corporations have a plethora of links with societies which are political in nature. The notion of citizenship, first, serves as a good descriptive framework to identify and characterize these links. Second, beyond this descriptive level, our analysis also provides an instrumental framework. In particular in the second half of the book, we have highlighted that in order to enact relevant aspects of what constitute contemporary political communities, corporations cannot be left out of the picture. Indeed, they are sometimes even pivotal in governing status, entitlements and processes of political participation in these political communities. Finally, our analysis has also exposed the normative dimensions of corporations being involved in the governing of citizenship. To govern, or participate in governing, normally involves some well-defined responsibilities within a polity. Identifying the political nature of the corporation through the citizenship lens has led us at numerous places throughout the book to raise crucial questions about corresponding duties and responsibilities of corporations as political actors. Citizenship in this multi-faceted view offers a variety of normative questions regarding the ability, desirability or even feasibility of corporations becoming political actors in contemporary society.

Dangers and limitations

It is at this juncture that we should reiterate some of the dangers and limitations of attempting to elaborate on corporate roles and responsibilities through the lens of citizenship. Critics range from, as it were, 'the right', who argue that corporations simply have a different purpose and role in society, to those on 'the left', who – while acknowledging the rising political influence of corporations – see this as nothing more than a threat to established notions of democracy and citizen's rights. Martin Wolf, chief economics commentator of the *Financial Times*, has put the first perspective neatly when he argued:

> The future of corporate accountability involves making managers accountable to owners, defining corporate morality, relating global governance to national sovereignty, dealing with fragile states and discouraging bad behaviour, such as corruption and arms dealing. But corporations are not political

institutions, accountable in the same way as governments – that would be to destroy their utility as engines of prosperity.[1]

This line of reasoning is predicated on the assumption that corporations are set up for economic purposes and that any political role will just impede their ability to produce goods and services in a profitable manner (see also Steinmann 2007: 23). Critics on the other side of the spectrum tend rather to point to the dangers of corporate political influence in society and argue that thinking about them in political terms amounts to legitimizing and justifying their 'corrupting' influence on existing democratic processes and institutions, thus leading to what, for instance, Tom Clarke refers to as 'the corporate state' (Clarke 1996). While we are sympathetic with both types of anxieties – indeed we have attempted to review and evaluate some of those throughout the book – we would still argue that these critics miss one fundamental point: that corporations simply *are* involved in the domain of citizenship in the various ways we have set out. Not talking about it, or not analyzing it, will not make it go away.

Admittedly, the academic debate on corporations as political actors is still young, certainly in the management discipline, which predominantly deals with corporations as objects of academic research. But there is palpable unrest in this literature about the framing or, as it were, the exposure of corporations as political actors (Hanlon 2008). Conceptualizing corporations through a citizenship lens has been brandished as 'an idea whose time has not yet come' (van Oosterhout 2005) or, even juicier, as something that 'amounts to little more than neo-liberal propaganda' (Jones and Haigh 2007). The reason for this reluctance to embrace corporations within the terminology of citizenship, and to conceptualize their current role in political terms, is that for some scholars this is tantamount to legitimizing their role in politics rather than simply analyzing it. Taking the notion of citizenship seriously, however, helps to analyze political roles that corporations already play, whether we agree with those activities or not, or even if we find this problematic or otherwise. Notably, avoidance of such analysis is by no means unique to the management literature; in fact, by and large, most of the literature on citizenship has so far more or less ignored the conspicuous role of corporations in shaping, enacting and transforming the concept. We will discuss this in more detail in the following section.

Understanding citizenship

The preceding chapters illustrate well both the richness and the complexity of the citizenship concept. In Part A, we drew on traditional notions of citizenship derived from liberal and republican schools of thought, and then in Part B, we explored key contemporary reconfigurations of citizenship based on identity, ecology and cosmopolitanism. This demonstrates quite clearly that citizenship is not a simple or uncontested idea that can be neatly summed up and then exported for analysis of the corporation. There is not, we would suggest, a robust concept of citizenship 'out there' that we can apply to our rather more stable concept of the corporation. Rather, we have shown that ideas about citizenship proliferate in different ideological and theoretical niches, and continue to inform an evolving and multi-faceted picture of what citizenship is and should be in contemporary society.

Despite the emergence of this variegated conception of citizenship, it is evident that the literature of citizenship has developed with little specific attention to the corporation. In many respects, corporations are something of a blind spot in a discourse that is still primarily oriented around individual citizens, governments and civil society. This, our analysis would suggest, is something of an oversight given the wide swathe of roles that corporations can inhabit in the realms of citizenship. Corporations can participate in societal governance, and they can provide citizenship entitlements. Corporations can also reflect, enable and inhibit the expression of citizenship identities, as well as export or erode existing notions of citizenship. Citizenship theory, however, has yet to identify and account for these roles. Moreover, while citizenship theorists have made in-roads towards understanding the role of the market in contemporary accounts of citizenship (e.g. Crouch 2003; Schneiderman 2004), there has been precious little attention to date on the rise in power and prominence of the corporation itself as an actor (as one of the few exceptions see Palacios 2004). And if corporations are allowed to enter the picture, the gist of the argument seems to be that they are a threat to existing notions of citizenship and their influence is conceptualized as incompatible with a rich enactment of status, rights and responsibilities of civic actors (e.g. Ikeda 2004).

Perhaps, then, the most significant conclusion that can be drawn from our analysis is that, contrary to existing assumptions, corporations and citizenship are not ontologically autonomous concepts – that individual citizenship is in many respects intertwined with the values, actions and impacts of corporations. We have shown that corporations have always been, and probably will always be, involved in the emergence, development and transmission of political ideas of individual citizenship and its governance across time and space.

In the previous section, for example, we discussed the role that corporations have played in blurring our ideas of what it is to be a citizen or a governor. Moreover, in Chapter 6 we showed how corporations such as the British East India Company were intrinsically involved in the exporting of the apparatus of liberal citizenship into India, just as, more recently, aboriginal concepts of citizenship, identity and place have been transformed by the property claims of corporations on traditional knowledge and land rights. In Chapters 5 and 7 we showed how the reconfiguration of citizenship in recent times away from traditional concepts of liberal and republican citizenship towards more identity, cultural and cosmopolitan concepts have been enabled, reinforced or inhibited by corporate activities of one sort or another. This ranged from the battles for political equality among women and racial minorities in the context of corporate hiring and promotion policies, to the reinforcement of gay and lesbian political identity through product marketing in the 'pink economy', to the enabling of global citizen communities through advanced information and communication technology services. Even in the arena of national citizenship, corporations have been shown to have played a role in the granting of 'de facto citizenship' status to illegal immigrants and other non-citizens by taking advantage of the poor enforcement of employment regulations.

Admitting corporations into the citizenship arena

The question here is not whether corporations have deliberately engaged in the construction and transformation of citizenship, or whether corporate managers have even been aware of such phenomena. These considerations are largely irrelevant to the more fundamental question of whether corporations (individually or collectively) have played a significant role in how we think about and valorize particular notions of citizenship. According to our analysis, they have. In this sense, corporations are transformative in and of political arenas. This goes beyond the relatively narrow remit of 'corporate political activity' where firms strategically seek to create a positive political environment for the advancement of organizational objectives (Getz 1997; Lord 2000; Wilts and Skippari 2007), to encapsulate deeper-level institutional effects around the meaning and enablement of particular forms of citizenship.

It is quite striking to see how many of the general issues discussed in this book are recognized and discussed by scholars in the citizenship field, yet the specific institution of the corporation has so far been afforded only scant attention. For example, in a recent assessment of the citizenship field, Isin and Turner (2007: 10) comment:

> The defining economic principles of Keynesian citizenship – high personal taxation, adequate pensions for retirement and a welfare safety net – are being eroded. The institutional framework of a common experience of membership of a political community – taxation, military service, a common framework of national education, and a vibrant civil society – is declining, and this development is the real basis of the erosion of social citizenship in modern democratic states. This decline is in fact the privatization of public identities following the privatization of public utilities.

It is significant to see that in all of these developments that Isin and Turner identify as having 'eroded' extant post-war notions of citizenship, corporations have played a pivotal role. They are a major basis for taxation (directly, and indirectly through providing the basis for income taxes), they have become providers of military services as erstwhile public institutions have become privatized (Singer 2003), in many jurisdictions their contribution to education is on the rise (Moon and Sochacki 1998; Riley *et al.* 1994) and private corporations now run many former public services. Clearly, corporations – for better or for worse – have 'invaded' the territory for citizenship, yet as actors they have received next to no attention in the academic debate on citizenship. The literature seems to have still a strong inclination to maintain a neat bipolar world of individuals as the 'subject of citizenship' (Yeatman 2007) on the one hand and governmental actors on the other, with maybe some growing attention to the rise of surrogate citizens such as non-governmental organizations (NGOs) (e.g. Linklater 2002: 326–9). The role of corporations, however, has largely been relegated to a broader, macro-analysis of transformations in consumer and labour markets and their role in new governance arrangements. This book is an attempt to redress some of this imbalance and sketch out basic features of the corporate involvement in the citizenship arena. However kaleidoscopic our picture might be, one key conclusion of our analysis is that the political nature of the corporation in participating in and governing citizenship can hardly be ignored any longer.

Where do we go from here? Towards a new research agenda for corporations and citizenship

It should be clear from our discussion so far that our conclusions are not meant to represent a point of closure in the debate about corporations and citizenship, but rather an opening up. Our insights do not in any way suggest that we have reached a point where we can fully elucidate new theories of the corporation or of citizenship, or that we can map out a clear new set of corporate responsibilities. Our contribution really has been to invigorate thinking about the political role and identity of the corporation, and to provide the necessary platform for informed scholarly analysis of corporations and citizenship across disciplinary divisions. As such, we will take this opportunity to outline five main avenues where our analysis has provided some important groundwork for future research to prosper.

First, our identification of an ambiguous political role for the corporation in society suggests that we need to rethink its existing status in political, legal and economic theory. At present, our view of the corporation tends to be predicated purely on its economic role as a value creator in society, which in turn has given rise to a legal status analogous to an artificial citizen. These are clearly outdated and unfit for purpose in the context of the political roles of the corporation that we have identified in this book. Corporations have effects that go beyond the economic (and indeed beyond even the social), and they occupy political roles that do not always bear much relation to their legal identity. Therefore, one important stream of further research will be to investigate ways in which we might redefine the corporation using insights from citizenship thinking. There is already a wide array of work addressing new conceptions of the corporation in management, law or philosophy, from the stakeholder model (Freeman 1984), to new approaches to corporate governance (Blair 1995) and social contracts theory (Donaldson and Dunfee 1999), just to mention a few. Based on our analysis, there is a substantial contribution, though, that could be made in exploring the potential for linking better the legal identity of the corporation with its political role. For those seeking to 'civilize' the corporation (Zadek 2007) and make it more 'citizen-like', there is a substantial task ahead in theorizing and conceptualizing the corporation as a political actor. While there is promising work currently emerging on various aspects of this venture (e.g. Levy and Kaplan 2008; Norman and Néron 2008; Scherer and Palazzo 2007), a serious debate on these issues – certainly in the management literature – is still in its infancy.

Second, our analysis in this book suggests that this rethinking of the corporate role in society will ask for a restating of corporate responsibilities. This will require several things, including the identification of a community of obligation, the identification of appropriate entitlements and the assessment of reasonable processes of participation by the corporation and by others in and around the corporation. Given the multiplicity of roles for corporations in the citizenship arena, however, our expectation is not so much to come up with one 'new' model of the corporation which would then allow us to state its concomitant responsibilities. Rather, we would expect research to look at temporally and spatially contingent models of corporate roles in specific contexts that would reflect the multifaceted and fragmented picture of contemporary citizenship.

Third, admitting corporations into the purview of citizenship does not only result in a re-conceptualization of the corporation and its responsibilities; this is after all a reflection of broader shifts in the roles and responsibilities of state and non-state actors, including local and international NGOs, government agencies, multilateral institutions, etc. It is therefore equally important to analyze what these shifts mean for other implicated parties and how new processes of governing citizenship need to be adapted and re-conceptualized.

Fourth, there is dire need for more interdisciplinary work on the political role of the corporation. Management, politics, law, sociology, philosophy and international relations – just to name the most obvious disciplines and fields – share an interest in facets of the phenomenon. We would suggest, though, that each discipline's 'toolbox' alone will not provide the necessary equipment to advance our understanding in this area. This book has demonstrated that the 'economic' actor that is the corporation has political significance too, with all the social, ethical and legal implications that this might bring with it. If the object of empirical investigation transcends disciplinary boundaries in this way, scholars interested in understanding these issues cannot afford to remain within the cosy confines of a single disciplinary home.

Fifth, given the conspicuous role of corporations in the citizenship arena we need more practical and on-the-ground research of how individual 'citizens' can respond to these shifts. In particular, we need more insight into practical avenues of how to 'use' corporations or exploit their political roles for positive social change. Such research will potentially reveal new ways in which political goals can be achieved by including corporations. So, for instance, there is no realistic hope of addressing global pandemics such as HIV/Aids or malaria without the active involvement of the research and development potential of pharmaceutical companies. These political spaces ask for new approaches and a new 'landscape' of participative governance between corporate, state and civil society players (LSE & Wellcome Trust 2005) in order to address this salient area of citizenship. At the same time such research would also identify the limits of the corporate role in this political context. In this book we have time and again pointed to potential anxieties with regard to corporations becoming involved in the citizenship arena, and research along these lines has to understand these limitations and map out potential avenues of addressing these. With active and engaged scholarship on the corporation's material impact on human citizenship, and how we can both harness and constrain this for the benefit of those that most need it, we have the potential to make a real contribution to our understanding of the political role of the corporation.

Note

1. http://www.ft.com/comment/columnists/martinwolf.

References

Akard, Patrick J. (1992), 'Corporate mobilization and political power: the transformation of US economic policy in the 1970s', *American Sociological Review*, 47, 597–615.

Albert, Michael (1991), *Capitalisme contre capitalisme*. Paris: LeSeuil.

Algesheimer, René, Utpal M. Dholakia and Andreas Herrmann (2005), 'The social influence of brand community: evidence from European car clubs', *Journal of Marketing*, 69 (3), 19.

Ali, Saleem H. (2000), 'Shades of green: NGO coalitions, mining companies and the pursuit of negotiating power', in *Terms for Endearment: Business, NGOs and Sustainable Development*, Jem Bendell, Ed. Sheffield: Greenleaf.

Altman, Barbara W. (1998), 'Corporate community relations in 1990s: a study in transformation (dissertation abstract)', *Business and Society*, 37 (2), 221–7.

Altman, Barbara W. and Deborah Vidaver-Cohen (2000), 'A framework for understanding corporate citizenship. Introduction to the special edition of *Business and Society Review*: "Corporate citizenship and the new millennium"', *Business and Society Review*, 105 (1), 1–7.

Andriof, Jörg and Malcolm McIntosh (2001a), 'Introduction', in *Perspectives on Corporate Citizenship*, Jörg Andriof and Malcolm McIntosh, Eds. Sheffield: Greenleaf.

Andriof, Jörg and Malcolm McIntosh, Eds. (2001b), *Perspectives on Corporate Citizenship*. Sheffield: Greenleaf.

Anon. (2005), 'TK debate puts pressure on patentees', *Managing Intellectual Property*, 1, http://www.managingip.com.

Archibugi, Daniele (2004), 'Cosmopolitan democracy and its critics: a review', *European Journal of International Relations*, 10 (3), 437–73.

Archibugi, Daniele, Ed. (2003), *Debating Cosmopolitics*. London, New York: Verso.

Ashman, Darcy (2000), *Promoting Corporate Citizenship in the Global South – Towards a Model of Empowered Civil Society Collaboration with Business*. Boston: Institute for Development Research Series of Occasional Papers, 16(2).

(2001), 'Civil society collaboration with business: bringing empowerment back in', *World Development*, 29 (7), 1097–113.

Bagozzi, Richard P. and Utpal M. Dholakia (2006a), 'Antecedents and purchase consequences of customer participation in small group brand communities', *International Journal of Research in Marketing*, 23 (1), 45.

(2006b), 'Open source software user communities: a study of participation in Linux user groups', *Management Science*, 52 (7), 1099.

Bakan, Joel (2004), *The Corporation – The Pathological Pursuit of Profit and Power*. New York: Free Press.

Baker, Gideon and David Chandler, Eds. (2005), *Global Civil Society*. London and New York: Routledge.

Baker, Jim (2004), 'Labour and the global compact: the early days', in *Learning To Talk. Corporate Citizenship and the Development of the UN Global Compact*, Malcolm McIntosh, Sandra Waddock and Georg Kell, Eds. Sheffield: Greenleaf.

Banerjee, Subhabrata Bobby (2000), 'Whose land is it anyway? National interest, indigenous stakeholders, and colonial discourses', *Organization and Environment*, 13 (1), 3–38.

(2003), 'Who sustains whose development? Sustainable development and the reinvention of nature', *Organization Studies*, 24 (1), 143–80.

Baron, David P. (2003), *Business and its Environment* (4th edition). Upper Saddle River, NJ: Prentice Hall.

Bartley, Tim (2003), 'Certifying forests and factories: states, social movements, and the rise of private regulation in the apparel and forest product field', *Politics and Society* 31 (3), 433–64.

Beck, Ulrich (1992), *Risk Society. Towards a New Modernity*. London: Sage.

(1994), 'The reinvention of politics: towards a theory of reflexive modernization', in *Reflexive Modernization*, Ulrich Beck, Anthony Giddens and Scott Lash, Eds. Stanford: Stanford University Press.

(1996), 'Risk society and the provident state', in *Risk, Environment and Modernity*, S. Lash, B. Szerszynski and B. Wynne, Eds. London: Sage.

(1997a), 'Global risk politics', in *The New Politics of the Environment*, Michael Jacobs, Ed. London: Blackwell.

(1997b), *The Reinvention of Politics*. Cambridge: Polity Press.

(1997c), 'Subpolitics, ecology and the disintegration of institutional power', *Organization and Environment*, 10 (1), 52–65.

(1998), 'Wie wird Demokratie im Zeitalter der Globalisierung möglich – Eine Einleitung', in *Politik der Globalisierung*, U. Beck, Ed. Frankfurt/Main: Suhrkamp.

(1999), *What is Globalization?* Cambridge: Polity Press.

Begg, Kathryn, Frans van der Woerd and David L. Levy Eds. (2005), *The Business of Climate Change. Corporate Responses to Kyoto*. Sheffield: Greenleaf.

Belanger, Jacques (1999), *Being Local Worldwide: ABB and the Challenge of Global Management*. Ithaca, NY: Cornell University Press.

Bendell, Jem (2000), 'Civil regulation: A new form of democratic governance for the global economy?', in *Terms for Endearment: Business, NGOs and Sustainable Development*, Jem Bendell, Ed. Sheffield: Greenleaf.

(2005), 'In whose name? The accountability of corporate social responsibility', *Development in Practice*, 15 (3/4), 362–74.

Bendell, Jem, Ed. (2000), *Terms for Endearment: Business, NGOs and Sustainable Development*. Sheffield: Greenleaf.

Benz, Matthias and Bruno S. Frey (2007), 'Corporate governance: what can we learn from public governance?', *Academy of Management Review*, 32 (1), 92–104.

Birchfield, Vicki and Annette Freyberg-Inan (2005), 'Organic intellectuals and counter-hegemonic politics in the age of globalization: the case of ATTAC', in *Critical Theories, International Relations and the Anti-globalization Movement*, Catherine Eschle and Bice Maiguashca, Eds. London: Routledge.

Black, Edwin (2001), *IBM and the Holocaust: The Strategic Alliance between Nazi Germany and America's Most Powerful Corporation*. New York: Random House.

Blair, Margaret M. (1995), *Ownership and Control: Rethinking Corporate Governance for the Twenty-first Century*. Washington, DC: Brookings.

Blair, Margaret M., Ed. (1996), *Wealth Creation and Wealth Sharing: A Colloquium on Corporate Governance and Investment in Human Capital*. Washington, DC: The Brookings Institution.

Blowfield, Michael and Jedrzej George Frynas (2005), 'Setting new agendas: critical perspectives on Corporate Social Responsibility in the developing world', *International Affairs* 81 (3), 499–513.

Boatright, John R. (2004), 'Employee governance and the ownership of the firm', *Business Ethics Quarterly*, 14 (1), 1–21.

Bock, P.G. and Vincent J. Fuccillo (1975), 'Transnational corporations as international political actors', *Studies in Comparative International Development*, 10 (2), 51–78.

Bohman, James (1996), *Public Deliberation: Pluralism, Complexity and Democracy*. Cambridge, MA: MIT Press.

Boli, John and Frank J. Lechner, Eds. (2000), *The Globalization Reader*. Malden, MA; Oxford: Blackwell Publishers.

Boli, John and George M. Thomas (1997), 'World culture in the world polity – A century of international non-governmental organizations', *American Sociological Review*, 62 (2), 171–90.

Bolino, Mark C. (1999), 'Citizenship and impression management', *Academy of Management Review*, 24 (1), 82–98.

Bolino, Mark C., James M. Bloodgood and William H. Turnley (2001), 'Organizational citizenship behaviour and the creation of social capital', *Academy of Management Review 2002 (OB)*, B1–B6.

Bondy, Krista, Dirk Matten and Jeremy Moon (2006), 'Codes of conduct as a tool for sustainable governance in multinational corporations', in *Corporate Governance and Sustainability – Challenges for Theory and Practice*, Sue Benn and Dexter Dunphy, Eds. London: Routledge.

Brammer, Stephen and Stephen Pavelin (2005), 'Corporate community contributions in the United Kingdom and the United States', *Journal of Business Ethics*, 56, 15–26.

Buckley, Christine (2007), 'Lambert warns of backlash over tax inequality', *The Times*, 11 July 2007, http://business.timesonline.co.uk.

Bulkeley, Harriet (2001), 'Governing climate change: the politics of risk society', *Transactions of the British Institute of Geographers*, 26, 430–47.

Calavita, Kitty (2005), 'Law, citizenship, and the construction of (some) immigrant "others"', *Law and Social Inquiry*, 30, 401–20.

Cannon, Tom (1994), *Corporate Responsibility*. London: Pearson.

Carroll, Archie B. (1991), 'The pyramid of corporate social responsibility: toward the moral management of organizational stakeholders', *Business Horizons*, 34 (4), 39–48.

(1998), 'The four faces of corporate citizenship', *Business and Society Review*, 100 (1), 1–7.

Cashore, Ben (2002), 'Legitimacy and the privatization of environmental governance: how non-state market-driven (NSMD) governance systems gain rule-making authority', *Governance*, 15 (4), 503–29.

Castells, Manuel (1989), *The Informational City: Information Technology, Economic Restructuring, and the Urban-regional Process*. Oxford, UK; Cambridge, MA, US: B. Blackwell.

(1998), *End of Millennium*. Malden, MA: Blackwell Publishers.

(2000), *The Rise of the Network Society* (2nd edition). Malden, MA: Blackwell Publishers.

Castles, Stephen and Alastair Davidson (2000), *Citizenship and Migration*. London: Routledge.

Chang, Tracy F.H. and Douglas E. Thompkins (2002), 'Corporations go to prisons: the expansion of corporate power in the correctional industry', *Labor Studies Journal*, 27 (1), 45–69.

Clarke, Tom (1996), 'Mechanisms of corporate rule', in *The Case Against the Global Economy*, J. Mander and E. Goldsmith, Eds. San Francisco: Sierra Club Books.

Coase, Ronald H. (1937), 'The nature of the firm', *Economica*, 386–405.

Coen, David (1999), 'The impact of US lobbying practice on the European business–government relationship', *California Management Review*, 41 (4), 27–44.

Coen, David and Wyn Grant (2001), 'Corporate political strategy and global policy: a case study of the Transatlantic Business Dialogue', *European Business Journal*, 13 (1), 37–44.

Cohen, Joshua (1997), 'Deliberation and democratic legitimacy', in *Deliberative Democracy: Essays on Reason and Politics*, James Bohman and William Rehg, Eds. Cambridge, MA: MIT Press.

Coleman, James S. (1990), *Foundations of Social Theory*. Cambridge, MA: Harvard University Press.

Coleman, William D. (1988), *Business and Politics: A Study of Collective Action*. Montreal: McGill-Queens University Press.

Collins, Andrea and Andrew Flynn (2005), 'A new perspective on the environmental impacts of planning: a case study of Cardiff's International Sports Village', *Journal of Environmental Policy and Planning* 7 (4), 277–302.

Collins, Denis (1995), 'A socio-political theory of workplace democracy: class conflict, constituent reactions and organizational outcomes at a gain-sharing facility', *Organization Science*, 6 (6), 628–44.

(1997), 'The ethical superiority and inevitability of participatory management as an organizational system', *Organization Science*, 8 (5), 489–507.

Cope, Stephen, Frank Leishman and Peter Starie (1997), 'Globalization, new public management and the enabling state. Futures of police management', *International Journal of Public Sector Management*, 10 (6), 444–60.

Cottier, Thomas and Marion Panizzon (2004), 'Legal perspectives on traditional knowledge: the case for intellectual property protection', *Journal of International Economic Law*, 7 (2), 371.

Courpasson, David and Françoise Dany (2003), 'Indifference or obedience? Business firms as democratic hybrids', *Organization Studies*, 24 (8): 1231–60.

Cova, Bernard (1997), 'Community and consumption: towards a definition of the linking value of product and services', *European Journal of Marketing*, 31, 297–316.

Cova, Bernard and Stefano Pace (2006), 'Brand community of convenience products: new forms of customer empowerment – the case "My Nutella The Community"', *European Journal of Marketing*, 40 (9/10), 1087.

Coyle, D., Ed. (2005), *The Impact of Mobile Phones, Moving the Debate Forward*. Newbury: The Vodafone Policy Paper Series, No. 3.

Crane, Andrew and Dirk Matten (2007), *Business Ethics. Managing Corporate Citizenship and Sustainability in the Age of Globalization* (2nd edition). Oxford: Oxford University Press.

Crouch, Colin (2003), *Commercialization or Citizenship. Education Policy and the Future of Public Services*. Fabian Society: London.

Cumming, Jane Fiona (2001), 'Engaging stakeholders in corporate accountability programmes: a cross-sectoral analysis of UK and transnational experience', *Business Ethics: A European Review*, 10 (1), 45–52.

Curtin, Deane (1999), *Chinnagounder's Challenge: The Question of Ecological Citizenship*. Bloomington: Indiana University Press.

Dahan, Nicolas (2005), 'A contribution to the conceptualization of political resources utilized in corporate political action', *Journal of Public Affairs*, 5, 43–54.

Dahan, Nicolas, Jonathan P. Doh and T. Guay (2006), 'The role of multinational corporations in transitional institutional building: a policy network perspective', *Human Relations*, 59 (11), 1571–600.

Dahl, Robert (1956), *A Preface to Democratic Theory*. New Haven: Yale University Press.

(1961), *Who Governs? Democracy and Power in an American City*. New Haven: Yale University Press.

(1972), 'A prelude to corporate reform', *Business and Society Review*, 1: 17–23.

(1985), *A Preface to Economic Democracy*. Berkeley: University of California Press.

(1989), *Democracy and its Critics*. New Haven: Yale University Press.

Davenport, Kim (2000), 'Corporate citizenship: a stakeholder approach for defining corporate social performance and identifying measures for assessing it', *Business and Society*, 39: 210–19.

David, Rhys (2000), *Business in the Community: BITC Awards Year 2000 (Financial Times Guide)*. London: Financial Times.

Davies, Iain A. and Andrew Crane (2003), 'Ethical decision-making in fair trade companies', *Journal of Business Ethics*, 45 (1–2), 79–92.

Dawkins, Cedric E. (2002), 'Corporate welfare, corporate citizenship and the question of accountability', *Business and Society*, 41 (3), 269–91.

Deakin, Nicholas and Kieron Walsh (1996), 'The enabling state: the role of markets and contracts', *Public Administration*, 74 (Spring), 33–48.

Dean, Hartley (2001), 'Green citizenship', *Social Policy and Administration*, 35 (5), 490–505.

Delanty, Gerard (2000), *Citizenship in a Global Age: Society, Culture, Politics*. Buckingham: Open University Press.

(2007), 'Theorising citizenship in a global age', in *Globalization and Citizenship*, Wayne Hudson and Steven Slaughter, Eds. London, New York: Routledge.

Diageo (2005), 'Knowing what's important', *3rd Diageo Corporate Citizenship Report*, http://www.diageo.com/report/index.asp.

Dickinson, Roger A. and Mary L. Carsky (2005), 'The consumer as economic voter', in *The Ethical Consumer*, Rob Harrison, Terry Newholm and Deirdre Shaw, Eds. London: Sage.

DiMaggio, P.J. and W.W. Powell (1983), 'The iron cage revisited: institutional isomorphism and collective rationality in organizational fields', *American Sociological Review*, 48, 147–60.

Dixon, Donald F. (1992), 'Consumer sovereignty, democracy, and the marketing concept: a macromarketing perspective', *Canadian Journal of Administrative Sciences*, 9 (2), 116–25.

Dobson, Andrew (2003), *Citizenship and the Environment*. Oxford: Oxford University Press.

Doh, Jonathan P. and Hildy Teegen (2002), 'Nongovernmental organizations as institutional actors in international business: theory and implications', *International Business Review*, 11, 665–84.

Donaldson, Thomas (1989), *The Ethics of International Business*. New York/ Oxford: Oxford University Press.

Donaldson, Thomas and Lee E. Preston (1995), 'The stakeholder theory of the corporation: concepts, evidence, and implications', *Academy of Management Review*, 20 (1), 65–91.

Donaldson, Thomas and Thomas W. Dunfee (1999), *Ties that Bind: A Social Contracts Approach to Business Ethics*. Cambridge, MA: Harvard Business School Press.

Dore, Ronald P. (2000), *Stock Market Capitalism: Welfare Capitalism – Japan and Germany versus the Anglo Saxons*. Oxford: Oxford University Press.

Driscoll, Cathy and Mark Starik (2004), 'The primordial stakeholder: Advancing the conceptual consideration of stakeholder status for natural environment', *Journal of Business Ethics*, 49 (1), 55–73.

Dryzek, John (1990), *Discursive Democracy*. Cambridge: Cambridge University Press.

Dunfee, Thomas W. (2006), 'Do firms with unique competencies for rescuing victims of human catastrophes have special obligations? Corporate responsibility and the AIDS catastrophe in Sub-Saharan Africa', *Business Ethics Quarterly*, 15 (4), 185–210.

Dunn, Debra and Keith Yamashita (2003), 'Microcapitalism and the Megacorporation', *Harvard Business Review*, 81 (8), 46–54.

Durán, José Luis and Fernando Sánchez (1999), 'The relationships between the companies and their suppliers', *Journal of Business Ethics*, 22 (3), 273–80.

Earles, Wendy and Jeremy Moon (2000), 'Pathways to the enabling state: changing modes of social provision in Western Australian community services', *Australian Journal of Public Administration* 59, 11–25.

Elliott, Anthony (2001), 'The reinvention of citizenship', in *Culture and Citizenship*, Nick Stevenson, Ed. London: Sage.

Engelen, Ewald (2002), 'Corporate governance, property and democracy: a conceptual critique of shareholder ideology', *Economy and Society*, 31 (3), 391–413.

Epstein, Edwin E. (1973), 'Dimensions of corporate power, Part 1', *California Management Review*, 16 (2), 9–23.

(1974), 'Dimensions of corporate power, Part 2', *California Management Review*, 16 (4), 32–47.

Eschle, Catherine (2005), 'Constructing "the anti-globalization movement"', in *Critical Theories, International Relations and 'the Anti-globalization Movement'*, Catherine Eschle and Bice Maiguashca, Eds. London: Routledge.

Eschle, Catherine and Bice Maiguashca, Eds. (2005), *Critical Theories, International Relations and 'the Anti-globalization Movement'*. London: Routledge.

ExxonMobil (2003), *Corporate Citizenship Report*. Irving, TX: ExxonMobil, http://exxonmobil.com.

Falk, Richard (1994), 'The making of global citizenship', in *The Condition of Citizenship*, Bart van Steenbergen, Ed. London: Sage.

(2000), 'The decline of citizenship in an era of globalization', *Citizenship Studies*, 4 (1), 5–17.

Ferner, Anthony and Richard Hyman (1998), *Changing Industrial Relations in Europe*. Oxford: Blackwell Publishing.

Fiorino, D.J. (1995), 'Regulatory negotiation as a form of public participation', in *Fairness and Competence in Citizen Participation*, Ortwin Renn, Thomas Webler and Peter M. Wiedemann, Eds. Dordrecht: Kluwer.

Fishkin, James S. (1991), *Democracy and Deliberation: New Directions for Democratic Reform*. New Haven: Yale University Press.

Fitchett, James A. (2005), 'Consumers as stakeholders: prospects for democracy in marketing theory', *Business Ethics – A European Review*, 14 (1).

Fort, Timothy L. (1996), 'Business as mediating institution', *Business Ethics Quarterly*, 6, 149–63.

(1997), 'The corporation as a mediating institution: an efficacious synthesis of stakeholder theory and corporate constituency statutes', *Notre Dame Law Review*, 73, 173–203.

Fort, Timothy L. and James J. Noone (1999), 'Banded contracts, mediating institutions, and corporate governance: a naturalist analysis of contractual theories of the firm', *Law and Contemporary Problems*, 62, 163–213.

Fowler, Penny and Simon Heap (2000), 'Bridging troubled waters: the Marine Stewardship Council', in *Terms for Endearment: Business,*

NGOs and Sustainable Development, Jem Bendell, Ed. Sheffield: Greenleaf.

Frankental, Peter (2002), 'The UN Universal Declaration of Human Rights as a corporate code of conduct', *Business Ethics: A European Review*, 11 (2), 129–33.

Freeman, R. Edward (1984), *Strategic Management. A Stakeholder Approach*. Boston: Pitman.

(1997), 'A stakeholder theory of the modern corporation', in *Ethical Theory and Business*, Tom L. Beauchamp and Norman E. Bowie, Eds. (5th edition). Upper Saddle River, NJ: Prentice Hall.

French, Peter (1979), 'The corporation as a moral person', *American Philosophical Quarterly*, 16.

Frenkel, Stephen J., and Duncan Scott (2002), 'Compliance, collaboration and codes of practice', *California Management Review*, 45 (1), 29–49.

Friedman, Milton (1970), 'The social responsibility of business is to increase its profits', *The New York Times Magazine*, 13 September 1970, 32–3, 124–6.

Frynas, Jedrzej George and Scott Pegg, Eds. (2003), *Transnational Corporations and Human Rights*. Basingstoke: Palgrave.

Fung, Archon (2003a), 'Associations and democracy: between theories, hopes, and realities', *Annual Review of Sociology*, 29, 515–39.

(2003b), 'Deliberative democracy and international labour standards', *Governance*, 16 (1), 51–71.

Fung, Archon and E. O. Wright (2001), 'Deepening democracy: innovations in empowered participatory governance', *Politics and Society*, 29 (1), 5–41.

Gabriel, Yiannis and Tim Lang (1995), *The Unmanageable Consumer: Contemporary Consumption and its Fragmentations*. London: Sage.

(2005), 'A brief history of consumer activism', in *The Ethical Consumer*, Rob Harrison, Terry Newholm and Deirdre Shaw, Eds. London: Sage.

Galbraith, John Kenneth (1974), *The New Industrial State* (2nd edition). Harmondsworth: Penguin.

Geppert, Mike, Dirk Matten and Peter Walgenbach (2006), 'Transnational institution building and the multinational corporation: an emerging field of research', *Human Relations*, 59 (11), 1451–65.

Gerencser, Steven (2005), 'The corporate person and democratic politics', *Political Research Quarterly*, 58 (4), 625–35.

Getz, Kathleen A. (1997), 'Research in corporate political action: integration and assessment', *Business and Society*, 36 (1), 32–72.

Ghosh, Shubha (2003), 'The traditional terms of the traditional knowledge debate', *Northwestern Journal of International Law and Business*, 23 (3), 589.

Giddens, Anthony (1990), *The Consequences of Modernity*. Stanford: Stanford University Press.

(1999), *Runaway World: How Globalization is Reshaping our Lives*. London: Profile.

Gilbert, Neil and Barbara Gilbert (1989), *The Enabling State: Modern Welfare Capitalism in America*. Oxford: Oxford University Press.

Goldblatt, David (1997), 'Liberal democracy and the globalization of environmental risks', in *The Transformation of Democracy? Globalization and Territorial Democracy*, Anthony G. McGrew, Ed. Cambridge: Polity Press.

Gossett, William T. (1957), *Corporate Citizenship*. Lexington, VA: Washington and Lee University.

Grahl, John and Paul Teague (1997), 'Is the European social model fragmenting?', *New Political Economy*, 2 (3), 405–26.

Gramlich, Jeffrey D. and James E. Wheeler (2003), 'How Chevron, Texaco, and the Indonesian government structured transactions to avoid billions in US income taxes', *Accounting Horizons*, 17 (3), 107–22.

Grant, Wyn (1984), 'Large firms and public policy in Britain', *Journal of Public Policy* 4 (1), 1–17.

(1987), *Business and Politics in Britain*. Houndmills: Macmillan.

Gray, Rob, Colin Dey, Dave Owen, Richard Evans and Simon Zadek (1997), 'Struggling with the praxis of social accounting: stakeholders, accountability, audits and procedures', *Accounting, Auditing and Accountability Journal*, 10 (3), 325–64.

Green-Pedersen, Christoffer (2002), 'New public management reforms in the Dutch and Swedish welfare states: the role of different social democratic responses', *Governance: an International Journal of Policy, Administration, and Institutions*, 15 (2), 271–94.

Grimsey, Darrin and Mervyn K. Lewis (2002), 'Accounting for public private partnerships', *Accounting Forum*, 26 (3), 245–70.

Grimshaw, Damian, Steve Vincent and Hugh Willmott (2002), 'Going privately: partnership and outsourcing in UK public services', *Public Administration*, 80 (3), 475–502.

Guler, Isin, Mauro Guillén and John Muir MacPherson (2002), 'Global competition, institutions and the diffusion of organizational practices: the international spread of the ISO 9000 quality certificates', *Administrative Science Quarterly*, 47, 207–32.

Habermas, Jürgen (1983), 'Diskursethik – Notizen zu einem Begründungsprogramm', in *Moralbewusstsein und Kommunikatives Handeln*, Jürgen Habermas, Ed. Frankfurt/Main: Suhrkamp.

(1989), *The Structural Transformation of the Public Sphere: an Inquiry into a Category of Bourgeois Society*. Cambridge, MA: MIT Press.

(1994), 'Citizenship and national identity', in *The Condition of Citizenship*, Bart van Steenbergen, Ed. London: Sage.

(1995), 'Citizenship and national identity: some reflections on the future of Europe', in *Theorizing Citizenship*, Ronald Beiner, Ed. Albany: State University of New York Press.

(1998), *Die Postnationale Konstellation*. Frankfurt/Main: Suhrkamp.

Hacker, Jacob S., and Paul Pierson (2002), 'Business power and social policy: employers and the formation of the American welfare state', *Politics and Society*, 30 (2), 277–325.

Hanagan, Michael and Charles Tilly, Eds. (1999), *Extending Citizenship, Reconfiguring States*. Oxford: Rowman and Littlefield.

Handelman, Jay M. (2006), 'Corporate identity and the societal constituent', *Journal of the Academy of Marketing Science*, 34 (2), 107–114.

Hanlon, Gerard (2008), 'Re-thinking corporate social responsibility and the role of the firm – on the denial of politics', in *The Oxford Handbook of CSR*, Andrew Crane, Dirk Matten, Abagail McWilliams, Jeremy Moon and Donald Siegel, Eds. Oxford: Oxford University Press.

Harding, Alan, Stuart Wilks-Heeg and Mary Hutchins (2000), 'Business, government and business of urban governance', *Urban Studies*, 37 (5–6), 975–94.

Harrabin, Roger (2005), 'Industry chiefs' environment plea', BBC News, 27 May 2005, http://www.bbc.co.uk.

Harrison, Jeffrey S. and R. Edward Freeman (2004), 'Is organizational democracy worth the effort?', *Academy of Management Executive*, 18 (3), 49–53.

Harrison, Rob (2005), 'Pressure groups, campaigns, and consumers', in *The Ethical Consumer*, Rob Harrison, Terry Newholm and Deirdre Shaw, Eds. London: Sage.

Harrison, Rob, Terry Newholm and Deirdre Shaw, Eds. (2005), *The Ethical Consumer*. London: Sage.

Hart, Stuart L. (1997), 'Beyond greening: strategies for a sustainable world', *Harvard Business Review*, Jan–Feb, 67–76.

(2005), *Capitalism at the Crossroads: the Unlimited Business Opportunities in Solving the World's Most Difficult Problems*. Upper Saddle River, NJ: Wharton School.

Hellman, Joel S. and Mark Schankerman (2000), 'Intervention, corruption and capture', *Economics of Transition*, 8 (3), 545–76.

Hellman, Joel S., Geraint Jones and Daniel Kaufmann (2000), 'Seize the day, seize the state', *State Capture, Corruption and Influence in Transition*. Policy Research Working Paper 2444. Washington: World Bank.

Henderson, Hazel (2000), 'Transnational corporations and global citizenship', *American Behavioural Scientist*, 43 (8), 1231–61.

Hertz, Noreena (2001a), 'Better to shop than to vote?', *Business Ethics: A European Review*, 10 (3), 190–3.

(2001b), *The Silent Takeover*. London: Heinemann.

(2004), 'Corporations on the front line', *Corporate Governance: an International Review*, 12 (2), 202–9.

Hettne, Björn (2000), 'The fate of citizenship in Post-Westphalia', *Citizenship Studies*, 4 (1), 35–46.

Higgins, Nick (2005), 'Lessons from the indigenous: Zapatista poetics and a cultural humanism for the twenty-first century', in *Critical Theories, International Relations and 'The Anti-globalization Movement'*, Catherine Eschle and Bice Maiguashca, Eds. London: Routledge.

Hilhorst, Dorothea (2002), 'Being good at doing good? Quality and accountability of humanitarian NGOs', *Disasters*, 26 (3), 193–212.

Hilson, Chris (2001), 'Greening citizenship: boundaries of membership and the environment', *Journal of Environmental Law*, 13 (3), 335–48.

Hippert, Christine (2002), 'Multinational corporations, the politics of the world economy, and their effects on women's health in the developing world: a review', *Health Care for Women International*, 23, 861–69.

Hirschman, Albert O. (1977), *The Passions and the Interests: Political Arguments for Capitalism Before its Triumph*. Princeton: Princeton University Press.

Hirst, Paul Q. (1989), *The Pluralist Theory of the State: Selected Writings of G.D.H. Cole, J.N. Figgis and H.J. Laski*. London: Routledge.

(1993), 'Associational democracy', in *Prospects for Democracy*, David Held, Ed. Stanford: Stanford University Press.

Hoffman, Andrew J. (2005), 'Climate change strategy: the business logic behind voluntary greenhouse gas reductions', *California Management Review*, 47 (3), 21–46.

Hoffman, Kurt, Chris West, Karen Westley and Sharna Jarvis (2005), *Enterprise Solutions to Poverty*. London: Shell Foundation.

Hopkins, Willie E. and Shirley A. Hopkins (1999), 'The ethics of downsizing: perceptions of rights and responsibilities', *Journal of Business Ethics*, 18, 145–56.

Howland, Dave and Rob Robertson (1999), 'Review of Chinnagounder's challenge: the question of ecological citizenship', *Journal of Political Ecology*, 6 (3), http://dizzy.library.arizona.edu/ej/jpe/Volume6/Volume_6_3.html.

Hudson, Wayne and Steven Slaughter, Eds. (2007), *Globalization and Citizenship*. London, New York: Routledge.

Ikeda, Satoshi (2004), 'Imperial subjects, national citizenship, and corporate subjects: cycles of political participation/exclusion in the modern world-system', *Citizenship Studies*, 8 (4), 333–47.

Isin, Engin F. and Bryan S. Turner (2002), 'Citizenship studies: an introduction', in *Handbook of Citizenship Studies*, Engin F. Isin and Bryan S. Turner, Eds. London: Sage.

(2007), 'Investigating citizenship: an agenda for citizenship studies', *Citizenship Studies*, 11 (1), 5–17.

Jacobs, David, Michael Useem and Mayer N. Zald (1991), 'Firms, industries and politics', *Research in Political Sociology*, 5, 141–65.

Jeurissen, Ronald (2004), 'The institutional conditions of corporate citizenship', *Journal of Business Ethics*, 53, 87–96.

Jingjing, Jiang (2004), 'Wal-Mart's China inventory to hit US$18b this year', *China Business Weekly*, 29 November 2004.

Jones, Ian W. and Michael G. Pollitt (1998), 'Ethical and unethical competition: establishing the rules of engagement', *Long Range Planning*, 31 (5), 703–10.

Jones, Marc T. and Matthew Haigh (2007), 'The transnational corporation and new corporate citizenship theory: a critical analysis', *Journal of Corporate Citizenship*, 27, 51–69.

Joppke, Christian (2007), 'Transformation of citizenship: status, rights, identity', *Citizenship Studies*, 11 (1), 37–48.

Kalberg, Stephen (1993), 'Cultural foundations of modern citizenship', in *Citizenship and Social Theory*, Bryan S. Turner, Ed. London: Sage.

Kaler, John (1999), 'Understanding participation', *Journal of Business Ethics*, 21, 125–35.

Kant, Immanuel (1970), 'Perpetual peace', in *Kant: Political Writings*, H. Reiss, Ed. Cambridge: Cambridge University Press.

Kerr, Jeffrey L. (2004), 'The limits of organizational democracy', *Academy of Management Executive*, 18 (3): 81–95.

King, Colbert I. (2001), 'Saudi Arabia's apartheid', in *The Washington Post*, 22 December, A23.

Klein, Naomi (2000), *No Logo: Taking Aim at the Brand Bullies*. London: Flamingo.

Kline, John M. (2005), *Ethics for International Business*. London/New York: Routledge.

Koenig-Archibugi, Mathias (2002), 'Transnational corporations and public accountability', *Government and Opposition*, 39 (2), 234–59.

Kolk, Ans (2000), *Economics of Environmental Management*. London: Financial Times, Prentice Hall.

Kolk, Ans and David Levy (2001), 'Winds of change: corporate strategy, climate change and oil multinationals', *European Management Journal*, 19 (5), 501–9.

Korten, David C. (2001), *When Corporations Rule the World* (2nd edition). Bloomfield, CT: Kumarian Press.

Kozinets, Robert (2001), 'Utopian enterprise: articulating the meanings of Star Trek's culture of consumption', *Journal of Consumer Research*, 28, 67–88.

Küng, Hans (2002), *Wozu Weltethos?* Freiburg: Herder.

Kurlantzick, Joshua. (2007), 'Beijing envy', *London Review of Books* (5 July 2007), 9–11.

Kymlicka, Will (1995), *Multicultural Citizenship: A Liberal Theory of Minority Rights*. Oxford: Clarendon Press.

Kymlicka, Will and Wayne Norman (1994), 'Return of the citizen: a survey of recent work on citizenship theory', *Ethics*, 104, 352–81.

Lambert, Susan J. (2000), 'Added benefits: the link between work-life benefits and organizational citizenship behaviour', *Academy of Management Journal*, 43 (5), 801–15.

Lamont, James (2002), 'Merck seeks wider private-sector coalition on Aids', *Financial Times*, 13 September 2002, 10.

Lamont, James and Frances Williams (2001), 'Campaigners attack drug companies on Aids patents', *Financial Times*, 17 October 2001, 14.

Lane, Christel (2000a), 'Divergent capitalisms. The social structuring and change of business systems', *Work, Employment and Society*, 14 (4), 813–15.

(2000b), 'Globalization and the German model of capitalism – erosion or survival? *British Journal of Sociology*, 51 (2): 207–34.

Leisinger, Klaus M. (2005), 'The corporate social responsibility of the pharmaceutical industry', *Business Ethics Quarterly*, 15 (4), 577–94.

Levy, David (1997), 'Business and international climate treaties: ozone depletion and climate change', *California Management Review (3)*, 54–71.

Levy, David and Daniel Egan (2000), 'Corporate politics and climate change', in *Non-state Actors and Authority in the Global System*, Richard A. Higgott, Geoffrey R.D. Underhill and Andreas Bieler, Eds. London: Routledge.

(2003), 'A neo-Gramscian approach to corporate political strategy: conflict and accommodation in the climate change negotiations', *Journal of Management Studies*, 40 (4), 803–29.

Levy, David and Rami Kaplan (2008), 'CSR and theories of global governance: strategic contestation in global issue arenas', in *The Oxford Handbook of CSR*, Andrew Crane, Abagail McWilliams, Dirk Matten, Jeremy Moon and Donald Siegel, Eds. Oxford: Oxford University Press.

Levy, David L. and Ans Kolk (2002), 'Strategic responses to global climate change: conflicting pressures on multinationals in the oil industry', *Business and Politics*, 3 (2), 275–300.

Levy, David L. and Peter Newell (2005), *The Business of Global Environmental Governance*. Cambridge, MA: MIT Press.

Lidskog, R. (2005), 'Siting conflicts – democratic perspectives and political implications', *Journal of Risk Research*, 8 (3), 187–206.

Light, Andrew (2003), 'Urban ecological citizenship', *Journal of Social Philosophy*, 34 (1), 44–63.

Linklater, Andrew (2002), 'Cosmopolitan citizenship', in *Handbook of Citizenship Studies*, Engin F. Isin and Bryan S. Turner, Eds. London: Sage.

Linneroth-Bayer, Joanne, Ragner Löfstedt and Gunnar Sjöstedt, Eds. (2001), *Transboundary Risk Management*. London: Earthscan.

Lister, Ruth (2003), *Citizenship: Feminist Perspectives*, (2nd edition). Basingstoke: Palgrave.

Livesey, Sharon (2002), 'The discourse of the middle ground: citizen Shell commits to sustainable development', *Management Communication Quarterly*, 15 (3), 313–49.

Logsdon, Jeanne M. (2004), 'Global business citizenship: applications to environmental issues', *Business and Society Review*, 109 (1), 67–87.

Logsdon, Jeanne M. and Donna J. Wood (2002), 'Business citizenship: from domestic to global level of analysis', *Business Ethics Quarterly*, 12 (2), 155–87.

Logsdon, Jeanne M. and Patsy G. Lewellyn (2000), 'Expanding accountability to stakeholders: trends and predictions', *Business and Society Review*, 105 (4), 419–35.

Lord, Michael D. (2000), 'Corporate political strategy and legislative decision making', *Business and Society*, 39 (1), 76–93.

Low, Christopher and Christopher Cowton (2004), 'Beyond stakeholder engagement: the challenges of stakeholder participation in corporate governance', *International Journal of Business, Governance, and Ethics*, 1 (1), 45–55.

LSE & Wellcome Trust (2005), *The New Landscape of Neglected Disease Drug Development (A Report from the Pharmaceutical R&D Policy Project)*. London: London School of Economics/Health and Social Care.

Luger, Stan (2005), *Corporate Power, American Democracy, and the Automobile Industry*. Cambridge, UK: Cambridge University Press.

Lunt, Neil, Paul Spoonley and Peter Mataira (2002), 'Past and present: reflections on citizenship within New Zealand', *Social Policy and Administration*, 36 (4), 346–62.

Maignan, Isabelle and O.C. Ferrell (2000), 'Measuring corporate citizenship in two countries: the case of the United States and France', *Journal of Business Ethics*, 23, 283–97.

Maignan, Isabelle, O.C. Ferrell and G. Thomas M. Hult (1999), 'Corporate citizenship: cultural antecedents and business benefits', *Journal of the Academy of Marketing Science*, 27 (4), 455–69.

Maitland, Alison (2002), 'Involvement by companies produces a ripple effect', *Financail Times*, 19 June 2002, 17.

Majone, Giandomenico (1997), 'From the positive to the regulatory state: causes and consequences in the mode of governance', *Journal of Public Policy* 17 (2), 139–67.

Manville, Brook and Josiah Ober (2003), 'Beyond empowerment: building a company of citizens', *Harvard Business Review* (January), 48–53.

Marsden, Chris (2000), 'The new corporate citizenship of big business: part of the solution to sustainability', *Business and Society Review*, 105 (1), 9–25.

Marshall, Thomas Humphrey (1964), *Class, Citizenship and Social Development*. London: Heinemann.

Matten, Dirk (2004), 'The impact of the risk society thesis on environmental politics and management in a globalizing economy – principles, proficiency, perspectives', *Journal of Risk Research*, 7 (4), 377–98.

Matten, Dirk and Andrew Crane (2005a), 'Corporate citizenship: toward an extended theoretical conceptualisation', *Academy of Management Review*, 30 (1), 166–79.

(2005b), 'What is stakeholder democracy? Perspectives and issues', *Business Ethics: A European Review*, 14 (1), 6–13.

Matten, Dirk, Andrew Crane and Wendy Chapple (2003), 'Behind the mask: revealing the true face of corporate citizenship', *Journal of Business Ethics*, 44 (1/2), 109–20.

McCraw, Thomas K. (1984), 'Business and government: the origins of an adversary relationship', *California Management Review*, 26 (2), 33–52.

McIntosh, Malcolm, Sandra Waddock and Georg Kell, Eds. (2004), *Learning to Talk. Corporate Citizenship and the Development of the UN Global Compact*. Sheffield: Greenleaf.

McIntyre, Alasdair (1984), *After Virtue: a Study in Moral Theory*. Notre Dame: University of Notre Dame Press.

Merchant, Caroline (1989), *Ecological Revolutions: Nature, Gender, and Science in New England*. Chapel Hill: University of North Carolina Press.

Meyer, John W. and Brian Rowan (1977), 'Institutionalized organizations', *American Journal of Sociology*, 83, 340–63.

Michael, Bryane (2003), 'Corporate social responsibility in international development: an overview and critique', *Corporate Social Responsibility and Environmental Management*, 10, 115–28.

Micheletti, Michele, Andreas Follesdal and Dietlind Stolle, Eds. (2004), *Politics, Products, and Markets: Exploring Political Consumerism Past and Present*. New Brunswick: Transaction.

Microsoft (2005), *Corporate Citizenship Report 2005*. Seattle: Microsoft Inc.

Mill, John S. (1946) [1861], *Considerations on Representative Government.* Oxford: Basil Blackwell.

Miller, William H. (1998), 'Citizenship that's hard to ignore', *Industry Week*, 2 September, 22–4.

Mitchell, Ronald K., Bradley R. Agle and Donna J. Wood (1997), 'Toward a theory of stakeholder identification and salience: defining the principle of who and what really counts', *Academy of Management Review*, 22 (4), 853–86.

Mitchell, William C. (1990), 'Interest groups: economic perspectives and contribution', *Journal of Theoretical Politics*, 2, 85–108.

Mokhiber, Russell and Robert Weissman (1999), *Corporate Predators: the Hunt for Mega-profits and the Attack on Democracy.* Monroe, ME: Common Courage Press.

(2001), *On the Rampage: Corporate Power in the New Millennium.* Monroe, ME: Common Courage Press.

Monbiot, George (2000), *The Captive State.* London: MacMillan.

Moon, Jeremy (1991), 'From local economic initiatives to marriages a la mode?: Western Australia and Tasmania in comparative perspective', *Australian Journal of Political Science* 26, 63–78.

(1995), 'The firm as citizen: corporate responsibility in Australia', *Australian Journal of Political Science* 30 (1), 1–17.

(1999), 'The Australian public sector and new governance', *Australian Journal of Public Administration* 58, 112–20.

(2002), 'Business social responsibility and new governance', *Government and Opposition*, 37 (3), 385–408.

Moon, Jeremy and David Vogel (2008), 'CSR, government and civil society', in *The Oxford Handbook of CSR*, Andrew Crane, Abagail McWilliams, Dirk Matten, Jeremy Moon and Donald Siegel, Eds. Oxford: Oxford University Press.

Moon, Jeremy and Kelvin Willoughby (1990), 'Between state and market in Australia: the case of local enterprise initiatives', *Australian Journal of Public Administration*, 49 (1), 23–37.

Moon, Jeremy and Richard Sochacki (1996), 'The social responsibility of business in job and enterprise creation: motives, means and implications', *Australian Quarterly* 68 (1), 21–30.

(1998), 'New governance in Australian schools: a place for business social responsibility?', *Australian Journal of Public Administration*, 57 (1), 55–67.

Moon, Jeremy, Andrew Crane and Dirk Matten (2005), 'Can corporations be citizens? Corporate citizenship as a metaphor for business participation in society', *Business Ethics Quarterly*, 15 (3), 427–51.

Moore, Chris, Jeremy J. Richardson and Jeremy Moon (1985), 'New partnerships in local economic development', *Local Government Studies*, 11, 19–33.

Moore, Geoff (2004), 'The Fair Trade movement: parameters, issues and future research', *Journal of Business Ethics*, 53 (1–2), 73–86.

Morgan, Glenn (2001), 'Transnational communities and business systems', *Global Networks*, 1 (2), 113–30.

Mullerat, Ramon, Ed. (2005), *Corporate Social Responsibility: the Corporate Governance of the 21st Century*. Boston, MA: Kluwer Law International.

Muñiz, Albert and Thome O'Guinn (2001), 'Brand community', *Journal of Consumer Research*, 27, 412–32.

Muthuri, Judy N., Dirk Matten and Jeremy Moon (2008), 'The creation of social capital through employee volunteering as a form of corporate social responsibility', *British Journal of Management*, in press.

Nelson, Jane (2000), 'The leadership challenge of global corporate citizenship', *Perspectives on Business and Global Change*, 14 (4), 11–26.

Nelson, Joel I. (1992), 'Social welfare and the market economy', *Social Science Quarterly*, 73 (4), 815–28.

Nestlé (2006), *Nestlé, the Community and the United Nations Millennium Development Goals*. Vevey: Nestlé.

Newell, Peter (2000), 'Environmental NGOs and globalization: the governance of TNCs', in *Global Social Movements*, R. Cohen and S. Rai, Eds. London: Continuum.

Nicholls, Alex and Charlotte Opal (2005), *Fair Trade. Market Driven Ethical Consumption*. London: Sage.

Norman, Wayne and Pierre-Yves Néron (2008), 'Citizenship Inc. – do we really want businesses to be good corporate citizens?', *Business Ethics Quarterly*, 18 (1), 1–26.

Ohmae, Kenichi (1990), *The Borderless World: Power and Strategy in the Interlinked Economy*. New York: Free Press.

Oldfield, Adrian (1990), *Citizenship and Community: Civic Republicanism and the Modern World*. London: Routledge.

Organ, Dennis W. (1988), *Organizational Citizenship Behavior: the Good Soldier Syndrome*. Lexington, MA: Lexington Books.

Orsato, Renato J., Frank Den Hond and Stuart R. Clegg (2002), 'The political ecology of automobile recycling in Europe', *Organization Studies*, 23 (4), 639–65.

Orts, Eric W. (1995), 'A reflexive model of environmental regulation', *Business Ethics Quarterly*, 5 (4), 779–94.

Osterberg, David and Fouad Ajami (1971), 'The multinational corporation: expanding the frontiers of world politics', *Conflict Resolution*, XV (4), 457–70.

Owen, David and Brendan O'Dwyer (2008), 'CSR: the reporting and assurance dimension', in *The Oxford Handbook of CSR*, Andrew Crane,

Abagail McWilliams, Dirk Matten, Jeremy Moon and Donald Siegel, Eds. Oxford: Oxford University Press.

Palacios, Juan José (2004), 'Corporate citizenship and social responsibility in a globalized world', *Citizenship Studies*, 8 (4), 383–402.

Parker, Julia (1998), *Citizenship, Work and Welfare*. Basingstoke: Macmillan.

Parkinson, John E. (1993), *Corporate Power and Responsibility*. Oxford: Oxford University Press.

Parry, Geraint (1991), 'Conclusion: paths to citizenship', in *The Frontiers of Citizenship*, Ursula Vogel and Michael Moran, Eds. Basingstoke: Macmillan.

Pateman, Carole (1970), *Participation and Democratic Theory*. Cambridge: Cambridge University Press.

Peñaloza, Lisa (1996), 'We're here, we're queer, and we're going shopping! A critical perspective on the accommodation of gays and lesbians in the US Marketplace', *Journal of Homosexuality*, 31 (1–2), 9–41.

Persky, Joseph (1993), 'Retrospectives: consumer sovereignty', *Journal of Economic Perspectives*, 7 (1), 183–91.

Phillips, Anne (2000), 'Feminism and republicanism: is this a plausible alliance?', *Journal of Political Philosophy* 8 (2), 279–93.

Phillips, Robert A. and Joel Reichart (2000), 'The environment as a stakeholder? A fairness-based approach', *Journal of Business Ethics*, 23 (2), 185–97.

Podsakoff, Philip M., Scott B. MacKenzie, Julie Beth Paine and Daniel G. Bachrach (2000), 'Organizational citizenship behaviors: a critical review of the theoretical and empirical literature and suggestions for future research', *Journal of Management*, 26 (3), 513–63.

Pollay, Richard W. (1986), 'The distorted mirror: reflections on the unintended consequences of advertising', *Journal of Marketing*, 50 (April), 18–36.

Post, James E. (2002), 'Global corporate citizenship: principles to live and work by', *Business Ethics Quarterly*, 12 (2), 143–53.

Power, Gavin (2006), *Who Cares Wins – the Convergence of Global Corporate Citizenship and Financial Markets*. Miami: Keynote Speech at the Investment Management Institute Conference, January.

Power, Michael (1999), *The Audit Society: Rituals of Verification*. Oxford: Oxford University Press.

Prahalad, C.K. (2005), *The Fortune at the Bottom of the Pyramid*. Upper Saddle River, NJ: Wharton School Publishing.

Prahalad, C.K. and Allen Hammond (2002), 'Serving the world's poor, profitably', *Harvard Business Review*, 80 (9), 48–57.

Pries, Ludger (2001), 'The approach of transnational social spaces: responding to new configurations of the social and the spatial', in *New Transnational Social Spaces*, Ludger Pries, Ed. London and New York: Routledge.

Pulver, Simone (2007), 'Making sense of corporate environmentalism: an environmental contestation approach to analyzing the causes and consequences of the climate change policy split in the oil industry', *Organization and Environment*, 20 (1), 44–83.

Reich, Robert B. (1998), 'The new meaning of corporate social responsibility', *California Management Review*, 40 (2), 8–17.

Reilly, Bernard J. and Myron J. Kyj (1994), 'Corporate citizenship', *Review of Business*, 16 (1), 37–43.

Renn, Ortwin, Thomas Webler and Peter M. Wiedemann, Eds. (1995), *Fairness and Competence in Citizen Participation*. Dordrecht: Kluwer.

Revill, Jo and Paul Harris (2004), 'Tackling obesity: America stirs up a sugar rebellion', *The Observer*, 18 January 2004, 20.

Riley, Richard, Sandra Feldman, Sofie Sa, Bruce S. Cooper, Diana Wyllie Rigden, Ted Kolderie, Hans Decker, G. Alfred Hess Jr. and Allyson Tucker (1994), 'Educating the workforce of the future', *Harvard Business Review*, 72 (2), 39–51.

Ritzer, George (2003), *The Globalization of Nothing*. Thousand Oaks, CA: Pine Forge Press.

Roberts, Sarah, Justin Keeble and David Brown (2002), *The Business Case for Corporate Citizenship*. Cambridge: Arthur D. Little International.

Ronit, Karsten (2001), 'Institutions of private authority in global governance', *Administration and Society*, 33 (5), 555–78.

Ronit, Karsten and Volker Schneider (1999), 'Global governance through private organizations', *Governance: an International Journal of Policy and Administration*, 12 (3): 243–66.

Rosen, Sydney (2003), 'AIDS is your business', *Harvard Business Review*, 81 (2), 81–97.

Royle, Tony (2005), 'Realism or idealism? Corporate social responsibility and the employee stakeholder in the global fast-food industry', *Business Ethics: A European Review*, 14 (1), 42–55.

Royle, Tony and Brian Towers (2002), 'Summary and conclusions: MNCs, regulatory systems and employment rights', in T. Royle and B. Towers, Eds. *Labour Relations in the Global Fast-food Industry*. London: Routledge. 192–203.

Ruggie, John Gerard (2004), 'Reconstituting the public domain – issues, actors, and practices', *European Journal of International Relations*, 10 (4), 499–531.

Sagoff, Mark (1986), 'At the shrine of our lady of fatima, or why political questions are not all economic', in *People, Penguins, and Plastic Trees: Basic Issues in Environmental Ethics*, D. VanDeVeer and C. Pierce, Eds. Belmont: Wadsworth.

(1988), *The Economy of the Earth: Philosophy, Law and the Environment.* Cambridge: Cambridge University Press.

Sassen, Saskia (2002), 'Towards post-national and denationalized citizenship', in *Handbook of Citizenship Studies*, Engin F. Isin and Bryan S. Turner, Eds. London: Sage.

Scherer, Andreas G. and Guido Palazzo (2007), 'Toward a political conception of corporate responsibility – business and society seen from a Habermasian perspective', *Academy of Management Review*, 32 (4), 1096–120.

(2008), 'Globalization and CSR', in *The Oxford Handbook of CSR*, Andrew Crane, Dirk Matten, Abagail McWilliams, Jeremy Moon and Donald Siegel, Eds. Oxford: Oxford University Press.

Scherer, Andreas G., Guido Palazzo and Dorothee Baumann (2006), 'Global rules and private actors – towards a new role of the TNC in global governance', *Business Ethics Quarterly*, 16 (4), 505–32.

Scherer, Andreas G. and Marc Smid (2000), 'The downward spiral and the US model business principles – why MNEs should take responsibility for improvement of world-wide social and environmental conditions', *Management International Review*, 40, 351–71.

Schneiderman, David (2004), 'Habermas, market-friendly human rights, and the revisibility of economic globalization', *Citizenship Studies*, 8 (4), 419–36.

Schneidewind, Uwe and Holger Petersen (1998), 'Changing the rules: business–NGO partnerships and structuration theory', *Greener Management International*, 24, 105–14.

Scholte, Jan Aart (2003), *Globalization. A Critical Introduction* (2nd edition). Basingstoke: Palgrave.

Schuck, Peter H. (2002), 'Liberal citizenship', in *Handbook of Citizenship Studies*, Engin F. Isin and Bryan S. Turner, Eds. London: Sage.

Schumpeter, Joseph A. (1965), *Capitalism, Socialism and Democracy* (2nd edition). London: Allen and Unwin.

Seelos, Christian and Johanna Mair (2005), 'Social entrepreneurship: creating new business models to serve the poor', *Business Horizons*, 48 (3), 241–6.

Seitanidi, Maria May and Annmarie Ryan (2007), 'A critical review of forms of corporate community involvement: from philanthropy to partnerships', *International Journal of Nonprofit and Voluntary Sector Marketing*, 12 (3), 247–66.

Sellers, Martin P. (2003), 'Privatization morphs into 'publicization': business looks a lot like government', *Public Administration*, 81 (3), 607–20.

Sender, Katherine (2005), *Business, Not Politics: The Making of the Gay Market*. New York: Columbia University Press.

Sennett, Richard (1996), *The Fall of Public Man*. New York, London: W. W. Norton.

Sethi, S. Prakash (1982), 'Corporate political activism', *California Management Review*, 24 (3), 32–42.

Sethi, S. Prakash and Oliver F. Williams (2001), *Economic Imperatives and Ethical Values in Global Business: the South African Experience and International Codes Today*. Notre Dame: University of Notre Dame Press.

Shelton, Dinah (1991), 'Human rights, environmental rights, and the right to environment', *Stafford Journal of International Law*, 28, 103–38.

Shiva, Vandana (1997), *Biopiracy: the Plunder of Nature and Knowledge*. Cambridge, MA: South End Press.

(2001), *Protect or Plunder? Understanding Intellectual Property Rights*. London: Zed Books.

Simons, Michael A. (2002), 'Vicarious snitching: crime, cooperation, and "good corporate citizenship"', *St. John's Law Review*, 76 (4), 979–1017.

Singer, Peter Warren (2003), *Corporate Warriors: The Rise of the Privatized Military*. Ithaca: Cornell University Press.

Singh, Val and Susan Vinnicombe (2005), *The Female FTSE100 Index*. Cranfield: Centre for Developing Women Business Leaders, Cranfield School of Management.

Smith, Mark J. (1998), *Ecologism: Towards Ecological Citizenship*. Buckingham: Open University Press.

Smith, N. Craig (1990), *Morality and the Market: Consumer Pressure for Corporate Accountability*. London: Routledge.

Somerville, Jennifer (2000), *Feminism and the Family: Politics and Society in the UK and the USA*. Basingstoke: Palgrave.

Soskice, David (1997), 'Stakeholding yes: the German model no', in G. Kelly, D. Kelly and A. Gamble, Eds. *Stakeholder Capitalism*. Basingstoke: Macmillan. 219–25.

Soysal, Yasemin Nuhoglu (1994), *Limits of Citizenship*. Chicago: The University of Chicago Press.

Steinmann, Horst and Albert Löhr (1994), *Grundlagen der Unternehmensethik* (2nd edition). Stuttgart: Schäffer-Poeschel.

Steinmann, Horst (2007), 'Corporate ethics and globalization – global rules and private actors', in *Business Ethics of Innovation*, Gerd Hanekamp, Ed. Berlin, Heidelberg: Springer.

Stephenson, Nick (2003), *Cultural Citizenship: Cosmopolitan Questions*. Maidenhead: Open University Press.

Stephenson, Nick, Ed. (2001), *Culture and Citizenship*. London: Sage.

Stigler, George J. (1971), 'The theory of economic regulation', *Bell Journal of Economics and Management Science*, 2, 3–21.

Stokes, Geoffrey (2002), 'Democracy and citizenship', in *Democratic Theory Today*, April Carter and Geoffrey Stokes, Eds. Cambridge: Polity Press.

Stoney, Christopher and Diana Winstanley (2001), 'Stakeholding: confusion or utopia? Mapping the conceptual terrain', *Journal of Management Studies*, 38 (5), 603–26.

Sule, Satish (2007), 'TRIPS (Trade Related Aspects of International Property Rights)', in Wayne Visser, Dirk Matten, Manfred Pohl and Nick Tolhurst, Eds. *The A–Z of Corporate Social Responsibility – The Complete Reference of Concepts, Codes and Organisations*. London: John Wiley, 484–5.

Sullivan, Rory, Ed. (2003), *Business and Human Rights*. Sheffield: Greenleaf.

SustainAbility (2006), 'Taxing issues: responsible business and tax' www.sustainability.com.

Swank, Duane and Cathie Jo Martin (2001), 'Employers and the welfare state. The political economic organization of firms and social policy in contemporary capitalist democracies', *Comparative Political Studies*, 34 (8), 889–923.

Tancredo, Tom (2004), 'Immigration, citizenship, and national security: the silent invasion', *Mediterranean Quarterly*, 15 (4), 4–15.

Taylor, Charles (1992), *Multi-culturalism and the Politics of Recognition*. Princeton: Princeton University Press.

Thompson, Grahame (2006), *Tracking Global Corporate Citizenship: Some Reflections on 'Lovesick' Companies (IIIS Discussion Paper No. 192)*. Dublin: Institute for International Integration Studies.

Timberlake, Lloyd, Ed. (2005), *Business for Development: Business Solutions in Support of the Millennium Development Goals*. Geneva: World Business Council for Sustainable Development.

Toyota (2007), *Sustainability Report 2006*. Tokyo: Toyota Motor Company.

Turner, Bryan S. (2000), 'Review essay: citizenship and political globalization', *Citizenship Studies*, 4 (1), 81–6.

(2001), 'The erosion of citizenship', *British Journal of Sociology*, 52 (2), 189–209.

US Small Business Administration (2001), *Minorities in Business*. Washington, DC: Office of Advocacy.

Unerman, Jeffrey and Brendan O'Dwyer (2006), 'On James Bond and the importance of NGO accountability', *Accounting, Auditing and Accountability Journal*, 19 (3), 305–18.

United Nations (2001), *2001 Report on the World Situation*. New York: United Nations Publications.

Useem, Michael (1984), *The Inner Circle: Large Corporations and the Rise of Business Political Activity in the US and UK*. Ithaca: Cornell University Press.

van Oosterhout, J. (Hans) (2005), 'Corporate citizenship: an idea whose time has not yet come', *Academy of Management Review*, 30 (4), 677–84.

Venetoulis, Jason, Dahlia Chazan and Christopher Gaudet (2004), *Ecological Footprint of Nations, 2004*. Oakland, CA: Redefining Progress.

Vogel, David (1983), 'The power of business in America: a re-appraisal', *British Journal of Political Science* 13, 19–43.

(1986), 'Political science and the study of corporate power: a dissent from the new conventional wisdom', *British Journal of Political Science* 16, 385–408.

Vogel, Ursula and Michael Moran, Eds. (1991), *The Frontiers of Citizenship*. Basingstoke: Macmillan.

Wackernagel, Mathis and William Rees (1996), *Our Ecological Footprint: Reducing Human Impact on the Earth*. Gabriola, British Columbia: New Society Publishers.

Waddock, Sandra A. (1988), 'Building successful social partnerships', *Sloan Management Review*, 29 (4), 17–23.

Wagner, Antonin (2004), 'Redefining citizenship for the 21st century: from the National Welfare State to the UN Global Compact', *International Journal of Social Welfare*, 13, 278–86.

Wagner, Cynthia G. (2001), 'Evaluating good citizenship', *The Futurist*, July-August, 16.

Waltzer, Michael (1983), *Spheres of Justice: A Defence of Pluralism and Equality*. New York: New York University Press.

Warhurst, Alyson (2004), 'Corporate citizenship', *Public Service Review: European Union*, Autumn, 12–14.

Warner, Michael and Rory Sullivan, Eds. (2004), *Putting Partnerships to Work. Strategic Alliances for Development between Government, the Private Sector and Civil Society*. Sheffield: Greenleaf.

Warren, Mark E. (2001), *Democracy and Association*. Princeton, NJ: Princeton University Press.

Werhane, Patricia H. and Michael Gorman (2005), 'Intellectual property rights, moral imagination, and the access to life enhancing drugs', *Business Ethics Quarterly*, 15 (4), 595–613.

Wettenhall, Roger (2001), 'Public or private? Public corporations, companies and the decline of the middle ground', *Public Organization Review: A Global Journal*, 1 (1), 17–40.

Wheeler, David, Heike Fabig and Richard Boele (2002), 'Paradoxes and dilemmas for stakeholder responsive firms in the extractive sector: lessons from the case of Shell and the Ogoni', *Journal of Business Ethics*, 39 (3), 297–318.

White, Stuart (2003), *The Civic Minimum*. Oxford: Oxford University Press.

Whiteman, Gail and William H. Cooper (2000), 'Ecological embeddedness', *Academy of Management Journal*, 43 (6), 1265–82.

Whitley, Richard, Ed. (1992), *European Business Systems*. London: Sage.

Williamson, Oliver (1967), *Economics of Discretionary Behavior: Managerial Objectives in a Theory of the Firm*. Chicago: Markham Publishing.

Wilts, Arnold and Christine Quittkat (2004), 'Corporate interests and public affairs: organised business–government relations in EU member states', *Journal of Public Affairs*, 4 (4), 384–99.

Wilts, Arnold and Mika Skippari (2007), 'Special issue: business–government interactions in a globalizing economy', *Business and Society*, 46 (2), 129–278.

Windsor, Duane (2001), 'Corporate citizenship: evolution and interpretation', in *Perspectives on Corporate Citizenship*, Jörg Andriof and Malcolm McIntosh, Eds. Sheffield: Greenleaf.

Wokutch, Richard E. and J. Lawrence French (2005), 'Child workers, globalization and international business ethics: a case study in Brazil's export-oriented shoe industry', *Business Ethics Quarterly*, 15 (4), 615–40.

Wood, Donna J. and Jeanne M. Logsdon (2001), 'Theorising business citizenship', in *Perspectives on Corporate Citizenship*, Jörg Andriof and Malcolm McIntosh, Eds. Sheffield: Greenleaf.

(2002), 'Business citizenship: from individuals to organizations', *Business Ethics Quarterly*, 12 (Special Issue on Ethics and Entrepreneurship), 59–94.

Wood, Donna J., Jeanne M. Logsdon, Patsy G. Lewellyn and Kim Davenport (2006), *Global Business Citizenship*. Armonk, London: M. E. Sharpe.

World Economic Forum (2002), *Global Corporate Citizenship: the Leadership Challenge for CEOs and Boards*. Geneva: World Economic Forum.

(2005), *Partnering for Success – Business Perspectives on Multistakeholder Partnerships*. Geneva: World Economic Forum Global Corporate Citizenship Initiative.

Yeatman, Anna (2007), 'The subject of citizenship', *Citizenship Studies*, 11 (1), 105–15.

Young, Iris Marion (1994), 'Polity and Group Difference', in *Citizenship: Critical Concepts*, B. Turner and P. Hamilton, Eds. London: Routledge.

Zadek, Simon (2007), *The Civil Corporation: the New Economy of Corporate Citizenship* (2nd edition). London: Earthscan.

Index